THAILAND BEYOND THE FRINGE

Robert Cooper

Author of *CultureShock! Thailand*

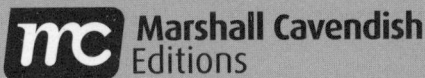

Marshall Cavendish
Editions

Cover design by Lock Hong Liang
Illustrations by Trigg

© 2007 Marshall Cavendish International (Asia) Private Limited
This edition with new cover reprinted 2009

Published by Marshall Cavendish Editions
An imprint of Marshall Cavendish International
1 New Industrial Road, Singapore 536196

Other Marshall Cavendish Offices:
Marshall Cavendish Ltd. 5th Floor 32–38 Saffron Hill, London EC1N 8FH • Marshall
Cavendish Corporation. 99 White Plains Road, Tarrytown NY 10591-9001, USA •
Marshall Cavendish International (Thailand) Co Ltd. 253 Asoke, 12th Flr, Sukhumvit
21 Road, Klongtoey Nua, Wattana, Bangkok 10110, Thailand • Marshall Cavendish
(Malaysia) Sdn Bhd, Times Subang, Lot 46, Subang Hi-Tech Industrial Park, Batu
Tiga, 40000 Shah Alam, Selangor Darul Ehsan, Malaysia

Marshall Cavendish is a trademark of Times Publishing Limited

National Library Board Singapore Cataloguing in Publication Data

Cooper, Robert George.
Thailand beyond the fringe / Robert Cooper. – Singapore : Marshall Cavendish
Editions, c2007.
p. cm.
ISBN-13 : 978-981-261-747-7

1. National characteristics, Thai. 2. Thailand – Anecdotes. 3. Thailand – Social
life and customs – Humor. 4. Thailand – Civilization. I. Title.

DS563.5
306.09593 -- dc22   SLS2007035395

Printed by Utopia Press Pte Ltd

Foreword

Foreword: The Smiling Backside

As a working title when putting this book together, I used *Thailand: the back side of the smile.* Not wishing to risk any offence, I asked a very educated Thai in English what he thought the reaction of Thais might be. He asked me to explain what the title meant. I used synonyms to 'back side' like 'reverse' and 'other' and 'obverse and 'bum' and explained that I wanted to go deeper into the darker side of the Thais and their changing cultural characteristics, remain sympathetic but approach with humour some of the areas that bother foreigners living in the country and wishing to integrate and understand more than they do. Because I think Thailand is only really appreciable when taken with a large dash of humour, I said I did not want to use 'behind the smile', which to me is not only too cliché but sounds kind of secretive. "Ah", he said, "The Smiling Backside. Great title." ... So, I changed the title to *Thailand Beyond the Fringe.* Thanks go to Acharn Suthep for his memorable suggestion, and of course a great inspirational debt must be acknowledged to all those forerunners of modern fringe humour for providing something for me to go beyond. Enjoy your trip to the outer fringes of this most amazing of countries...

Robert Cooper, 2009

What this NEW book might do to you:

Make your smile extra white

Make your skin deep down stunningly sparkling white

Help you trade age spots for teenage spots

Resolve your cuckolding problem

Explain sudden nether-region irritation

Assist your handling of persistent khatoeys

Hone skills of ingratiation and integration

Keep you considerate of others while masturbating

Help you market your suicide and assassination

Teach you to love your mother-in-law

Encourage you to bide your time and plan your revenge privately

Enlighten you on the social benefits of giving your money away without any thoughts of eventual reward

Inform you of the advantages of doing nothing

...and ever so much more...

01

On a Big Rough Dog Falling in Love with Your Leg

This can be a subject of extreme amusement to the Thais. Unlike rabies, such untoward sexual advances are not considered hazardous to your health and the laundry of your trousers or panty-hose may therefore not be claimed against insurance.

There is of course, no guarantee that an enamoured dog is not also a rabid dog, so it is wise to examine the mouth of the animal before directing your view to its private parts. If the former, a rapid visit to your doctor or veterinary surgeon seems appropriate. If the latter is frothing, you might have the consolation that your ordeal by dog might soon be over. Nonetheless, you are on the edge of a very embarrassing public situation in which you could lose important points of social standing — and your trousers are on their way to the cleaners in a plastic bag.

Of course if you are one of those shorts-wearing people with extremely hairy legs, fleshy calves, knobbly knees, and an English spouse, the naked contact between man and beast might well appeal. If such is your case, you may be saved the laundry bill; but rather than sell tickets to a live show, it is polite behaviour to curtail the public entertainment and make a private arrangement to meet man's best friend behind the back wall of the nearest disco. You might even suggest he bring along a companion for the other leg.

If you are not into that particular kind of ménage, or if for one of any number of reasons you simply wish to project an image of one who does not enjoy being leg-rogered by a big shaggy dog, disengagement tactics are in order. It is your action of disengagement that will be scrutinised by the Thai public behaviour judging panel and by which you may either gain or lose social prestige. So enter the activity not lightly and never shoot the dog, at least not in public view and not without an effective silencer.

Presuming the ground is not littered by canine or other faeces — rainy-season mud puddles just have to be endured — sit down upon the animal sharply. With any luck your admirer will immediately transfer his affections to the leg of the chap or chapess nearest your own irresistible appendage. After all, to a dog, one leg is much like another — Thai dogs are like that, don't take it personally.

To be safe, retain a cross-legged sitting posture for the time it takes for nature to take its course. Under most circumstances this action, which neither hurts the dog nor offends the owner, if owner there be, will avoid any confrontation, human or canine, and will thus raise your status in the minds of the sniggering Thais who are witness to the leg-rogering of the *farang*.

High points have been scored for conflict avoidance. However, if you are in direct company of a big man, perhaps having *dejeuner sur l'herbe* with the *Nai Amphur* who happens to be the owner of Rover the Roger, while listening to the local Abbot's *khao phansa* message on how to behave, sitting in cross-legged equality will lose you many of the points you have just gained. To maximise your social standing: as you sink quickly to the ground make sure both your legs, even if one has a dog attached, are tucked away out of sight under your body and sit, tottering, in the sideways stance of respect. This may give you muddy pants, but will increase your social standing by precisely 29.7 points and should finally resolve your problem. *Should*. But... an unlikely event is that the dog is not immediately humbled by your respect for Thai norms and does not immediately desist and excuse himself; instead he transfers his cuddles to your outstretched arm, which is now precariously holding you upright and cannot be moved without your toppling, depending on the season, into the mud or dust, leaving your whole body in apparent total subjugation and invitation to all and every canine watching the show. And in an even more unlikely event, the *Nai Amphur* does not come to your aid by calling out to his shaggy mongrel, "Hey, Cutie, that's enough. Down, boy. Good dog. Let the *farang* alone now. You don't know where he's been." Only in such unlikely circumstances, and *only* when the attention of everybody is taken by the appearance of a lucky elephant on the scene or an opportune pile-up collision of six motorcycles, is it permissible to release your strongest leg from under your body, stand rapidly erect and, making sure that Cutie's teeth are nowhere near your throat, launch an almighty kick to his randy scrotum. Then, as Cutie whimpers off to complain to the *Nai Amphur*, you sit back down with a look of complete innocence on your sangfroid features. Take an extra 100 points.

Bottom line:
Even under trying circumstances, avoid any conflict with big men or women, or with their canine or affinal extensions. Resolve a problem without resort to public violence and you streak ahead.

02

On a Tall Red Man Cuckolding You Daily

On discovery that a tall red man is cuckolding you daily, and in your own bed too, best take it lying down.

This tall red man was standing over me. I was lying in bed and couldn't see his face. I don't know why. I think I never looked up, or just looked away, but I never saw his face. It was just before dawn because after it was over and he had gone, the sky was beginning to get light. He just stood there looking at me for a time. He was a sort of bright red, as if he had been painted with that paint that glows in the dark. I was on my back. He reached down and put his hand on my tummy. He was naked and his erection was red too, he was all red. At first he had a huge erection, then when he put his hand on my tummy and squeezed, it seemed to shrink until it was quite small, then it got big again, then small again, then absolutely huge. I couldn't move. I don't know why. I think it was his hand on me. He was so strong. I couldn't call out for help. He climbed on me and raped me. I closed my eyes. When I opened them, he was gone. He comes every morning. Before you wake up. And he rapes me. Never says a word. And there is nothing I can do to prevent it.

This account is edited, but it is absolutely real. I didn't make it up. Registered it on a voice recorder and translated it. Left the recorder running on slow all night and never heard a thing the next day. Made sure the *farang* husband was awake all night, had him text every hour. He was beside his Thai wife all night every night. And every morning the wife would wake up and say she had been raped.

Just dreaming? Undoubtedly. But the girl was sure as she could be that the same rape scene was happening over and over again and that it was not a dream but a *phi* who was really raping her. She was afraid of getting pregnant and having a red baby instead of a half-white one.

A case for the shrink's couch? Undoubtedly. Who knows what was really worrying the young wife. But the not-so-young *farang* husband was getting a bit fed up with the story. And he couldn't really work out why his wife seemed rather upset on waking up but, by the time she had eaten her *khao phiak*, she was as right as rain.

The wife was from a small village. She had a basic education, but knew little of the world. The husband reasoned that there was no point in taking her into the strange world of psychiatry. So, with her consent, he took his wife to see the abbot of the *wat* nearest their house. The abbot listened. He asked no stories about the wife's background and did not see the wife alone. He blessed some water and shook it over the couple. The wife said she felt much better. But the next morning she had the same story, and back they went to see the same abbot.

Now, like Christianity, Buddhism has little to do with the darker side of the spirit world. And, like Christianity, it can assist in exorcism if required. Such exorcism seems to be required a lot more in Thailand than in countries where people can go to counsellors or psychiatrists — or to their local doctor for a supply of the latest addictive wonder drug. Thus, the abbot asked if the rape-dream woman had gone through the proper rituals for pleasing the *phra phum*, the spirits who live on the land, when moving into the new home. She had not, she said, because there was no spirit house on the property, and having no garden, she had not set one up. The abbot did not have to speak again. The wife explained to the *farang* husband that they needed the permission of the spirits who owned the land on which their house was built to live in it, and the permission of the same spirits to have sex in it. No permission, statutory rape. The husband went along with things, but very doubtfully. Off they went, bought a nice little spirit house and asked the neighbour where best to set it up. Some flowers, alcohol, rice and bananas, a couple of dancing girls modelled in clay and a little Mercedes car, presented along with burning incense to the *phra phum*. The spirits are fairly basic in their requirements — much like men really. The next morning, the Thai wife was not raped, and was never raped again, and the *farang* husband delighted in telling how he had aided and abetted the red spirit who had regularly raped his wife.

While most *phi* do not personify themselves as tall, strong, red men, or for that matter little, weak, green men, all can and do get themselves involved in every aspect of Thai life, and being a foreigner does not exempt you from their attentions. Look around you. You won't see them. But you will see offerings to the *phi* on every corner, in every garden, on the verandah if there is no garden, on a shelf if no garden or verandah, or simply stuck into the ground. And you will find such offerings in all businesses. No house will be constructed nor business opened until the *phi* have given their consent. Move the Embassy flag pole one metre to keep the flag out of a tree's branches and you need a little ceremony of flowers and incense before you do. No construction workers would work on a pile-driver until the spirits in the ground are bought off. A monk may bless the nose cone of a new jumbo jet before it goes into service with Thai, but the *phi* will have been consulted before work ever began on it, and if anything goes wrong, it is the *phi* who get the blame, or, more likely, those people who should have made sure the *phi* were happy before things got started and were kept happy throughout the undertaking. The *farang* manager of any enterprise which goes bottom-up skimped on the opening rituals, didn't listen to the advice of his Thai colleagues, or behaved on the premises in a way likely to annoy the spirits. Down you go, might as well have thrown a spanner in the engine, it is clearly all your fault. Whoops, there goes your status... and your company's profit... and perhaps your job.

So, when your colleagues, above and below your status level, tend to ignore you when they play the spirit game, don't you ignore them. They think you will not understand, and at first you won't. Maybe you never will. Never mind. Giving your secretary or maid a few baht now and again to buy flowers and incense for the *phi* may be the cheapest investment of your life. Not only will the Thais respect you the more for it — a good plus point already — but you get flowers that look nice and have practical value in keeping everybody, visible and invisible, happy. And your building may be the only one standing after the next earthquake, bomb blast or tsunami. You may not see them, but they see you. Just like any other beings in the country, those *phi* not actively on *your* side are likely to be on or beyond the fringe. Few are neutral. That's their mischievous nature.

Bottom line:
You need all the help and good offices you can get, so don't antagonise anybody or any spirits. Your best move is to placate them and get them all on your side from the start. If you failed to do that, remedial action is always possible. But don't skimp.

03

On Accepting and Giving Gifts

Thais love to receive and give little gifts, and there is every reason for the non-Thai to join in this game. Such gifts often have no practical or functional value and may be recycled without embarrassment — although do try not to give them back to the person who gave them to you.

Real little bits of 25-baht supermarket bargain shelf stuff need not be wrapped. The rule could be: if the paper costs more than the gift, don't bother to wrap. It is perhaps difficult to think generously "well, it's the thought that counts" when someone obviously has thought that you, a person of refined taste, would ever want such an item of dubious standing in your home. Or is that just your interpretation? Yes, it probably is. The giver probably never gave any thought to what you would like in your home, just wanted to drop in on you and happened to be shopping. Don't make the mistake of considering that the Thais are working everything out; action is more often based on spontaneous thought with no great meaning.

But it really *is* the thought that counts. Small gifts — or larger ones for that matter — show that the giver was thinking *of you*, not *what* the giver was thinking of you. There is a difference. Do the pair of small plaster figures, that you would associate with a 10-year-old's idea of something they would like on their bedroom shelf, look any better now? Probably not, but maybe you can see behind them a little easier.

Cheap gifts are more likely to come from those below you in the social structure and wealth bracket. Something more to make you feel bad. How could you have been so uncharitable in your thoughts? Being unwrapped, you can't just put such cheap gifts to one side. On the other hand, a verbal thank you is quite enough — don't belabour it. Don't feel you have to stand whatever it is on the TV or in the front window. When the visitors are gone, off goes the gift into the maid's room — you certainly don't want to recycle such stuff among people that matter, do you? — and the maid will probably enjoy getting a little gift from her employer; it showed he was thinking of her, not *what* he was thinking of her.

Most other gifts that come unwrapped are not really wrappable and have immediate use: flowers and fruits fall into this category, and sometimes cakes, although these will often be put into a nice box with a bow at the place of purchase. Gifts on occasions such as birthdays will usually be wrapped, but might also end up with your maid. Accept such gifts — you can't refuse them anyway, and you should never say "you shouldn't have", even if you really wish they hadn't. NEVER unwrap these in front of the guest, unless strongly requested to do so; this might be the case when your staff members have clubbed together to buy you a goodbye present to take back to your country — a nice hardwood full-sized eagle with wings spread that weighs twice your weight allowance and would completely dominate your small sitting room back home. They want it in the group photograph for you to remember them by.

The reason you simply take a wrapped-up gift, say thank you or *wai* or give some sort of sign of acknowledgement, and put it aside unopened is because waxing lyrical about how lovely it is, is to Thai ears very much like saying you want more of the same — and you just might get it! Just regard putting wrapped gifts aside as a convenience. It saves you and the giver embarrassment. You can open such gifts when alone later and have a quiet laugh all on your own. Or maybe there is something really quite nice and expensive — which will no doubt make you wonder what the giver wants out of you, which could be another misinterpretation. Gifts are more often associated with demonstrating appreciation for things in the past than actively seeking future favours.

You do not send little notes saying how much you liked the painting of two fish fighting, even if you did. Indeed, you probably will never mention it, and this might be just as well.

A very different kind of gift is that which comes in a white envelope, either left on your desk or passed through your assistant. Such really should be opened when alone. This really could be a gift given in expectation of reciprocal favour.

The non-Thai should also be aware that giving gifts can serve a major function of neutralising animosity in Thai society. If, in spite of all the warnings in this book, you do let rip with a publicly unacceptable or personally insulting statement or action, apologies alone are unlikely to heal the rift; a nice present, sincerely given, just might do so. If the "excuse me" present works, normal relations will be established and there is no need to go into the embarrassment for both sides of a formal *khor thort* (excuse me/please punish me) and a formal *yok thort* (acceptance of the excuse/lifting of any punishment). If the present is refused, no amount of verbal excuse is likely to have any effect. The value of such a present should fit both the gravity of the social "insult" and the status or power of the recipient. It can therefore be as small as a box of chocolates or a bottle of Black Label or as high as a 3-baht (weight) necklace. Money is not generally acceptable as an excuse-me present, unless you have insulted a policeman or a government official. If you have seriously done something very naughty, don't delay in trying to make amends.

Bottom line:
When receiving gifts, don't necessarily read too much into them. There are categories of gifts that do require some serious thought, but generally don't expect too much or think too much and you will not be disappointed.

04

On Acting on Anger

In Thailand, anger is either suppressed in the interests of conflict avoidance (90 per cent of the time), or acted upon. Far less frequently is it expressed. But even if not expressed or publicly evident, anger may be felt, and felt for somewhat different reasons than in the West, acted upon differently, and expressed if at all in very different ways. In all societies, anger indicates a feeling of injustice. The Thai deals with this privately, the *farang* more often goes public with an expression of the feelings that victims of injustice suffer, and often continues in the public arena with an act to redress the perceived injustice.

The Thai may be simmering through with anger but keeps cool while revenge is planned, privately, and executed, privately or if necessary in public. In 99 per cent of cases, to leap to public violence would cause a huge loss of face to the Thai, whether the anger was justified or not. For many foreigners, on the other hand, some well-aimed insults followed up with a fist in the face might — as long as the face was not on a person clearly unable to retaliate — be seen as a public resolution of the problem, an expression of anger felt, and a point-gaining defence of honour. Perhaps okay in your country, almost certainly not in Thailand.

Different responses are partly cultural. "Private" does not always mean the same thing for Thai and *farang*. The private "internalisation" of feelings of injustice is, for a Thai, quite likely to be discussed with Mother or another significant influence. The Thai Mother is an escape valve for the emotions. Few *farang* have such an escape valve, and many would think of it as childish or sissy to run to mummy with their problems. For the *farang*, who more often than not prides himself on independence of decision and the ability to stand alone against the tide, keeping things private often means keeping things pent up within the head and heart. The *farang* who has "nothing to hide" is much quicker to "go public" with his feelings and actions.

Although the Thai rarely gets angry if the public street outside his front door is dirty, visitors should take off their shoes when coming into the Thai's private world. Even soldiers and tanks in the streets are not going to raise too much concern as long as there are no soldiers in the Thai's living room, and no threat to his family. The *farang* thinks the Thai too tolerant of public wrongs. The Thai often cannot understand why the *farang* is getting all steamed up over something that may concern him only in passing.

Two cups of coffee in a row, brought cold to his table, could blow a fuse in a *farang* head — unless, of course, that head is a wise old English head, which can tolerate ten cups of cold coffee rather than cause a fuss. On the other hand, even the polite English gentleman might get incensed at something a Thai would likely shrug off. Simple contravention of the code of the road is often enough for the *farang* to feel *personal* anger: a car passing another on the wrong side, or coming out of a turning a little close, or whizzing over a zebra crossing. The Thai is not likely to hoot, give chase and force his adversary to a halt. If he noticed, a shrug of the shoulders and a comment to his passenger would be the extent of expression. There is unlikely to be any personal insult felt and therefore no face to retrieve. The *farang* car-chaser, inevitably a big guy who does 99 press-ups each morning but can only roger his wife on Saturday, would be out to humiliate his adversary, who saves himself from violence only by abject and public apology. Even then the offender is likely to get a very loud verbal warning never to travel this road again, and a kick in the right wing of his car instead of a punch in the face. *Farang* adversaries are usually men, and violence will be much more likely if either's or both's girlfriends or wives are present.

Thai road habits are changing with the introduction of compulsory insurance on motor vehicles. A few years ago, accidents were settled in the first instance by Thai drivers themselves. There was a general principle, not based on any reason or substantive logic, that the car driver was responsible for the damage and injuries to a pedestrian, bicyclist or motorcyclist. He was bigger, superficially richer and should have taken more care of little people. It was, just a few years back, cheaper to run down and kill than to run down and maim. Kill, and the family of the deceased would accept monetary compensation to an amount pretty well established and that was that. Cripple, and the driver could be responsible for the crippled for life, in addition to huge hospital bills. Insurance companies are now, like those anywhere in the world, keen to apportion objective blame.

Thais will feel every bit as angry as the *farang* at being slighted, being passed over for promotion, or losing a lover to a rival. Expression of such anger is governed by the *jai yen* philosophy. True feelings are kept under wraps, especially if the anger is felt towards a person of superior social position. Revenge might be such a long time coming that the rival has forgotten the reason for it. It might, in the meantime, be expressed through use of charms, potions and manipulations of black magic, still very prevalent in Thai society. Should the adversary fall sick or have any sort of bad luck during this time, that might be enough to satisfy the injured party that the laws of *ka'ma* or the manipulation of magic has taken its course and justice has been done. If not, accidents can be arranged, premises might suddenly blow up or catch fire, and, as a final recourse, there is the professional lone avenger from Petburi.

The foreigner intending not only to survive but to climb up the social ladder in Thailand will need to look to his temper. There are times to show anger, but this is a skill that needs lots of practice if it is to result in action rather than aggression avoidance or a complete freeze-up. Get it into your head that you are never going to show anger to those of senior social standing, even if they have caused you the most serious inconvenience or heartache. There are other ways of getting even. And sometimes you might happily forego the getting-even stage if the big man, heartened by your generosity and arse-licking when other *farang* might have been shouting through the roof, puts some goodies your way and invites you to dinner at his club — at which invitation you jump to attend, no matter what you think of him and no matter how much swallowing his food will give you indigestion.

Showing measured anger to those of lesser social standing than yourself can be productive, but it must remain constrained. The gloves stay on. Try to give the impression, which is not going to be hard to do, that you are bottling up a volcano of anger — you have it under control but it might blow at any minute, *unless* the airline check-in clerk gets you onto the plane that his airline has over-booked. Very low growls, like distant rumblings of a tsunami about to break over everything, are perfectly appropriate. And when he does get you on, you are all smiles, he is an excellent fellow, you will write commending the service, so could you have his name?

You manipulate people, they manipulate you. This is the way it works. Reasoning has a place, but not much of one compared to other factors. Be careful of showing anger to the big man because he has the power to crush you. Be constrained, as brief as possible, and avoid personal criticism in the anger expressed to the little man or woman. Some people are beyond the expression of any anger — the bar girl who nicks $100 from your shirt pocket, the taxi driver who gets so lost you have to get out and take another taxi. All people can suddenly snap. Deal with the bar girl cleverly and in private, making sure there are no sharp implements on hand. If you can get your money back without force, maybe that is victory enough (maybe even half the money back...?). Making enemies for life, even if you never intend to return to the scene of confrontation, is very bad policy. Bad Thai pennies always turn up, and they turn up in the *farang* world. Thailand is not a particularly violent society as things go on the world stage, but the Thais are proud people. They can swallow their pride when necessary, but it will eat away at their insides... until it finds a way out. Try to be elsewhere when it does.

Bottom line:
Lose your cool, lose your face, lose the battle, lose your life. Keep your cool, keep your face, win the battle, advance your life.

05

On Arse-licking for Beginners

Licking arse, or to put it another way, exaggerated deferential behaviour, is one of the cardinal procedures of social advancement in Thai society and you must perfect both performance and reception of this act.

It is of the utmost importance to lick the right arse and to have the right kind of people queuing up to lick yours. Indiscrimination in this most important of social actions will relegate you to the poignant ranks of those forever licking, with no real chance of ever licking your way to the top. Which is fine if you want it that way.

The licking of arse is comparable to the pecking order of chickens, but unlike the situation with chickens, no pecking takes place from top downwards. All actions of ingratiation are bottom up — quite literally so in some cases. This is indeed what lifts the human society above that of the animal equivalent. Only the number A-one chicken has no other chicken pecking a hole in his head, until of course his place in the Politburo and Central Committee is taken by another. The Z-10 chicken at the bottom of the ladder has nobody to peck at. Human beings, on the other hand, may democratically lick their way upwards from the very bottom of the stack, and almost before they know it, they will be basking in received ingratiation.

There is no direct reciprocity in licking arse. When someone licks your arse, you do not lick his or her arse in return. This principle is found throughout Thai social structure, and not just because direct reciprocity would involve advanced yogic configurations. You pay for your insubordinates, your superior pays for you. Your insubordinates initiate all routine social encounters: they smile first, they are the first to raise their hands in a *wai*, they initiate dialogue with questions designed to penetrate your intellect and demonstrate your superiority, "Why you come Thailand?" Learn how to grovel by studying those who grovel to you; repeat the performance to your superior on the social ladder.

While the bar hostess might tell you, "You number one", or "You number ten", depending on the overflow from your wallet, the whole of Thailand is really numbered from 1 to 63 million. You are a foreigner with more money than most of the 63 million, even if you have little else going for you. So, you do not fit in at the very bottom. When it comes to

licking arse however, the bottom is a very good place to start. Doing so will help you determine your placement number with the smallest amount of offence to those of superior ranking to you. You can do this exercise with a minimum of Thai language. Watch for the deferential actions: the *wai*, the stooping pass of body, the handover of objects, the order of walking, talking and decision making. Watch for the agreement with everything you say and the unbridled praise of everything about you. And as you begin to feel confidence in your superiority, even if it is costing you money, notice at which points in the world around you the cracks appear. The much repeated *khrap* is replaced by *urh* as an agreement with what you say. The social manners of deference begin to reverse. You find yourself waiting for the familiar signals to come, then do them yourself and receive acknowledgement. You have found your level.

Patterns of deference are complicated by friendship. See the same Thai two or three times and familiarity breeds a softening of deference. But it is still there. The smiles come almost at the same time, but not quite at the same time.

Bottom line:
If, at first, getting ahead seems an impossibility, console yourself with the thought that there are only 63 million between you and the zenith.

06

On Arse-licking for the Advanced Practitioner

Having found your level in the Thai order of things, notice that it has a very flexible relationship to friendship. While you will not want to be friends with the scum of the earth and while you will not be acceptable as a real friend at the other extreme (the one you are trying to get to), be aware that the two extremes do interact. The Thai system is not a simple pecking order. And while deference is always there, and always proceeds from below, a social group — a *puak* — may contain the big boss and his driver; and if the driver or the driver's job is threatened, the big man will intercede to protect him. The big man is the patron of the small man; the small man gets protection from above and will jump whichever way the big man decides — almost.

This is very important for you to know. Being within a *puak* is a way for social advancement. When evaluating a prospective *puak*, look at the top person within it. More often than not, he is the one who pays and the one who appears to ignore all Thai norms of social etiquette, turning up at a luncheon in shorts and a baseball cap when everybody else had polished their shoes before coming. While impersonation may be a form of flattery, do not model yourself on this big man, but defer to him. Should you find he defers to you, especially when the time comes to pay, consider changing your *puak*. But don't throw away links you have made, even after you have outgrown them. Thai *puak* are like the ripples on a village pond when the rain begins to fall. They overlap and change with the weather. The top man in one may be the middle man in one other and the lowest member of yet another. So, you do not have to leave one group to join another — just try to remember where you are in each group.

Your advance will depend on more than simple deference to the big man, although he will be inclined to support you and say nice things about you if you do the same for him. To this extent reciprocity is direct. Material and social opportunity may come your way through such association, without any of you belonging to the Masons.

As you get into things, the various gestures and language, which of course will have to be Thai (although a Chinese dialect has its uses), become second nature. This presents another danger to the dedicated social climber. You may find you plateau out at a level where you feel comfortable. Well, plenty of Thais do exactly that. You can too if that's what you want. But, as long as your behaviour is publicly acceptable and you remain a decent chap, you can't help but advance, albeit more slowly than you might have hoped at first. As you grow in kinship relations, age, and social connections, a slow advance within the system is almost inevitable — even if you want to stay where you are. Wealth too helps a lot; even if yours stays static, you can't avoid some sort of social advance, just by being around and not offending anybody. The licking of arse continues, but becomes second nature.

Some occupations and honorary positions come equipped with a high status, even if the salary is low. Teachers, for example, command a very high level of respect. They get called by the same name as monks — *ajarn* — and they may ride a bicycle but their status is in situational terms, probably the same as a businessman who drives a Mercedes. Their students will lick the arse of any *ajarn*, within the teaching situation and outside of it. This only applies on a society-wide basis if somebody knows you are an *ajarn*. Many Thai *ajarn*, especially those teaching at university level, will have a high education and traditionally would come from an established and wealthy family. Thus, there are complex reasons for their status that go beyond standing in front of a blackboard. Down on their luck *farang* teaching English and hanging from bus straps do not get the same status, although within the classroom some expression of it may be apparent on a superficial level. And if they wear a clean white shirt, have tidy hair and act in a Thai way, these superficial aspects of respect may increase. But unless you have substantial means — which probably means you will not be teaching English — such occupations are most unlikely to give you a head start on the status ladder. Honorary Consuls fare rather better, with many Thai business men and organisations only too happy to be associated, even in a lopsided way, with a foreign embassy. If you do have such a title, or an academic prefix like Dr, use it on your business or visiting card. It's all part of the package, and we do have to package you as well as possible if you are to get anywhere at all in the Thai status stakes.

One word of caution on your way to the top. A few of those who have advanced reasonably in the art of arse-licking find, often much to their surprise, that they enjoy the humility that comes from licking arse more than the esteem that comes from having one's arse licked. Thus there is a masochistic element in the process. If you feel this coming on, don't worry, but don't get too carried away and forget which way you are going. Of course, if you want to go the other way, that's okay too. But, heaven forbid that you are seen as a deviant. Thus, if a masochist at heart, try to bridle your enthusiasm a bit.

Over-enthusiastic licking down when you should be licking up could smack of sarcasm and therefore come across as sadism rather than masochism. The paradox is that these over-enthusiastic arse-lickers often make it through to higher levels of society in spite of themselves. It seems there is no point at which the licking has to stop. Like most things, the more you enjoy it, the better you do it, and the better you do it, the further you go.

Bottom line:
If arse-licking is your forte, turn the other cheek. It is more blessed to receive than to give.

07

On Assassination and Conflict Avoidance

This book might serve very little purpose if the reader were to get rubbed out as he or she walked out the front door of the bookshop with the tome flicked but unread, tucked under an armpit. Although, looking on the bright side, we must admit that the royalties to the author at purchase would be the same and a very clean second-hand copy would be made available to the public, reducing the publisher's immediate print runs perhaps but assisting in the preservation of forests. On the even brighter side, if the rubbed-out would-be reader were a person of some note, the assassination might merit some free widespread publicity resulting in a rush to buy and read what was so thoughtfully tucked under the armpit of the assassinee at the moment the fatal bullet struck home.

So, there are definite pros and cons to keeping you alive. But on the whole, you are probably not of rubbing-out publicity status, and be you ever so influential, and adequately alive, you might actually recommend the book to your upwardly mobile friends. Thus, after due thought and reflection, and in full recognition that most if not all assassinations are 50 per cent accidental, the author has come down on the side of saving a reader or two from a premature rebirth. This warning piece will therefore be slipped in at the front somewhere, presuming that most readers of English tackle a book from the front to the back, and glance at the first few pages before they part with their cash. This is quite a presumption, considering this book has an alphabetical format; indeed, there is a natural inclination on the part of the bookshop-flicker to thumb through the back pages and to look for what the author found to put under the letter Z. Well, you can try that, but the substantive substance of the book, as well as the English alphabet, leads up quite cunningly to the *Zenith*. But you won't get to that zenith if you are going to be terribly *farang* and spend your time with this book looking for things to criticise, and enjoy it only if you can find fault in it. Why you should do that, I don't know. Do you? Isn't it enough that I am trying to keep you alive... *and* help you prosper?

Be assured, wary reader, that Bangkok is not an assassin's playground any more than, say, Central Park in New York. In fact, Bangkok has been called the safest place in the City of Angels. So, not to worry.

Assassination is best seen as a part of life, admittedly a rather extreme and final part. Like military coups, assassinations exist as an ideal more than a reality. Without them the rest of existence wouldn't have quite the same meaning. I suppose I have to explain that. Life, marriage, business, diplomacy and war trundle along quite nicely most of the time, and as long as there is mutual gain and exploitation, there is a willingness to compromise and contain aggressive instincts in the name of common wealth, as long as everyone feels they are getting a bit ahead of everybody else. That's the encouraging carrot — upward mobility. The opposite state is not so much downward mobility, which is reversible, but assassination, which is lateral immobility. Assassination, or the possibility of it, stops you becoming too bored with trundling along... and keeps you on your toes. Have you really *never* dreamed — when standing on a crowded pier on the

River of Kings, side by side with a nagging spouse or a misery-making boss, almost lost in the crowd as the river bus churns its back towards you and the waiting multitude —+have you *never* dreamed of a simple, unperceived, hate-driven knee to the thigh and a follow-up prod to the kidneys? And as the well-insured partner or the boss whose chair you will inherit trips into the whirling propellers, you, the poor, traumatised, dumbstruck survivor emits a barely audible, "Oh dear. Help, help." Just dreams of course, but far from idle ones.

Given such dreams, you will readily appreciate the importance of trust. Trust is oft said to be the real stuff of marriage and business. Fair enough. Both institutions have contractual agreements associated with them, but given that contracts are broken well over 50 per cent of the time, one might as well rely on trust. In the nature of the beast, trust only grows through time. Unfortunately, *all* things that grow over time contain the seeds of their own destruction. Trust can grow to fruition over years or generations and vanish quicker than you can say in Thai, *yet mae.* So, if you are going to move upwards, but not towards the saints, do not *really* put your faith in trust.

When trust flies out the window and all *appears* lost in the winds of suspicion, hostility and violence, all is not *quite* lost. Two options remain to you: suicide and assassination. Even if you happen to be Japanese and feel a natural proclivity towards the first option, be informed that in your new circle of Thais and Thailand, it will gain you no points at all. Suicide is therefore not recommended for the average upwardly mobile foreigner. (Suicide must never be confused with Assassination; see the "suicide" section under letter S.) Assuming, for the moment that suicide is a way out of society and not a way into it, and that you have an interest in getting ahead in Thailand, assassination might be the only real alternative that can earn you points. It is, of course, a double-edged sword and, if you are to gain points *and* be around to benefit from them, it must be handled with extreme care.

Some of the most revered people on earth have been assassinated. Such individuals achieve the pinnacle of status. If that is your aim in life, fine; martyrdom will carry you that extra mile into the league of immortals who have a pretty indefinite hold on the ranks next to god. But, to get into that most exclusive of clubs ever, you have to be already at the Social Zenith at the time of being assassinated, so timing is everything: too early and, quite frankly my dear, nobody will give a damn; too late and you will have passed your prime and be on the way down, and if anybody bothers to assassinate you, it will be almost an act of charity.

If faced with the choice between suicide and assassination, you will, having a basic grasp of economics and not having an exceptionally generous and liberal insurance policy (at least not one known to your trusted beneficiary), readily appreciate the cost-benefits of making a killing of another than yourself. At a stroke, it can remove the major source of competition and thereby invoke good fortune. It is also, in Thailand, much cheaper than in the more industrialised countries — although of course, nothing these days is as cheap as it used to be — and it leaves the cleaning up to people other than your beloved family and friends, even if one of those beloved individuals is the assassin.

Knocking somebody out for keeps is not to be contemplated lightly. That would be immoral. It is not done, therefore, to leave such things until the last moment. The astute man or woman of affairs, like the considerate spouse, will make his or her contingency plans at an early stage in a developing relationship — probably when shaking hands or sniff-kissing a cold cheek over the wet ink on the first or only contract in what promises at the time to be a long and mutually profitable relationship. Such "just in case" planning, while the champagne is still bubbling in the glass, is amoral and logical. It helps avoid the messiness of on-the-spot improvisation, epitomised by the poor husband waking in the middle of the night to find a duck swallowing his member and his wife standing over the scene, red-bladed knife in hand. Like the nuclear deterrent, careful planning assures assassination may never be necessary, while at the same time giving you the chance, if it comes to it, to nuke first rather than last.

The act of assassination has simple and logical ground rules, written down by Machiavelli a few hundred years back and available today at WH Smiths, Borders and other non-terrorist bookshops. Do the deed as quickly as possible after realising that your trust has been broken. Never, ever, do it yourself, no matter what heights of satisfaction you might get from direct involvement. And if more than one nasty piece of work is in your sights, do all your killings at once — they will be sooner forgotten and, more importantly, there will be nobody around to get back at you.

The deed itself follows a well-tested, if somewhat unimaginative, formula, at least where business or political rivals are concerned. A hired gunman from the beautiful little town of Petburi draws up on a motorcycle alongside the target's traffic-bound Benz. At that precise time you are alibied up to the hair-tips at the sixtieth birthday party of the most influential person you know. Or, if you want a nice safe place a couple of hours away from the action, try Petburi town itself; gunmen never dirty their own doorsteps.

Red-light assassinations have been greatly aided by the introduction of count-down traffic lights. Now as the red numbers drop, 5... 4... 3... 2, the Man from Petburi coolly pulls his gun from his shirt and sprays the target, driver and anybody who happens to be in the way.

The hit man spends years in training in darkened rooms. This allows him to see, aim and shoot with great accuracy. This is essential given the usual brightness of a Thailand day and the total obscurity of black glass windows on a big man's Benz, an obscurity multiplied by the gunman's own shades, thoughtfully mirrored on the outside to give the victim a final view of himself. This view should be one of surprise.

If invited to ride with a big man in the deep soft amber leather of his deep black automobile, you won't turn down the offer, as rubbing shoulders with quality is the only way some of it might rub off onto you. Worth a good few points, but not worth dying for. Do not say you'd rather take the sky-train. Take instead a few precautions.

In Thailand, vehicles usually drive on the left. This regulation is very flexibly interpreted by buses and motorcycles. You are very unlikely to be ambushed by a bus. Buses are very rarely seen snaking in and around traffic and positioning themselves for the perfect kill. Look out for the gunman, therefore, on a motorcycle. Not a Harley-Davidson or even a Honda Gold Wing, nothing fancy — the gunman does not measure status in the same terms as you. Along with his training in night vision, the gunman has learnt to blend into the herds of motorcycles, fully aware that the best place to hide a book is in a library. He has also learnt the basics of protocol. Thus he is fully aware that drivers pull into the left-hand side of the road to load and unload their big men or big women, who therefore occupy the kerb-side rear of the vehicle. While drivers might vary their routes and times in the interests of security, in-car seating-status habits are rigidly adhered to. This is fine, as long as you are sitting offside. You may get a few small shards of window glass and a good smattering of blood, but these are invaluable status enhancers, so make sure you do not clean up before the TV cameras arrive. Indeed, it is worth keeping the numbers of a few cameramen on your mobile phone and ringing them as soon as you can get your head up off the floor. As a short-cut to attention-seeking status building, being cheek-in-jowl with an important assassinee at the moment of demise rates very highly, as you will become aware if and when released from police questioning.

Bottom line:

What, you might ask, does assassination, which sounds pretty much like the epitome of conflict, have to do with conflict avoidance? Well, I can understand you asking that question: you are still seeing things in the farang way. In time, indeed by the time you have read this book, you will understand that assassination is in fact conflict avoidance taken to the extreme. After all, a fellow cannot conflict with you if he has just been shot between the eyes.

08

On Avoiding Avoidance

If you find Thais avoiding you, it probably has nothing to do with your toothpaste or deodorant — although it might just be that simple, so check first that you are reasonably clean; a shit, shower, shave and a clean shirt can sometimes do wonders for your status.

Thai tolerance allows almost anything except affronts to Buddhism and the monarchy. Tolerance is *not* the same as approval. The Thai may disapprove strongly but will rarely interfere in the life of others, particularly if they are not family members and even more particularly if they are strangers who pass in the night. The main weapon a Thai uses to cope with what he or she does not like or understand is avoidance. If you find Thais, one of the most gregarious people in the world, avoiding you, you have to ask yourself, very seriously, why. Not much point in thinking you can integrate into and prosper in the Thai social system if the Thais, or at least those Thais you want to impress, are avoiding you. So, what's your problem?

Are you developing a bad reputation? You might be the last to know. You might even think that you are doing everything correctly and enjoy many things about living in Thailand. But if Thais are avoiding you to the point of not wanting any social interaction, even a chit-chat as you pass in the street, something is wrong. And since we cannot blame an entire people, something must be wrong with you.

What could it be? You will not find out by asking a Thai — if you can find one that will speak to you beyond superficial and bland responses to your overtures. Maybe it's time to look at your behaviour.

• Sex? Not a problem in itself. Although many foreigners get quite the wrong idea regarding Thai attitudes to prostitution and playing around. Repeated public offences will be enough to encourage avoidance. There is a place for everything and some discretion is appropriate. Thailand is not a promiscuous society, neither is it really a macho society.

• Meanness? Did you invite your neighbours out for dinner and not pay the bill? Or worse still, pay only your part of it?

• Conflict? We all know that Thais are masters at conflict avoidance and the best way of avoiding conflict is to avoid aggressive or drunken personalities. You might be surprised that anyone can think of you as aggressive: a brusque accent and manner, quite all right in the north of England, can be enough to make Thais afraid of you. Get into lots of conflict situations and you are no fun to be with — questions of right and wrong do not come into it.

• Boredom? You would need to be extremely boring for the Thais to notice. But some *farang*, with their thoroughly intellectual questioning of everything, dialectical conversation and extended world-view, do manage to bore the Thais, while the simple soul from a Belgian chocolate factory, who is constantly offering Thais his *khwai* to eat, may be considered lots of fun.

• All of the above plus some?

Thais are great gossips and even if you have done nothing terribly wrong, an accumulation of minor faults can give grist to the mill of a Thai, perhaps a member of the opposite sex, who doesn't like you. Without going over the hill into paranoia, is there anybody out there who particularly dislikes you? Are you sure?

What to do to recover from the situation? That's not so easy. Time may heal all wounds, but time can be awfully elastic in Thailand and even if you behave impeccably from now on in, it might take forever just to get back to square one — and that's not your objective at all. By far the best way of avoiding this dilemma is to *avoid* avoidance. This means conforming to Thai ways and standards from the off. Remedial action such as buying your way back in is possible but is not guaranteed and cannot be done more than once or twice.

Bottom line:

If you want to be respected in Thai society, respect Thai ways from the start. Bide your time, do not appear too ambitious. Do not strike while the iron, or anything else, is hot. In Thailand, cool is better.

09

On Becoming a Walking ATM Machine

On becoming a walking ATM machine, you become available to all Thais on the very edge of Thai society. They may poke their numbers into your mouth, nostrils and eyes, press enter and collect the money. If the ATM does not pay out, they may try giving it a kick or two before moving onto another ATM machine that works the way they think it should.

This is not correct behaviour. Both Thai and ATM are at fault. It is behaviour which has nothing to do with social climbing. Paying through the nose in this way creates no real patron-client relationships. It almost certainly results from some form of prostitution. Those Thais who use you in this way are simply exacting exaggerated payments for their services when you used them. They also make your life very boring; you have better — and cheaper — things to do and better and more interesting Thais to meet. It is only too easy for a foreigner to enter a *puak* of such people, but this is a *puak* likely to overlap with *puaks* of police and criminals. Close the ATM and the group will disappear. Members of it will be back periodically as individuals to see if you have changed your mind, but eventually you will be well rid of them. If you want to stay precisely where you are in terms of social status, marry one, or establish a fixed relationship with one. That one will most likely keep away the rest, but this will not help you at all in terms of status, since he or she will tend to keep everybody away.

Many foreigners get the impression that all Thais will do anything for money. Indeed, this is why many come to Thailand. It is true that a large number of Thais will provide sexual services in exchange for money. It is not true that they will do *anything* for money. They may indeed sell their little sister or brother, as they might themselves have been sold earlier, but they will do nothing to hurt or offend their mother. Neither are they likely to do much, apart perhaps from trafficking the occasional Buddha image or artefact, to offend Buddhism. For them, as for just about all Thais, mother and religion are the paths to status within their communities — which usually exist a long way from the temporary anything-goes groups to which they belong and into which you may so easily buy your way in the urban environment.

The money spent on good Thais — paying for dinner and the occasional *thio*, little pocket-money type gifts, that sort of thing, no paying through the nose — should not be confused with abuse of the foreigner as an ATM machine. Of course, if you do develop romantic attachments, you can expect to give a series of presents, starting small and getting bigger, to girl/boy and mother. These are reasonably institutionalised and, in theory at least, are to establish a basis for a lifetime together. To confound these payments with the money given to a whore is to make a grave mistake — but many a foreigner does just that.

> *Bottom line:*
> *If you are being used as a walking ATM and feel you are not getting your money's worth, there is something wrong. Hang a sign on your nose saying sia, "Out of Service", and see what happens.*

10

On Behaving Badly

Going out every night, getting drunk in your own neighbourhood, picking up an obvious sex partner, walking back arm-in-arm, fondling her or him on your doorstep, is behaving badly.

Going out every night, getting drunk in a different neighbourhood, picking up an obvious sex partner, having sex in a private room in a bar or short-time hotel, walking home alone or with a friend of the same sex, arm-in-arm if you like, is behaving well enough.

The difference is not so much a qualitative one as a perceived one. What you do in private is up to you, what you do in public, particularly on your doorstep, goads social judgement by your neighbours, even if you don't know them. In this, Thais are pretty much like most people worldwide — although in Thailand nobody will ever suggest you make too much noise when crashing your car into the lamppost, or even hint that your indiscretions are observed and disapproved.

The great tolerance, for which the Thais are rightly known, is essentially a reaction of non-interference — the safest and surest way to avoid conflict. Nobody cares what a *farang* and a prostitute get up to, just as long as they are not involved. And even if you are invited to a party at your Thai neighbours, and you take along a Thai prostitute, nobody will say a word

— not to your face that is. But you are unlikely to be invited again, and if you invite them, maybe just a couple of the men will come and drink your beer and suggest they get you a girl or a boy. A bit like Goose Green back home really, except for the last bit.

So, with your Thai friends or on your own, play away or under wraps. People will say what an upstanding person you are. Even the wife of the big man you were in the massage parlour with will say you are a *khon dii*.

> *Bottom line:*
> *Play away from home, be tactful, careful, watchful, alert, vigilant, guarded, wary, precautious, respectful, and fun to be with and you really can do no wrong — if you can do anything at all.*

11

On Being Alone and Loneliness

However much you might scream to be left in peace, the Thais know you don't really mean it. They know you really want to be with them. A person alone is to be pitied. It can, of course, happen that even a Thai will find him or herself alone on unfortunate occasions. But even going to the toilet in a restaurant is best done with a friend. Being alone is simply not Thai. Eat alone and the food, however fancy and expensive, Thai or *farang*, is not tasty. Live alone and who will squeeze spots from your skin and who will pluck unwanted hairs from your nose? The most inner-looking and meditative of Thais wear saffron robes and renounce the temporary pleasures of life — but how often do you see a monk alone?

If a person alone is contrary to the social norm and, in a Thai way, to be pitied, a person who *wants* to be alone is a danger to society. To the average Thai mind, there is definitely something deviant about a person living alone and wanting to do so. You need not rush into marriage or a monastery — well, not immediately — but being alone, even if you are a number one great guy or girl and gay as they come, is in itself something of a negative and loses you points at each turn. If you try to avoid losing points by avoiding turns, you travel in a straight line, and going straight in Thailand is extremely difficult for a butterfly; quite apart from the fact that going straight from A to B is the most dangerous thing you can do when the spirits are abroad and waiting to jump into somebody who doesn't have the sense to twist and turn.

Fortunately, the Thais will be only too happy to help you out of the miserable state you got yourself into. This is not to say that all of them, or even any of them, will be your real friend, but most of them will, if given the chance, be your companion. Just as the Thais say: "Eat alone and the food is not tasty", so they say: "A friend to eat with is easily found, a friend unto death is rare indeed". Fortunately, to build your status in the Land of Smiles, you need companions to eat with rather than friends unto death. And almost any companion is better than none. Almost.

If you're intent on building your status in Thailand and integrating into Thai society, spend as little time alone as possible. You cannot award yourself social status points: by their nature, such non-subjectives are awarded by others. Being alone all the time is not neutral, it is a socially negative act. So mingle. Unless you mingle, you will have no hope of mingling well. And even the lowly play a role in your grandeur. You need somebody to recognise that you are better than them.

You may be surrounded by Thais, but through no fault of theirs or of yours, you may feel lonely. Something more than homesickness or culture shock is involved. You miss meaningful interaction in your own language. You might be in a better position than a Thai in your country in that you can watch the news and occasional movies in English, French or German, use the Internet in your language, get European food quite easily, and a daily newspaper in English. But you do most of these things on your own and can't talk about what is happening in the world with anybody apart from maybe a few other foreigners. Your best friends are likely not to be Thai but people from your own country or those who share a common native tongue. But the foreign community is constantly changing, so maintaining real friendships among those who share your background and likes is also difficult, particularly if your spouse doesn't really like the spouse of your friend, or vice versa. You don't dislike Thais, in fact you like them, but you miss real friendship and all that goes with it. At the same time, what used to interest and excite you in Thailand has become quotidian and may be as boring as anything back home. In the end, you feel not so much alone, but lonely.

This can be a dangerous situation. A surprising number of foreigners commit suicide, or are reported as having committed suicide. Many of those have spent years in the country, appear to have integrated into Thailand well, perhaps entering the monkhood, marrying a Thai and having Thai children, even taking on Thai nationality and feeling at home in the Thai language, even those who are respected by Thais and know that they would be unhappy if they left Thailand.

I'M ALWAYS ALONE DOCTOR

A parallel may be drawn with the main character in George Orwell's *Burmese Days*. That British Businessman, after many years in the East, overcomes the *orientalism* through which many Europeans saw and interpreted the East; he steps out of the colonial view and is sympathetic to the "natives". At the same time the "natives" all around him (Burmese of course, not Thai) are far from the beautiful Orientals of tropical dreams and fantasies; in fact, almost all seem to have as many failings — greed, corruption, immorality thinly covered by surface morality — as their colonial masters. The story ends with this sympathetic and understanding Englishman shooting his dog before killing himself. Now, *this definitely is **not** recommended as a final solution.* I happen to like dogs.

There is no glib answer to cope with this situation. Often, by the time real loneliness and depression hit home, you have burnt the bridges that connect you with the home country. Your money, your way of life and even your family is in Thailand, and *you* are in Thailand, probably to stay. It's not that you have any illusions that there are better places to be, it's just that you feel lonely. If this is your case, there is really little to be done about it except to confirm that you are likely to feel even lonelier back home and to suggest that you rekindle your interest in Thailand and try to come to terms with the Thais as they really are, no better and no worse than they are.

If all this sounds rather depressingly familiar, you have perhaps plateaued out socially. Maybe you think you have done whatever there was to do and only old age, sickness and death await you. This is *never* really the case, even if you *are* old, sick and will die sooner rather than later. It is perhaps time to pass a new threshold and really *think* Thai to jog yourself out of the sort of depressive state of mind into which Thais are less likely to fall and which, even if they really like you, they will find hard to understand. If you find yourself withdrawing into general scepticism about Thailand, the Thais are likely to think you don't like them. But the really important thing at this stage is not for the Thais to understand the way you feel. Thais have words for depression, but no special medicine for it. You have to learn to laugh at yourself. Laughter really is the best medicine. It is extremely hard to kill yourself when you are laughing, as long as you are not playing with loaded guns or primed hand grenades, or walking across Sukhumvit without a care for the traffic.

It sounds facile trite, but count your blessings not your regrets or misfortunes. And if you are not comfortable in your rut, change it for another rut. Thai society may be boringly homogeneous in many ways, but it does allow individuality, so work on that aspect and rebuild your individuality within the Thai structure. If Buddhism and reincarnation require too much faith, try reading up on existentialism. It allows for the fact that social paths may be so wide that at times whole nations can lose their way, and that at other times, the path towards personal understanding is so narrow that each must walk alone. There is a difference between the intellectual dogma of Thai Buddhism and Western existentialism, but maybe not that much. In the end, both teach that you have a choice, that you have responsibility for your actions, and that you may, if you wish, choose to be alone. It's all up to you. If you are happy to be alone, you are a rare individual. For most people, anywhere in the world, one thing is true: the more you spend time alone, the lonelier you will become.

Bottom line:
Alone, you are always in bad company — although there is always worse.

12

On Being Invited to Eat

"*Gin khao!*" Come eat, they say as you pass by, but don't mean it. "*Gin layo!*" Already eaten, you say but don't mean and turn into a restaurant for your lunch. Just social convention. Just saying "Hi". When people are passing by, they almost *have* to say something to people they know, even if they don't know names and have barely interacted socially. "Hot, isn't it?", "Dusty", anything will do, but something to do with eating is the most usual.

When people really want to invite you to eat, they often say nothing at all. You don't have to be a mind reader. Convention has it that if somebody invites you to their home, they feed the guest, or at very least have food available to feed the guest. Usually on such occasions, the food will be set out, or brought out without asking you, and placed in front of you. It is polite not to begin until the host says the token *gin khao*; no formality, this is like an English speaker saying "tuck in". It's also polite to say you are full, *im layo*, a bit before you really are, so that the host can urge you to eat more and you can do so. Leave a bit on your plate, or a good host will keep filling it up.

While on the subject of table manners, here are a few other bits and pieces to help you make a good impression — which has a lot to do with getting on in Thailand.

First, never step over food or people. This is easier to do than you might think if eating at floor level. It's fine to take a break and go to the toilet — no taboo against saying you want a pee-pee — just walk around people, not through them.

Second, say *bon appetite*. The English-speaking world doesn't have a phrase for it and has to use French, but very often doesn't say anything at all — exactly the same with Thais.

Third, there is no real order to eating and everything is usually brought out at once, or whatever happens to be cooked and ready first is brought first. You just take from anywhere. Soup is served along with the rest. There might or might not be a sweet, served after; if there is, this is more a Bangkok/Western influence. Central Thailand's excellent sweet dishes have now spread everywhere, but it is still rare for people to include a dessert in daily fare. Sometimes people eating in a small group at home will go out for the sweet.

Fourth, it is fully in order to say the food is *aroy*, tasty. And if you don't say it quickly enough, or often enough, someone will ask if you like it.

Fifthly, Thais do not normally drink alcohol with their food at home, but when a guest is present they might offer some beer. If not, it's water or water with coloured syrup in it.

Sixth, not obligatory but on parting, you can thank the host for the excellent food. This does carry none too subtle indications that you would like some more of it sometime, but in this circumstance that is okay.

Okay, that's the easy bit. When you invite Thais to *your* house, don't just sit them down with a drink and a packet of peanuts in a bowl. If you do, they will wait for the food to come. They might wait a very long time and go home hungry, wondering why you bothered to invite them when you are such a cheapskate. Inviting for drinks alone just doesn't work. If you can't get something in for people to eat, invite them to a restaurant — Thais do all the time.

When inviting a big man you are trying to impress to your house, think not only of the food but of the other guests. They should ideally not be of higher status than your guest of honour, but certainly should not all be too low. If He really is big, don't be offended if He doesn't stay long and maybe doesn't eat more than a token; He has graced you with His presence. His coming will impress the others, but you might all feel something of a collective relief when He has gone.

Bottom line:
Compared to other cultures, eating with Thais is very simple and should be relaxed, with nothing obligatory and little really taboo. At the same time, the status of the host is involved in the quantity and quality of food, and making a relaxed atmosphere can sometimes be hard work.

13

On Being Sworn At

It won't happen every day, and indeed hopefully it will never happen at all, but it might. In spite of your praiseworthy efforts to toe the Thai line, bestow gracious smiles on those below you, not lust after your neighbour's wife or your neighbour, keep your cool when your heart is pumping red hot venom, and read *CultureShock! Thailand* every day of your life, some bugger will swear at you from the shadows.

You must first be sure you have been sworn at and have not, for example, been invited to taste a piece of cake. No much point in asking your Thai companion, he or she will just say "never mind" and hustle you away none the wiser — although perhaps a whole lot safer. Instead, consult the Words Which Must Not be Said section at the back of this book, which you should carry with you everywhere.

Having determined that you have indeed been sworn at in Thai and not complimented in English on your "he man" stature, do not immediately reach for your shooting iron, or even for your waffle iron, the chances are the man, or indeed the woman, has a death wish and swears at everybody in the hope of being put away for keeps. And why help out somebody who swears at you?

The only appropriate reaction is to stand rigidly to attention and sing at the top of your lungs and in absolutely fluent Thai, the Thai national anthem. This will drown out subsequent swearing, prevent any verbal riposte on your part, and establish you publicly as a jolly good fellow who knows how to behave. If it happens to be eight in the morning or six in the evening, so much the better.

Should the provocations stinging your ears be in the English language, first ensure that they do not come from a *farang* who has fallen through a hole in the road and is simply expressing his general dissatisfaction at his awfully inauspicious *ka'ma*. If it is indeed a Thai, and if indeed the insults are aimed at you and not at the tarty thing in the skimpy see-through and bright red mouth holding your hand, there is one appropriate response that should give you satisfaction and give Nit Noy plenty to talk about at the beauty parlour. Singing the British, American or Australian national anthems, even at the top of your lungs, will have no effect at all. A rapid karate chop to the throat, on the other hand, should bring the vilifications to an immediate end. In case the vilifier might be tempted to raise the ante from the strictly verbal, this can be discouraged by following through

with a sharp knee to the groin. As your detractor sinks to the ground, the flat of your shoe should push him or her onto his or her back before grinding his or her nose into his or her face. You may then allow yourself to break your silence with, "And may that be a lesson to you". Should the vile-mouthed creature under your shoe be a woman, do take care there are no Norwegian Knights of the Round Table in the immediate vicinity. Should there be one, and even if his understanding of Thai plunges the depths of depravities, he will certainly intervene with, "How dare you treat a lady that way?" Resist the temptation to say, "easy".

Should, by chance, you be one of those people who do not have a black belt in the martial arts, or if there is indeed a large Norwegian lurking in the shadows waiting to defend the honour of a damsel in distress, an alternative solution to the problem is to do what your Thai companion suggested and just walk away without a word.

Bottom line:
On being vilified, reasoning that sticks and stones may break my bones but names will never hurt you, will only result in sticks and stones. You must either react with overwhelming force or flee the scene.

14

On Being Told Thais are Quiet People

There is a lot of noise about how quiet Thais are and how a foreigner should whisper in their company to avoid disturbing their finely-tuned yin-yang spiritual balance. True, if you are talking to a big man (or woman) you are trying to impress, talk quieter than him or her. But that's not too difficult since he or she will usually be talking at full volume, punctuating a monologue with shouts into his or her mobile phone. Whatever you have read about it being polite to talk quietly might not have stated that only the social inferior has to be polite to the extent of being practically inaudible. This is because the social inferior has nothing of significance to say. The superior doesn't necessarily rant and rave, although that is up to him. In the immigration office and the police station, it comes close to a loud snapping. You don't snap back, not if you want your visa extended or only a small fine for driving at 200 km an hour in a 30 zone. You bow and, if it is possible to do so in the close confines in which immigration and police choose to work, you scrape. Make sure the only audible word you say is *crap* (aka *khrap) crapom* or, if you happen to be female, *ca-ca.*

Thai officials particularly like to hear foreign women say *ca-ca.* If you are a young and pretty foreign woman, you have all the qualifications needed to get served first, but as compensation for the privilege you have to tell your life story and say how charming Thai officials are. Whatever your sex, you wait until you are snapped at, then move rapidly to the table of the snapping official, taking a chair only if it is indicated by the slightest nod of the head, a grunt, or a wave of a ballpoint pen. Under no circumstances place yourself between the official and his TV, and never suggest he turn the volume down. Continue to speak in an unintelligible whisper, except for those magic words *crap* and *ca*, which can be spoken at near normal volume. The language you speak is immaterial. Continue like this until told to speak louder. Then speak barely audibly until told again to speak louder. Then speak normally, compensating by holding your body at a grovelling 35 degrees.

During your time in Thailand, either at work or play, you will also be faced with the reverse situation: let's say the female student coming to see the professor. While she might be a dedicated follower of fashion out of school, to the point of simulating or even practising sexual freedom within her *puak* and beyond, chances are you will be looking at the top of her head and unable to hear a word said. While it is difficult not to do so when leaning over to try to catch a few words, it is considered opportunist to pick this time to look down the top of the blouse in your search for inverted nipples.

Just about all social interaction in Thailand, at least between Thais, follows the deference system formerly known in Germany as the Leader-principle (*Fuhrerprinzip*). There are some special occasions when polite quietness is maintained, seemingly against all the odds. One of these is on a speeding Bangkok bus, not the quietest of vehicles. There the little boy or girl collecting your fare and expertly chopping your ticket into shreds, will occasionally whisper *pai* (falling tone), which means stop, or *pai* (mid tone), which means go. The driver always discerns the tonal and vowel length difference and acts accordingly, even when the conductor notices there is nobody worth picking up at the stop and says in quick succession *pai (*stop) and *pai* (go). Whether the system could sustain more than two words, neither of them *crap*, is open to question, although nobody has raised the question so far.

You do get marks for speaking softly — no matter if you are unheard and ignored — perhaps more so because you will be the only one who knows how to behave. And if unsure of your Thai, it works wonders, as the addressee will repeat what you possibly said, asking for confirmation. This is not only a free language lesson for you, but the repetition is always a significant improvement on what you actually said, and it is repeated in excellent Thai and very polite. This technique can be used repeatedly in official meetings and seminars. Having a Thai echo your humble mumbles, and interpret them into brilliant pronouncements, is a free service provided to all visitors spending some time in Thailand; and believe it or not, it actually comes with status points given by your hosts with no effort on your part. So, go softly... and never mind the infernal noise.

Bottom line:
Through the thundering traffic, sit quietly and you will hear the tinkling sounds of tiny bells and cymbals keeping time with the steps of dancing girls and hear the soft and plaintive whine of a mor lam *singer. These things exist like a flower blooming deep in the forest. If no human ear witnesses it, it still exists. Pity about the f'ing noise 'though.*

15

On Being Touched Up By a Homosexual in a Hetero Porn Show

On accidentally entering a live show of the most crudely vulgar kind, especially one with a ringed donkey present, go cautiously, aware that you are undoubtedly in the company of visiting nobility from foreign lands, airline executives, leading government personnel, the socially recognised, and people you don't want to rub up the wrong way. You could gingerly back out, not having seen a single face in the dimmed audience lighting, but why miss the chance of showing them you're just as good in the crudity and discretion department as are they?

Seating on such occasions will be horseshoe-shaped to allow performers to enter the circle without groping. Audience-groping of artistes engaged in live acts is indeed considered vulgar in any establishment with seats; although, if you are all closely packed arm-to-arm or even sitting on the floor, and if audience participation is the speciality of the house you are in, a gentle fondle is permitted if a tasty handful comes your way. And you don't have to stretch over your neighbours' laps, which in this situation is a particularly perilous undertaking. Look for signs stating "No Groping" or "Groping Welcome".

Look also for a suitable place to sit. If you recognise any hoi polloi, try right behind them if sure you can avoid groans and gusty breaths down their necks. Do not tarry on the sitting, for you block the views of others. But it is best not to cross in front of a man, or woman, in the throes of what seems to be Parkinson's Disease, or indeed two people afflicted by the disease attempting to help each other control the shakes. Since it is difficult to check the seating during a non-stop performance, when the lighting is correctly and directly on the performers and there is no flashlight-bearing usherette to guide you in, it is advisable to place a cheap handkerchief, or even a Tesco-Lotus plastic bag between your trousers and the seat they will occupy.

Should you be a woman, or possess marked womanly features and movements, you will be in a very small minority at such exhibitions, but you will be perfectly safe, unless wearing only a G-string and mistakenly taken for a performer.

Such shows are intended to stimulate sexually, so a loosening of clothing to accompany expansions is permissible. However, if hands wander across to help you in this or other tasks, you must quickly assess whether you are a homosexual or bisexual, in which case the cautionary notes so far will not apply to you; or a heterosexual, in which further case you must quickly assess whether these hands accord you deference and come from beneath your social station, or if indeed they are the hands of a very notable Thai patrician temporarily slumming it.

> *Bottom line:*
> *Should you feel arousal, ask yourself if this is because of the close proximity of patrician power, in which case you may choose to exchange business cards as soon as your hands are free. Test the telephone number while in the toilet and if it is a bummer, conclude that so are you.*

16

On Blaming the Maid for Everything

There is one little person who is so far below you in the deference stakes, she shouldn't really be anywhere near your beautiful persona. But there she is, party to your innermost secrets, possibly the object of mutual envy for foreigners of the female variety, possibly the object of sexual fantasy for foreigners of the male variety, allowed free run of your home and gardens and undergarments, daily interaction with your children who love her more than they do you, mastery over what comes into the kitchen, and trusted by necessity with handling much more money than she gets paid at the end of the month. Usually young, usually attractive, usually female, usually in her pyjamas.

This is the young thing who is responsible for absolutely everything that goes wrong in your household. Well, of course she is. *Under-educated*, "Do you know dear, she can hardly read in her own language, let alone English? She put the Milk of Magnesia down the toilet and the bleach into John's birthday cake"; *under-privileged*, "She lives miles from anywhere... I don't think there is a school in her village... eleven brothers and sisters... no wonder she's so skinny and always tired... we had her de-wormed of course."; *under-experienced*, "I had to teach her everything, you know, everything. I don't think she had even seen a toilet before coming to us. And she has

absolutely no idea where America is, you wouldn't believe it.";
under-developed, "Well, I couldn't believe it, she told me she
had her first period only last year. Childish. Almost retarded
really. Not a thought in her head. Caught her trying on my bra.
Of course I got angry, but can't blame her really, I mean she
has absolutely no breasts, at least none to talk of."

Now where did the remote control for the TV go? *The
maid hid it under the pillow.* Has anybody seen John's
briefcase? He'll be late for his meeting. In the Kitchen?
What's it doing there? *The maid did it.* Why are the goldfish
dead? Who turned off the oxygeniser? *The maid did it.*
"I've got the runs, what could it be?" *The maid of course.*
"No f'ing paper in the toilet!' *The maid strikes again.*

Foreigners, who have never had domestic help before
coming to live and work in Thailand, get far more in a maid
than just somebody to clean the house, wash the clothes, do
the ironing, cook the food, answer the door and telephone,
wash the car and bring glasses of water or beer to visitors.
They get a human being who is responsible for every little, or
big, thing that goes wrong in the house.

"And always walking around in those pyjamas, dear. Quite
funny really. They stick right *into* her buttocks. She doesn't
even seem to be aware of it." Maybe. Bet your life John's aware
of it 'though.

"Never mind, dear. You just go to sleep. I'll put the cat
out tonight." And down goes John, in his pyjamas, with
the cat. And there, behind the house is the skinny little
underdeveloped maid washing her long hair, wearing just
a very wet and very clinging sarong. And John watches her
as he lets the cat go. And as she looks up... their eyes meet
as they have met a thousand times ever since John's fantasy
world began to revolve around the maid. And pyjamy-clad
John is getting very excited...

"Well, would you believe it?! After all we did for her? She was trying to get off with *John*! Lucky I arrived just in time. Poor John, quite embarrassing for him. To imagine that skinny thing with no tits thought John would be interested in her! Of course he wouldn't, not my John; he likes a woman built like a woman, not like a boy. Shaken my confidence in the Thais that has. I mean, we gave her far more than she has ever had before and how does she repay us? Can't even let your husband put the cat out at night without the maid trying it on. I'll be a bit more careful with the next one. Nobody under 45. And the cat's going to."

Poor John.

Bottom line:
Once the maid enters the family, nobody in it will ever be the same again. And you'll never find anything either, because only she knows where everything is.

17

On Calling for Help

When calling for help, the Thais are very polite. Whether sinking into the Mekong River or into quicksand or being attacked by ruffians, there is one set phrase to be used and one only. It is this: *Chuay Duay*. These two little words are rarely introduced into courses of "Survival Thai".

Considerately, these two words are both high falling tones, which tend to come naturally to those screaming at the top of their lungs. However, given that should you need to utilise these words you will most likely be in a situation of stress and distress, it is important to note that water entering the lungs or protracted punches to the stomach can seriously impair the production of clear and unequivocal Thai tones. Lest a passer-by think you are politely requesting the passing of the salt, a substantial measure of pre-performance practice is recommended. To prevent unnecessary call on the security services, this should preferably be in a soundproof room.

It is important, given that the cry is likely to be repeated, possibly many times, to sustain conviction and despair while maintaining unambiguous falling tones and a correct initial "ch". One way, but not the only way, of accomplishing this is to grip the scrotum tightly. Women could find difficulty in doing this, but gripping the scrotum of another person is unacceptable, as calls for help are in the majority of cases made by the unaccompanied. It is also important to practise in all conditions. Sitting comfortably at a desk is not really distress simulation. Much better is to make repeated cries of *Chuay Duay* while attempting to float in a large jacuzzi turned on full, while in a smoke-filled room with the doors tightly sealed and triple-locked from the outside and flames licking at your ankles, while naked in sub-zero temperatures and being menaced by a very large policeman and his German Shepherd (a make of dog), and while hanging upside down from a high fan bracket supported by snapping parachute cords (the fan should be on slow to optimise realism).

If you cannot make a convincing *Chuay Duay* under these circumstances, it is advisable to record the voice of a person of your race and colour who can make very acceptable calls for help in Thai. This should be done on a small but powerful voice recorder that you will need to carry with you at all times in a waterproof container. Do not get a Thai to make this recording, as passers-by who might otherwise help will be looking for a Thai, not a second-generation immigrant to the East End of London. Unfortunately there is, as yet, no commercially available distress signal in Thai; the nearest you will come to it is a high-pitched whistle, which is excellent for calling every dog in the vicinity but which requires the lungs to be free of water or fists.

A brief sojourn into etymology is at this point is necessary, lest this section become overly pragmatic.

Chuay means "help". It is also used as a polite particle in many phrases like, "*Please* pass the fish sauce", in which case it translates as "please".

Duay means "with". It is also frequently used as a polite particle in many phrases like, "Pass the fish sauce *please*", in which case it also translates as "please" in the sense of "if you

wouldn't mind", or "if it's not too much trouble" (this will be instantly recognisable to the truly English reader over 60).

Because these words are both intrinsically polite, there is no need, when drowning, to embellish *Chuay Duay* with further particles of politeness like *crap* and *kha* (although you still have to add them when requesting the fish sauce). In fact, to do so might diminish the immediacy of your request. *Chuay Duay* alone is all that is needed, and the two diphthongs may be repeated without any other word or words as many times as you are able before the waves take you. There is no need to add a clause of explanation. For example, it is not required to say, "Help, I am drowning". The fact that you are drowning should be quite evident enough to any observer intelligent enough to offer any assistance. You can, if it makes you feel better, throw in the occasional "Help!" in English, just in case a Norwegian has his eye on you (but only if you are a damsel, or are damsel-looking). But in Thai, don't try to get away with

Chuay all alone. That's a bit like saying *"Aidez"* without the *"moi"* in France. People will watch you sinking beneath the ruffian's fists and scratch their heads wondering why they should help ruffians engaged in dubious activities. Similarly, using *Duay* alone will sound more like an invitation to join in the fun than a cry of distress. And, whatever you do, don't mix them up and say *Duay Chuay.*

> *Bottom line:*
> *On requesting people to save you from certain death, it is a good idea to respect their linguistic conventions.*

18

On Committing Adultery

In Thailand, nobody commits adultery. Also, nobody takes life, nobody steals, nobody tells untruths, and nobody gets drunk or stoned. At least, they try not to do so in public.

All of these actions together form the basic Five Precepts of a Buddhist life. So, the ordinary Thai, man or woman or child, has but five basic commandments to observe, not the ten maintained by Christianity, and not the multitude required by Judaism, Islam and Hinduism. So, being a Thai Buddhist should, on the face of it, be a relatively easy job when compared to other religions. Were the temptations not so ubiquitous in the Land of Smiles, perhaps it would be.

There is absolutely no basis for assuming Thais cheat on their spouses any more than married couples of other nationalities. Admittedly, not all countries have quaint hotels, where you can drive your car into a bay and have a young boy run around it pulling a ceiling-to-floor curtain about your car, to keep off the dust. And not all countries have such convenient hotels, where there is no need to pass through a reception area; just step out of your car and into a nice windowless room with thoughtfully mirrored walls and ceiling so you can remember who you are with. And not all countries have hotels with such a fair payment system, where you are charged only for the hours you occupy the premises.

And if you step out of your dark-glass windowed car alone and are feeling lonely, a call from the bedside phone will usually bring you whatever you want.

Many Thai men might be offended if you accused them of adultery. Were you to do that, which of course you will *not* do, you might get the reply that (a) the girl was selling her body — it is not for the customer to ask if she is married or not; or (b) the girl is not married, even if the man is, thus it is not really adultery; or (c) we only had oral sex; or (d) you're being silly, "I don't even know her name". Very rarely would an ordinary man feel a pang of conscience at "betraying" his wife. And he certainly would not think it considerate of her feelings to tell her all about it and claim it didn't count because he didn't enjoy it and that it will never happen again. If she did find out about it — and Thais do gossip if fed the raw material — he is likely to feel more than the pangs of conscience, as attested by the numerous male members chopped off and fed to the ducks by women scorned.

Discretion is once more the key to doing what one pleases while avoiding conflict. Going out for a drink with the boys in a bar with naked dancing and sex shows is not even close to adultery, although if a wife or anybody should ask, all are out at a meeting. Popping into a private room above such a bar for a quick forty winks, or even occupying the special chair out of sight around the corner of the bar, is a lapse so temporary, can it really be considered as adultery? After all, we were all lusting after the girl on the pole, and I paid for her.

The idea of payment regularising relationships and illegalities is frequently found in Thai society. Should the somewhat errant husband be caught by the power of gossip, there is a good chance he could buy his way back into his wife's affections, at least as far as the public world is concerned. It would, however, cost him a lot more than the immediate price of his infidelity — at least that single infidelity that came to his wife's attention. Time for another gold necklace.

Infidelity and adultery is a two-way process and a man does need a woman to complete his peccadillo. The female partner might indeed feel she is not party to adultery if she is not married, particularly if she has some sort of status as *fan* (regular companion) or *mia noy*, minor wife, which indicates a consistent relationship with an older, married man. Sometimes the first wife might agree to such an arrangement, sometimes not. A minor wife has accommodation and an allowance provided for her and may have children by her man, whom she may refer to as husband, although she is not married according to the law. The husband of a minor wife need not divorce his first wife, but should continue to provide for her and any children. If he has the means to support two wives and their children, he may be seen anywhere in public with the minor wife, particularly if she has born him a son. Inheritance is likely to be taken care of during a man's lifetime rather than after his death. Instead of trying to incorporate the minor wife legally into the will, if any (not all Thais make one), he is more likely to make her regular presents as the relationship continues — monthly stipend, house, car, education for the children, care of her parents and siblings, trips within Thailand and overseas. A man who treats both wives correctly loses no social status, and indeed may gain some. Such a man will be older, although not necessarily in his dotage, and certainly richer and more powerful than most in his entourage. His relationships with the two wives are *not* looked upon as adulterous (but a relationship with a third party might be). When looking for powerful people to increase your status, the existence of a minor wife is often taken as the mark of success in life.

The apparent power of a man when it comes to extra-marital affairs and appendages to his first marriage might appear to contradict the role of the woman, particularly the bride's mother, in controlling family matters. That might be so. It might also be the case that the close relationship between a woman and her mother squeezes the man out to the extent that he looks outside for the kind of affection he used to get from his own mother. But that's a Freudian-Portnoy way of looking at things. In reality, whether a man is simply unfaithful to his wife or whether he takes a second wife, the object of his affection and/or lust will almost always be a cute little thing, usually of his children's or grandchildren's age. And if that is acceptable publicly, why not?

In Thailand, public acceptance legitimises some things that are, strictly speaking, against the law. Public disapprobation, on the other hand, stigmatises some things that are fully within the law. There are good reasons for regarding Thailand as "loosely structured" with a large measure of individual decision and social movement, but only a fool would ignore the importance of public opinion.

Bottom line:
It takes two to tango. Or sometimes three or four or more.

19

On Death by Traffic Light

On finding your *tuk-tuk* driver oblivious at the traffic lights, it is permissible to ascertain if he is dead, in apoplectic seizure, meditating, or merely having a nap. This is done by pushing him from the left shoulder, gently increasing the angle of incline to 25 degrees. At this point, he should either awake into the world or fall more evidently out of it. If the latter, you are perfectly within your legal, moral and social rights to leave the vehicle and enter any other *tuk-tuk*, after assuring yourself that the new driver is awake and alive. While Thai law does not specifically forbid a person whose spirit is hovering or departed to pilot a *tuk-tuk*, it is inadvisable to continue your journey with such a driver, unless you want to go where he is going.

Death by traffic light happens more often than you might think. And at some of the busiest intersections of Bangkok, it might be hours or days before the fact is brought to the attention of the police, who will then rush to the scene and charge the driver with obstruction. It is a possibility because of the long hours *tuk-tuk* drivers work and because the red lights are among the longest in the world. The digital red countdowns offer assurance that nobody is going anywhere soon and provide a soporific for drivers and passengers alike. This soporific allows an escape from the prison of Bangkok traffic and, occasionally, a more permanent escape from the cares of city life.

> *Bottom line:*
> *It is not done to take advantage of a driver's slumbers or temporary meditative absence to sneak away without paying the fare. This is, however, permitted in cases where the driver has jumped the lights for the very last time.*

20

On Declining Children

Khun Meechai, also known as Mister Condom, popularised the use of condoms by getting everybody in Thailand, including those in the religious orders, to use them or promote their use in birth control, and later in disease control. Thanks to him, the population of Thailand, which might have outstripped its resources, has been maintained at just over the 60 million mark and condoms are on display along with Kit-Kat at every supermarket checkout. This promotion of birth control was done through public campaigns that were even more fun than sex. All very Thai, public parades promoting birth control included *khatoeys*, gays and others unlikely to conceive anyway, plus bar girls, political figures and representatives of the religious establishment. Lots of Thais together, party time, condom blowing contests, must be fun, let's all wear condoms, even if only on nose or thumb. Sex unites (usually) only two people, campaigns unite everybody. For poorer families, there was also an incentive element: they were given a piglet if they agreed to space their pregnancies. This led to two of the greatest advertising slogans of all time: "Pace your pregnancies with a pig" and, a straight adaptation of Buddhist teachings, "Many births cause suffering".

This increase in the pig population was concomitant with a sharp decline in the number of children. Many of the pigs were painted, "I wear condoms", a message that got home to the remotest villages. Thirty years or so ago, Thai women had five to seven children. Then they decided they would rather have pigs. Today's families average 1.7 children per household. And although at weddings the guests will still wish the couple "children to fill the house", it is possible to find women who say they want no children at all in their nice high-rise apartment. These women, somewhat paradoxically, also say they want no pigs in their apartment. No pleasing some people.

Outside of much richer Singapore and Japan, this is a rather unique situation in Asia. Some women, and their husbands, are able to think this way without much pressure from the family as long as somebody in the family group is producing children, and as long as there is a general sharing of childcare among Mother's larger family unit. Such care is no longer needed for the welfare of the children but for the welfare of the adults, who must have children to cuddle and coo-coo. The 1.7 children clearly get more of everything than children in their parent's generation, and there is some dilution of norms when it comes to teaching children to respect, honour and obey their elders and betters. They get much more in terms of schooling, health care, technological aids to modern isolation, and, most notably, food to make one fat. They are also pampered, almost to the point of being spoilt. That they stop short of spoiling (in most cases) says something for Thai ways; most of the 1.7 are growing up just as polite and friendly as their parents, but significantly taller and fatter. As Thai buses, doorways and theatre seats come up for renewal, they are replaced with higher and wider; this is perhaps the true indicator of economic progress, but one as yet unrecognised by any development agency.

At the moment, the majority of the Thai population is in the working range, which is great for the economy. But in a few more decades, that 1.7 will be caring for ageing elders, accumulating merit for the rebirth of parents and selves, and looking after their own children, if any.

> *Bottom line:*
> *If the trend over the past quarter-century continues, there will be just two Thais left in the world by the year 3000. Both* khatoeys. *So hurry, Thais will increase in scarcity and the price is bound to rise.*

21

On Deliciousness and the Insect World

Thais have a special relationship with the insect world which may be different from your own. *Really* Thai traditional food, not the haute cuisine that originated in palace circles or was Chinese before it became Thai-ised and is now universal, can be a rite of passage in itself. If you do share the full Thai view on deliciousness, you have a head start in the integration process. If you don't enjoy foraged food, Thais will understand, but this will be another wedge between you and the full Thailand waiting on the far side.

You have been invited by someone in your *puak* — or just maybe you have seized the initiative and invited them — for a *tio* a bit *bahn nok* to eat, drink and sleep the afternoon away at a real Thai restaurant with the kind of Thai food you can't find at your club in Kensington. This could be a real bonding experience, so if you want to be bonded, don't hesitate to accept. *You* won't have a lot to do — Thais are great arrangers. And even if what they arrange is often the opposite to what you thought it would be, it is usually better than you thought it might be, and everybody needs a magical mystery tour sometimes. You will have to be prepared to drink and eat *real* Thai; how much you sleep is up to you, and if *you* invited *them* you will have to pay at the end, but a whole lot less than inviting them all to dine at the pub back home.

What to take with you? If you want to appear Thai while retaining some non-Thai precautions, you could do worse than pop into your breast pocket a tube of *yaa dom* to stick up your nostrils and inhale, and share with your friend's nostrils, and a wad of toilet paper tactfully tucked in the back pocket of your blue jeans. As with any trip upcountry, a card of paracetamol tablets and a blister pack of Imodium can be useful for any member of your party — headaches and runny tummies are not just for the non-Thai. Try not to wear shorts or a skirt, particularly if you are male, as there will be sitting, lying and stretching exercises to punctuate the afternoon, and you should never show off private parts purely by accident. A can of spray-on insect repellent is these days acceptable and will not destroy the Thai-ness of your temporary environment. Do be careful, however, not to spray onto your food, as this may cause its premature death. And please spray away from the ozone layer.

Ready to *tio?* Boonpop knows just the place. Leave it to him. If it all goes bottom up, he loses face, not you.

Nicely settled? You will know you are in a real Thai place when there are no chairs or tables in sight, where cobras, *tookgers* and scorpions stare eternally at you from the inside of large glass bottles, where nobody knows the name of the place, where there are precisely the same number of dogs as customers, and where there is absolutely no menu. Ideally, there will also be cushions on the floor and a huge poster of tulips in Amsterdam covering the cracks on the wall.

This will be more than a trip into the gastronomic unknown. On this day you will encounter delicacies that should take your psyche nostalgically back to the days when your own ancestors foraged for their supper. Chaps and chapesses have been out knee-deep in muddy fields, ditches, swamps and forests, scavenging for the myriad of creatures that fly, crawl, hop, swim, burrow, or do all of these evasive actions at once in a futile attempt to escape being served up to you as not just any old source of protein but a source still occasionally wriggling to demonstrate to your 21st century green mentality that absolutely no pesticides were used in their capture. Your conservationist conscience can thus be at ease, knowing that there are a lot more of whatever it is out there and that by eating the wildlife, you help preserve it.

Now, as you settle into the drinking, the choice is yours. Do you want god's little creatures thrown alive into the boiling oil? Or do you prefer them raw but well chopped up, so the collective bits hardly look like what they were, and served in a nice red-hot chilli sauce or a *nam jim* on the side? Or maybe you'd like them steamed in banana leaves? This has the advantage of taking longer before they are quite ready, but they may lose much of their crispiness and there is always the danger that a scorpion or two will be brought out as *gap gam* to satisfy your demanding palate while waiting.

Etiquette for eating black scorpions might be new to you; fortunately, it is much the same as attacking crabs (the edible variety). First, make quite sure your snack is dead, otherwise it might end up eating you. The way to do this is to pull off a leg or two and look for any movement before crunching a small bunch of severed legs between the molars. You may then proceed to the claws and tail. Since scorpions are usually smaller than crabs, there is no need to crack claws open with empty beer bottles. Just pop it all in, crunch, crunch, crunch, extract from between your lips and teeth the unwanted shell, and wash down the rest with a large Sang Som whisky-soda, with a large twist of lime added and plenty of ice. In fact, two or three very large Sang Soms are recommended before the feast begins and will definitely, like the finest claret, add much to the appreciation of the delicacies to follow, helping lift you over the threshold of preconceived prejudice. And here it comes.

Various venomous arachnids, plates of grasshoppers, crickets and water beetles. A plate of more familiar-looking eggs. Deceptively familiar. These are *khay luuk* and each has a pre-hatched baby chicken inside. Don't confuse with *khay luak*, which are lightly boiled eggs with no chicks. These all fall into the category of *gap gam*: snacks to accompany inebriation. And while you are at the cesspit, *shooting the rabbit*, your friends, seeing the obvious delights the insect world holds for you, will be thoughtfully setting up a wok under a bare light for the early-evening gift of the gods. Termites and other winged creatures, instead of a suicidal flutter into your sundowners, will on this occasion perform a final ballet around the naked bulb until their wings buffet off and their long little bodies fall conveniently into the boiling oil, to be scooped up periodically by a noodle sieve, tossed onto a painted enamel plate and presented to you like the finest caviar.

If you are very, very lucky, the end of festivities will be marked by the confection of Elephant's Penis Soup. This delicacy has increased in rarity in recent years, as the essential ingredient is darned difficult to obtain. It is preferably served in a *galaman* and accompanied by a large measure of alcohol taken from either the scorpion bottle or the bottle containing the cobra in full strike. These all serve to put lead in your pencil, although by this time you might have forgotten what your pencil is for.

If capable of speech, ask that more of everything be *say thung*, for consumption later. And while your party bag is being prepared, lots of praise for the food, *aroy dii maak*, and, however drunk you are, pay the bill — if no other has already done so — with a generous tip for the fine food, for more of which you will certainly *clap ma*.

End of the day, if you never had before, you now have a *puak* — just don't suggest stopping for a Big Mac on the way home. Your group will support you, right or wrong, whenever you need their help. At least that's the theory. A circle of friends to live and die for, until you waft yourself, or get wafted, into a circle of higher status. When that happens, remember that *puaks* are additive not exclusionary. This is not the old country. Class here is an entirely different matter to class back home. There is movement, rise and fall. *Puaks* are not set in stone; over time people come and go, and come again. In Thailand, as you move up to even higher things than sucking on scorpion claws, you don't have to abandon your old friends to acquire new; although those who drop by the wayside need not necessarily be helped out of the gutter.

Bottom line:
Never mind your principles, stick with your party.

22

On Doing as the Thais Do

Should one do as the Thais do? Yes and no. It all depends. What Thais? Doing what? Where? When?

It is not at all the thing to do for you to squat by the kerbside grilling squid over a charcoal burner and wearing only a bra and ragged sarong, particularly if you are a man. On the other hand, it is absolutely fine and you're a really decent chap who knows how to muck in and pull together if you are wearing that bra and sarong at your gent's club *khatoey* night. Some of Thailand's most imminent men have enjoyed dressing up in women's clothes. Perhaps the most famous was the great statesman and author, Kukrit Pramoj, who won a cross-dressing contest and went on to win the premiership of the country — although there is no connection between the two competitions.

No wonder foreigners trying to get ahead, or simply to stay where they are and integrate, sometimes have a difficult time knowing who they should emulate. Having three wives or more can be fine if you can afford it and can handle them; but having just one good one and treating her well clocks up your social points. Being homosexual is often a short cut to the top — although it can also cause your fall once you get there. Giving and taking presents is part of Thai life, but at what point does it become bribery and corruption?

Sexual opportunity is all around, in the car park behind the disco, in the massage parlour, in the bar, in the guest house and club, and in the shopping centre, in the supermarket, on the bus, and along the road. Most of the clients, you know, are Thai. So why all the fuss about being discreet? Thais aren't, are they? Well, yes, they are, most of them. And if you really want to do what the Thais do, that's okay, but do it the Thai way.

Doing as the Thais do involves doing things the way Thais do them, and short of masturbation, very little is done alone. You need to be in one or more groups. You have to have your *puak*. Then, in company, any indiscretions will be nipped in the bud or covered up. In order to do as the Thais do, you simply have to be with Thais, otherwise whatever you do is not going to be done the way Thais do it.

Thus, get into a group that is of your social grade or preferably contains some members of a higher grade, conform, and they will take care of you. Simple as that.

Or is it? Thais do things in groups, true. But groups are not Masonic lodges. They don't usually meet at the back room of the pub every Tuesday night and they don't swear undying comradeship; but a Thai will help somebody in his group, and go to him for help. The individualism comes in with movement between groups or "membership" of more than one group, even of a number of groups that at times appear as concentric circles and at other times as overlapping Olympic rings.

Thais (men and women) have their *puak*. Each also has his or her family, with a network of kin and classificatory kin that forms a support group at the same time as requiring support from any member able to give it. With occasional movements through marriage and divorce, the family does not change much. It is the basis of any individual's identity, security, respect and social welfare. "Honour" seems a reasonable word to describe the family in larger Thai society. A good family, a good individual. An individual is defined by his or her family, for good or bad. And the good do different things, or the same things differently, to the bad.

The foreign transplant exists, more likely than not, without a Thai family. This is a neutral situation. He or she is not dragged down by relatives, neither can he or she claim an automatic status that goes with a family's surname, which differs from every other surname in the Kingdom, or with being known and respected in an area. The lack of relatives leaves you free to develop your group networks more than most Thais can do. Bide your time. Look where you are going. Follow all the cautious qualifications on action, and wash your dirty linen in private, rather than in public.

Bottom line:
Do as your group does and you are doing what the Thais do.

23

On Doing Nothing

The most respected people in the land spend large amounts of their time sitting quietly doing nothing. This is meditation. It involves the spontaneous or directed mental activity required to move towards the great void of nirvana, where desires are no more. It is recognised that desiring to achieve nirvana is an act likely to push it further away, so a monk takes his time and before he starts, knows that he is never going to achieve this perfect spiritual state. This doesn't make his journey any less useful than any other journey, for example your journey to and through Thailand and your desire to get ahead in a new culture. As the English put it and try to believe, it doesn't matter if you win or lose, it's playing the game that counts. Doing nothing is a process, a quality in itself. And one much better than doing anything else. Got it?

You don't have to be a monk to meditate, in fact you don't have to be anything at all. And plenty of people meditate, either alone or, being Thai, in groups of like-minded people.

It is important to signal your meditations. If you are sitting on the floor with feet drawn up under you, still, eyes closed, it is pretty obvious what you are doing. But this typical attitude is not required and many a busy businessman opts out for 20 minutes without leaving his comfortable executive's chair. If you are so engaged, it is rather distracting to have somebody prod you in the shoulder and ask, "Are you all right?" Thus, if you have a secretary, tell her that she is to tell all callers that you cannot be disturbed as you are meditating. Then lock the door. You hear her answer the phone and say, "He cannot be disturbed for 20 minutes. He's meditating." You have won on two fronts at least: you have opted out of work and social interaction for a time, which is positive, even if you are masturbating not meditating, or nodding off into a dream that has little to do with general perceptions of nirvana, since it gives your mind a little trip out of the office confines, *and* your interlocutor knows that you are a serious person capable of ordering his life to incorporate the really important. Meditation is not confined to Buddhism, and is not even a religious activity, although some do get a buzz out of it and generally it is regarded as pleasant, so by saying you are doing it when you are not is no sacrilege. In fact, since there are so many forms of meditation; and in Thailand, you do not even have to sit, you can walk, hop, wash dishes, and still meditate on what you are doing. But it is best to start at the bottom, and sit, although not necessarily cross-legged on a hard floor if you find your soft, leather armchair more conducive to a calm nothingness.

It is not a good idea to drift off into another world when in a meeting with your investment bankers or when tripping across Ploenchit Road without using the overhead crossing. At least not until you have a certificate in nirvana. Better at first to stay within friendly environments.

Maybe your 20 minutes is really forty winks. Never mind. You have done nothing, and that's all that really matters.

There are limits to doing nothing, but these are perceptual limits. Stop shaving (not advised, particularly if you purport to be female). Go into work as usual and wait for some smart aleck to ask why you are growing a beard. You can then reply in absolute honesty that you are doing nothing.

Bottom line:

If you can't do nothing right, how on earth do you expect to do anything right?

24

On Economising the Truth

The substance of this section is censored.

Bottom line:
The Thais never tell falsehoods. They are simply economical with the truth.

25

On Fidelity

Here I shall refer not to the quality of reproduced sound compared to its original source, but to the quality or state of being sexually faithful. Both qualities are generally thought to be desirable, but both are considerably more expensive as the quality increases.

It *is* possible to find sexual fidelity in Thailand. However, for the average foreigner, don't expect it to come easily — or particularly cheaply.

Three things are necessary:

• The partner comes from a family that holds fidelity to be a virtue worth maintaining as a value, although even the most virtuous family is unlikely to be fanatical about it.

• The foreigner has to reciprocate fidelity in return.

• The foreigner has to love and cherish — even if this is not part of the marriage contract. This means a degree of financial support for partner and family and the granting of extra-territorial rights to the partner's family.

Thais are fun-loving people, and some rural Thais are easily persuaded or cajoled into somebody's bed, especially if the cajoler is an important person, or gives that impression. Such simplicity is not a sound basis for protracted virginity, but it can be a basis for fidelity. There is little that is more true and lasting than the love of a simple person. Simplicity does not have to be absolute — IQ can be perfectly normal. It is evident in a shallow range of interests and skills, the ability to stare at the TV screen without knowing what is on it, an obsession with some point of personal beauty: skin colour, hair, breast or penis size, an ability to live with a foreigner they might like but do not understand. Simplicity does not mean your partner will not know or care if you are unfaithful, and it is quite untrue that in Thailand, men can do anything they want while women cannot. On the other hand, opportunities for infidelity are comparatively more easily found for men.

The real fidelity-cement is all in the mind. Thais can be terribly romantic. Almost everyone *wants* one partner who is faithful and all that goes with that: stable family life and so on. Many, indeed a great many, Thais feel that *farang* are a better bet in the fidelity game than are Thais. True or not, very debatable; but no need to debate it, use the fact to your advantage — if you want a faithful partner that is. If you get someone at their early stage of development, where hope still springs eternal, you are lucky — feed the feeling and you are on fairly safe ground. Early development does not necessarily coincide with tender years, as physical and emotional development can come comparatively late in Thailand. But there can be no guarantees. For Thais, as for everyone else, once trust is broken, it is more difficult to build or rebuild real trust with the partner or next partner, and a person who has had a string of partners is unlikely to place a high value on fidelity. So, sorry, but expecting your Suzie Wong bar girl/ boy suddenly to revert to the model of fidelity is unrealistic. The first time she or he says, "If you don't give me the money, I'll have to get it elsewhere", kick her or him out and change the locks as well as the sheets. Or, much better still, don't waste your time, money and reputation on bad bets in the first place. Believe it or not, the average Thai girl or boy does *not* work in some form of prostitution, so don't look for the good ones in a bar.

Family and close friends of a Thai will always support their own should it come to an argument over fidelity. However, while animosity towards his partner may not be immediately evident to a male foreigner, Thais do collect enemies and rivals as well as friends. It is these enemies who will phone you to let you know what your partner is up to. Of course, they may be lying. It really does help to speak the language.

On a perhaps brighter note, fidelity is harder for the male foreigner playing away than for the Thai partner, playing at home. Until, that is, you take her back home, where poles of attraction and scarcity are reversed — and not in your favour.

Bottom line:
Arguments between foreign men and Thai women occur much more over money than over infidelity. But there is a link between the two and one thing can easily lead to another.

26

On Finding Your Wife Dancing
Naked in Your Pub

On finding your wife dancing naked on the bar of your local watering hole, reach immediately for those hidden reserves of phlegm, but do not direct them in her direction as you are certain to miss, and thereby compound a basically simple situation. Such superfluous encounters can be a bit of a surprise, even a blow, for any man, and mishandling the situation can aggravate the loss of face that she has already caused you. But even in this unhappy situation there is a natural progression of action. You may, hopefully, never have to take any of these steps, especially if you follow the guide to finding the perfect Thai partner (see page 154 *On Marriage as a Hazardous Undertaking*), but it is just as well to have them somewhere in a pocket of the mind, for ready reference should the sad day come.

First, make sure it's really your wife. There is absolutely nothing to be gained by getting yourself killed by a hulking Norwegian for whopping his bird with a bottle of Chang beer; it will only compound negatives to waste a perfectly good bottle of beer by smashing it into the face of somebody else's tart. So, particularly if you're in your cups at the time, do make sure it's not the missus' little sister or the twin you didn't know about, or just another girl who has a similar birth feature on the left buttock, a rose tattooed on the right breast and King Kong nostrils.

Second, cast your mind back to the day you first saw her, does she look as fine dancing up and down the reflective chromium pole as she did then? If not, isn't it time for a trade in?

Third, would the extra money come in useful?

Fourth, have you secreted her ATM number and card? And are you able, even before she can get her knickers back on, to empty any accounts in her name or — fools are born every single day at the rate of 99 to one wise man — any joint accounts she has not already pillaged? And can you readily pocket any of the gold you gave her? You will need it for the next one.

Fifthly, do you have the technical skills and determination to burn to the ground any property you put in her name together with all she possesses, and the means and motivation to flee the scene forever?

Those familiar buttocks are continuing to gyrate to familiar music, the football game on TV has finished, all eyes have turned to you. You have to do something and you feel too inexperienced or unprepared to tackle the five-point plan set out above.

Know that in this conflict-avoidance society, crimes of passion happen every day and none are recognised as such by the Thai legal system. A reaction that the French would consider fully justified in the heat of the moment could therefore lead you to the firing squad or death by lethal injection. And even if you confess and help the police with their enquiries, you will be lucky to get a commutation to 30 years in a Thai prison, during which you will have to start all over again, licking arse, probably quite literally, as you work your way up through the prisoner hierarchy.

Thus, if ever there was a time to keep your cool, this is it.

For those of you who find five-point plans too difficult to remember, or feel the need for some sort of instant action, here's a simpler plan on what to do. Ring the bar bell loudly and call out, "Drinks on me for everybody in the bar, including all the girls". This act of selfless altruism will be taken as a warning of impending calamity by all who know you and your naked, dancing wife, and those who don't will have the facts of the situation quickly whispered in their ear. Your offer will be taken up by only a tiny proportion of those present; most of the others, Thai and non-Thai, will be reaching for their clothes or reaching for the door handle, following the well-tested practice of conflict avoidance through fleeing the scene.

Never mind that your foreign friends are gone and that you have no support group left and two heavy bouncers are moving into your sides as you belly up to the bar. Down the stiffest drink you can think of and call for another round for everyone and pay on the spot. You will not have to do a thing. The management will take care of that troublesome little tart on the bar, making sure she gets the message to steer well clear of the premises. By the time she is out the door, word will have gotten round the neighbourhood that she is trouble. You, on the other hand, are the very nice guy who didn't deserve any of this. However much it rankles, shake hands (don't *wai)* with the manager and the heavies and ask them to be so kind as to have a drink with you. Slowly the customers will dribble back, curious to know what happened. Hesitantly, the other girls will resume their activities.

The next step in the procedure is the same as getting thrown by a frisky horse. Get right back on another horse. Preferably the cute little new number you have been looking at for a few days now, but done nothing about because of your fire-breathing missus in the wings. If the new cutie is hesitant, perhaps understandably wary of getting her eyes scratched out, the manager will persuade her. He will even wave the bar fine.

> *Bottom line:*
>
> *On finding your wife dancing naked in your local, don't change the bar, change the wife.*

27

On Flattery

Thailand is the most beautiful, interesting and amazing country you have ever been to. And the Thais, always smiling, always friendly, always hospitable, always kind and gentle, always calm. Always. All ways. The Thais — by far the most beautiful people you have ever met. Beautiful skin, beautiful eyes, beautiful mouths, beautiful hair, beautiful nose, beautiful shape, beautiful legs, beautiful arms, beautiful hands, beautiful feet, beautiful backsides, beautiful knees, beautiful ears, beautiful elbows, beautiful eyebrows, beautiful eyelashes, beautiful tongues, beautiful language, beautiful toenails. And you, o beautiful one, you are the most beautiful of the beautiful.

Repeat this at least one hundred times a day, in public, to every Thai you meet. And never forget it.

Bottom line:
Flattery will get you everywhere. But do you want to go there?

28

On Fleeing the Scene

Your taxi driver is first away from the lights with a clear run until the next set. He steps on the gas. Foot to the floor. Adrenalin flowing. See the glint in the driver's eyes. See the empty bottles of M-150 on the floor beside his feet. See the policeman stepping out on the street whistling for the driver to stop. See the policeman jump for his life as your taxi speeds on. See the traffic lights ahead change to orange and red. See the motorcycle in your way. See the taxi driver swerve. Hear the crunch as the motorcycle disappears. Feel the spin out of control. Feel the collision with the police car. Feel the sudden jolting halt as you ram a bus. See the taxi driver... where's he gone?

You go down to put the cat out. Now where's that sweet little maid in her pyjamas? Hear her in the kitchen outback. Hear the voice of the man with her. Hear the voices raised. Hear the smack of fist on skin. See through the window the maid on the floor. See the man tearing at her pyjamas. See the maid scratching his face. See the maid lunge for the kitchen sink. See the flash of the meat cleaver. See the man fall. See the cleaver in his head. See the maid... where's she gone?

You buy a bargain air-conditioner with a three-year warranty and free service every six months. Feel the cool air at night. Wonder about paying much less than the supermarket price. Hear the noise from the condenser. Feel the hot air. Drive to the shop where you bought it... where's it gone?

When caught in an imminent situation of high conflict. When there is no obvious way out. When all the beautiful smiles and flowers, *wais* and compliments in the world will not help. Then conflict avoidance can materialise instantly into fleeing the scene. Getting out of the way, out of the situation, until things cool down.

> *Bottom line:*
> *If you are not around, you can't conflict. If things get too much, you can always flee the scene.*

29

On Getting a Male Fertility Test at
Your Local Hospital

On getting a male fertility test at your nearest Thai hospital, come prepared. That is to say, find out precisely how to say "fertility test" in Thai, carry with you a large dictionary, and ejaculate a sperm "sample" into an empty honey jar, bucket, egg cup or thimble, as appropriate, which you should ideally wash and dry before use and cover with cling film after use. Alternatively, in the comfort of your own bed, a condom may be applied and attempts made to fill or part fill it. Please knot at entry end, after removal. On this occasion only, you may ignore the admonitions to use once only, if second use is for a further fertility test, in which case you wash the receptacle between uses and hang it on the line to dry. It is suggested that you also hang a few plastic bags on the line to dry at the same time, to deflect any curious enquiries or advice on use from your neighbours.

Take the dictionary and the sample to your hospital. You have an absolute maximum of three hours between the moment of ejaculation and the moment a young girl looking through a microscope will count how many of your sperm are born dead, how many have broken tails or are otherwise deformed and how many, if any, might just gasp their way through to be decapitated by an egg. Because of time constraints, having a second try, in the hope of impressing the hospital staff with a full receptacle is not recommended. Remember that within the time margin, you have to explain at the hospital front desk exactly what you want, and the girl who will look at your sperm has to finish breakfast and get herself into the correct clinical mood. If you think , given the time available, you cannot make it on the sky train or tuk-tuk, with a knotted condom warm in your breast pocket, you can always use a hospital toilet cubicle on arrival, although you have to bring your own pornography.

Failure to come properly prepared will require your explanation — without the help of a large dictionary — that you have come for a fertility test. There is no special desk for discreet enquiries tucked away in a quiet corner of the lobby, and no experienced old ladies who know exactly what you have come for by the furtive look in your eyes. You must get through this front-desk hurdle at even the very best hospitals, each of which has reception staff who speak fluent English, French, German, and Japanese and have no clue what "fertility test" means. It probably does not help that the hospital front desk, like any other front desk, has to attract customers and places its sexiest and youngest girls on duty to welcome you. Their function is to fit you into one of the slots within which hospitals categorise patients. So what is your problem? Heart? Legs? Plastic adjustments? Teeth? Eyes, nose and throat? The list is long but you just don't seem to fit into any of the slots.

It doesn't help much that all around you people are having no trouble at all; they all come with coughs or diarrhoea or want bigger or smaller boobs. You try explaining, "Can I have a baby? I mean, can my wife have a baby?"

"Ah," says reception with a broad smile of understanding. "Which ward is your wife in?"

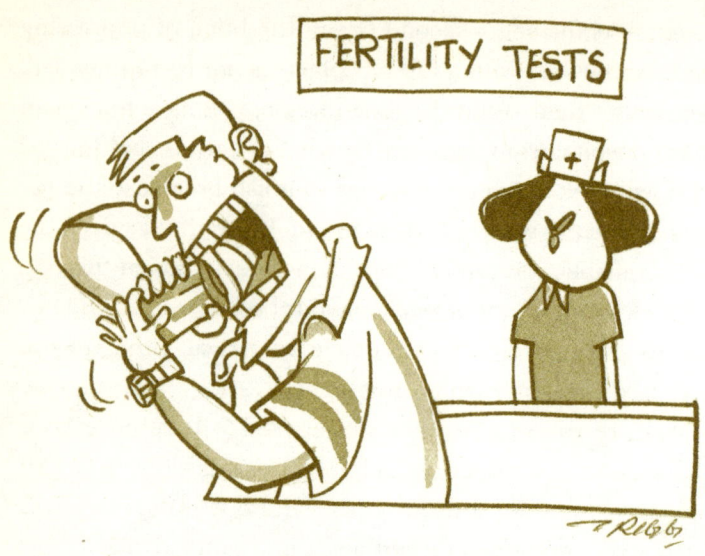

"No, my wife is not here."

"Never mind. Here is the brochure. When your wife wants to give birth, try to call before hand."

You are not allowed hand actions, and anything more than a diplomatic nod of the head downwards towards your lower regions could lead to the intervention of the heavy door keeper, whose real job is to prevent people leaving, even to go to the bank, without paying their bill, but who, if required, can encourage a rapid departure.

Never mind the subtlety. "Sperm. Good? No good?"

The girl looks at you, aware that you have asked a question and expect, sometime soon, an answer. So she smiles again and says, "Good," wondering, what is saperm?

You draw little snakes on a piece of paper provided, lots of little wriggling snakes. The girl looks over at the doorman.

"I want baby!" You exclaim with an air of finality.

The girl looks at you doubtfully, turns and giggles with her friend. "You man," she says.

Finally, somehow, perhaps by a day-long process of elimination, you make yourself understood. The girl hands you a small transparent cup with no lid and points you to the toilets. You return in half-hour, red-faced, and say you cannot do it and do they have any magazines. She points you to the piles of reading matter provided for those waiting the results of tests far less complicated than yours. You pick a couple of fast car mags and again repair to the toilet, returning triumphantly an hour or two later, having had a break for lunch and a stimulating beer or two in the excellent hospital restaurant before consummating a platonic relationship with a very sexy Aston-Martin. Proudly you place the little transparent cup on the reception desk. The girl has changed. "Can I help you?" asks the new girl.

Bottom line:
Many Thai hospitals are of an international standard with doctors trained in the West. But don't expect your ideas of tact and privacy to be any more prevalent in an establishment that looks reassuringly familiar and caters for foreigners than is general in Thai society. Private room or public ward, Sir?

30

On Getting Your Teeth Done

While at the lovely hospital, and after your fertility test, pregnancy test, and sex-change consultation, why not get your teeth done? It's either that or go next door to the guy with an open-air oral treatment centre nicely shaded by a leafy treetop from which hangs a giant plaster of Paris tooth over a chair full of character stains. He does a good job too, considering his anaesthetics are confined to a large bottle of Sang Som whisky. It helps to be advanced enough in techniques of Thai Buddhist meditation that you can transcend dental medication.

But why sit under a tree by the side of the road awaiting enlightenment and adding to local colour? You can have the best treatment in the world in half the time, at half the cost, at half the pain of the same treatment back home, and at a time suitable to you, not at a time when the dentist has a cavity in his appointment lists. No blood-stained bowls in the toilet — the whole surgery gets a mouthwash every few hours. And all dentists in Thailand seem to have been trained in the Mid-West (of Thailand). Some foreigners are so impressed with dental care in Thailand, they have all their teeth out and a whole new whiter than white set put in that automatically defrost and automatically flash a welcoming smile up to a distance of 10 km.

And if you happen to think you have perfect teeth apart from all those yucky, smelly stains that come from ten years of smoking before you quit and twenty cups of coffee a day, have them painlessly cleaned using the latest US formulas in 90 minutes of relaxation, nice music, CNN, Cosmopolitan. You go in dingy and polluted and come out a gleaming white virgin. Doesn't work on skin 'though.

Got some kids all with too many teeth for the spaces available? Two years of braces treatment will set you back a tad over the $1,000 mark. And if you are not going to be around that long, a Thai dentist will pop in the braces, give you the X-rays and let your dentist back home finish the job.

"Hey! Katie. Where'd you get those super sexy teeth?"

"Thailand. My Dad got them for my birthday. Cool aren't they? Never seen multi-coloured braces before."

Better believe it, people fly to Thailand and, having booked on the Internet, spend a week in a VIP room in a luxury hospital, getting that hernia sorted out that has been trussed up for years in the UK, getting that face, chin and tit lift they had been saving up for in France for so long that by the time they had the ready to pay for it they would have forgotten why they wanted it, nipping out any unwanted piles, warts, birthmarks and varicose veins, getting a state-of-the-art new pair of multi-focals, and getting their teething problems well sorted. Then, ten years younger, they hit the town.

Bottom line:
Yes, that can be tucked in as well.

31

On Giving Flowers to Soldiers

Now, let's agree on this: the Thais are tolerant people, given to conflict avoidance rather than conflict resolution; people who have a nice gregarious nature and therefore like to do things together, and like what they do together to be full of *sanuk* — bundles of fun. They are also riding a high wave of economic prosperity, have a dramatically declining birth rate, have an enviable education rate with slightly more girls than boys going to university, are currently balanced between residence in rural and urban areas, look like they have had the sense to place a brake on HIV-AIDS infections, can meet and overcome national tragedies like tsunamis with the required mix of fatalism and energy, and have developed a democratic system to resolve political disagreements through parliamentary debate and elections. They are a leading force within ASEAN and teeter on the brink of developed nation status. Europeans and Japanese love Thailand for their holidays and the United States loves it as a friendly ally in the long fight against the enemies of democracy. The Thais are friendly people who can say *may pen rai* — never mind — when faced with a disturbance they can't do much about, who can often smile in the face of adversity, and find meaning and hope and strength in their religion and respect for individuals in their all-pervading deference system. The Thais seem to have it all sassed out a lot better than most peoples, enjoying economic prosperity, a strong family life, political freedoms and social lives that see no great divide between serious endeavour and fun. Can't ask for much more, can you?

Then, in September 2006, the armed forces suddenly had a *coup d'état*, removed the Prime Minister popularly selected in an uncontested election six months earlier, and declared they were defending order and democracy. They set up committees to investigate corruption, to revise the constitution and to select a new prime minister who would uphold democracy and Thailand's constitutional monarchy. The ousted prime minister, in New York at the time, was told he was free to return. The nation was a bit surprised to wake up to find their television programmes interrupted by the announcement of the takeover, tanks and soldiers in position at all important buildings and traffic ways, and the banks and financial markets closed. However, within 24 hours, the world's media was happily covering the military presence and pointing out by way of explanation that this was "a very Thai coup".

A whole generation of Thais had grown up without seeing a single coup, and they were curious. So out they went onto the streets, not in protest or support, but because their friends were also going out on the streets, and within a few hours the international television channels were carrying footage of Thai civilians and Thai soldiers smiling at each other. The soldiers had guns, but they had yellow ribbons tied around the barrels to harmonise with the yellow shirts and bracelets worn by the majority of the Thai public throughout most of 2006 as a mark of love for the King and celebration of his 60 years on the throne. As TV cameras filmed, the Thais, presumably including those who had recently voted for the ousted Prime Minister and put his Parliamentary majority in power, were taking photographs of their children in army uniforms, complete with toy guns, being lifted up onto tanks by happy soldiers. As the days went on, the public affection for the coup seemed to grow, and troops were almost embarrassingly inundated with flowers, food and refreshments. Did that mean the ordinary Thais supported the coup? Those interviewed by foreign TV mostly said they were not in favour of *coups d'état*, but now it had happened...

Where was the loyalty and fidelity that one might expect voters to show for their elected representatives? It certainly was not on the streets in Bangkok or elsewhere. But loyalty and fidelity were not entirely absent. They were simply redirected to a higher order and ideal. Unwittingly, the Thai public was acting in complete agreement with Thomas Hobbes, one of the leading political thinkers of 16th century England, who had argued that the citizen has a duty not to resort to violence to change the political system, but that if that system were changed without the involvement of that same citizen, that citizen had a duty to support the new order. Hobbes saw a greater loyalty as being to the country and its institutions. A very pragmatic view and one that argued for the least disruption of life and the least risk to the commoner, placing the responsibility clearly on those who really controlled the system.

The soldiers regaled with flowers never demanded them or asked for them. They never asked for the smiles either. And they certainly did not ask to be presented with a nation's children to cuddle and fuss over. No more than the average Thai asked for a coup to resolve the conflicting views of politicians and a few giants in the economy. But when presented with a *fait accompli*, they certainly made the best of things and responded with the old Thai adage: one smile makes two.

It is tempting to see the Thais as rather shallow people who can not see beyond the fun of the temporary situation on their streets to the permanent treasures of democracy. This view would be quite wrong. The Thais did not rally in support of their democratically elected prime minister because it did not seem important at the time to do so. They were far more interested in avoiding any possibility of conflict by *disarming* the soldiers with their smiles and flowers. It was all a bit 1960s flower power generation. And what's wrong with that? And the coup presented an opportunity that could not be missed to socialise children in the ways of conflict avoidance: what to do when there are men around you with the power of guns. The fact that it was more *sanuk* to go along with the coup and treat it as theatre of the absurdly real was fully in keeping with the principles of conflict avoidance; it was also in keeping with a greater loyalty than was owed to a politician elected under the existing constitution, the loyalty to one's family, country and king.

Okay, the common people could not do much about the coup, so they tolerated it, smiled and went out of their way to neutralise any potential disturbance to their peace. But why have a coup anyway? The armed forces seem to have gone out of *their* way to risk creating a conflict situation — or did they? They avoided immediate conflict by taking action when the person they were ousting was out of the country. They neither encouraged nor forbade that person's return to Thailand. They interrupted banking and stock market activities only for 24 hours and they were very quick to promise a return to democracy and get the King's post-facto agreement for their actions. They apologised to the population for any inconvenience and explained they had acted only to end the political dispute which had been slowly boiling for months. No excuse perhaps for circumventing the democratic process after 17 coup-free years, but the coup was probably more fun than the elections — and rather less violent.

A parallel may be drawn with Thailand's successful anti-AIDS campaign. Nothing funny about AIDS and nothing funny about armed soldiers taking power into their own hands. But the Thais appear to have treated both in much the same way. Such things existed and required neutralisation. To neutralise the powerful, smiles and flowers on this occasion proved effective. And they did indeed make the event into a very Thai coup.

Bottom line:
If faced with an impossibly more powerful force than yourself, say it with flowers.

32

On Going to a River City Auction

On going to an antique auction at the plush River City, treat the occasion like any other theatre, except that you don't come fashionably late, you don't have to pay to go in and the lights are on full all the time, allowing those who matter to be seen by and to see the upwardly mobile and the fakers.

Unfortunately, these same circumstances attract any passing foreigner and you must therefore be careful to keep close to any Thais present. It's a fair bet that, unless they are trying to sell fake rubies to gullible farang, Thais at the auction either have come to see how much their heirlooms are fetching, or belong to that small minority of wealthy Thais who appreciate old things or pretend to do so. Watch out particularly for any who actually buy at the high prices commanded by the combination of glossy surroundings and pretentious attendees.

Wear smart casual, that is to say come as you left your Benz convertible and as you will continue after the auction to the yacht club. Should you possess one, this is the occasion to sport a blue blazer with a corner of the lapel sewn with the tactful threads of the Legion d'Honneur. Harmonise this with a lapel pin of your old regiment but avoid like the plague those medals you picked up at Chatuchak market. Ties are taboo and neckerchiefs offer a dash of panache only if knotted as tightly as your red neck can sustain, never folded and tucked in. One or two oil stains on your deck shoes are acceptable. Such dress sense counters the biting cold of the auction room and cuts you out nicely from the humdrum short-sleeve tourists and foreign residents who pop in because it is conveniently near the all-you-can-eat buffet in the hotel attached. You absolutely need to distinguish yourself, not simply as a connoisseur of Thai-Chinese-Burmese art, but as a species worth a knowing smile as a fake vase goes for twenty times its value.

When viewing the antiques and objets d'art, move slowly, lingering next to any well-dressed Thais and overhearing their conversation, even if it is so liberally laced with southern Chinese dialect as to be incomprehensible. Try to resist giving the china a ping with your middle finger, and if another person does so, do not frown deeply at the resonance when a slight frown and barely perceptible shake of the head is quite sufficient.

Should your eyes meet other eyes over a Ming vessel, a gist of a smile will indicate that you recognise a fellow expert. Should that expert choose to exchange a few words with you, measure his or her brevity. "What do you think?" should be the extent of unsolicited comment. An upward movement of the eyebrows is entirely adequate as reply. The well-connected Thai, no less than the European equivalent, does not rush into social intercourse in such reserved circumstances, which approach the British Museum reading room on a noisy day. Make your viewing immediately prior to the auction; rarely does any Thai of consequence bother to come the day before. Use the viewing period wisely and you will know where to sit as the auction begins. Do not sit right beside your targeted big-shot, but directly in front and one or two seats to the side of direct line of vision. This will allow the big shot and his comely companion full view of your dandruff-free grooming and frayed shirt collar, worn sportingly, if a trifle passé as current fashion goes, over your jacket neckline. Always take a bidding paddle, although you have no intention of buying.

Flies like to pop in from the searing heat in the ordinary people's world of Bangkok outside, much as you have done. They seem to be attracted to the cool atmosphere, which makes them prone to sleepiness. Should one settle on your long nose and instantly fall asleep there, do not attempt to swat it with a wave of the paddle. And certainly do not use the paddle to scratch any part of the body. You will use it to bid at the opening range, but only if you see from the corner of your eye your social target bid first. When bidding, do not shoot the paddle in the air, call out, or slap your knee; a single wave of the paddle with absolutely no hint of commitment or enthusiasm is the appropriate action for somebody who goes to these things all the time. Stop as soon as that socially-attractive person just behind hesitates. Should another bidder take over, turn slightly in your chair, catch the eye of the person outbid and give a slight nod to indicate recognition of fellow shrewdness. This is quite enough to establish a feeling of complicity, which is the stuff of the upper classes. Should your target win the bid, replace the slight nod with a more enthusiastic and pronounced movement, with light smile attached, to demonstrate congratulation on a brilliant move. Later, when the show is over, do not hesitate to verbalise your congratulations, adding, "You are obviously an expert on the period." If the reply comes that you can have it at the bid price, or that your social interlocutor's comely assistant is not having her period, retreat rapidly and mark up an experience gained. If, however, your profound conversational gambit leads to a beer at the hotel bar or even an invitation to view similar pieces at home, exchange cards — the one naming you as a buyer of a well-known international auction firm — and consider you have won the day. You may indeed walk out with a skip in your step and turn to give a small wave and half-smile; but don't then climb into a tuk-tuk.

Bottom line:
If all your subtlety and status craft gets you nowhere, you are at least handy for the all-you-can-eat buffet next door.

33

On Going to the Lavatory with a Hose Pipe

Should you find yourself in a modestly modern bathroom, with a sit-down toilet, there is a good chance it will also have a hose pipe curling up from a wall water inlet or from the depths below the system and hooked onto the wall at a convenient height for you to reach with one hand. On the head of the little hose pipe will be a lever which, when depressed, will shoot a continual spray of water until released. The primary purpose of this pipe is to relieve the hand of the need for wiping the backside. Do not depress the lever while looking into the nozzle. While still sitting on the porcelain, direct the nozzle upwards towards the natural orifice. Under no circumstances treat this as an enema wash; while pleasure may be taken during its use, and while use may without any guilty feeling be reasonably extended to maximise this pleasure, resist any temptations to poke the nozzle into your outlet. The correct operational distance is 3–5 cm. From 11 am until dusk, this may be extended to 20 cm for the first 15 seconds, to avoid any shocks should the cold water supply pipe be in the direct rays of the sun. However, should you like it hot, the distance cannot be shortened. In consideration of those who come after you, any contact with the rear passage is to be studiously avoided. When operating, follow usual directions for high pressure water washing of the underside of your car.

Given the paucity of bidets, the hose may be used, mostly by women, to spray-clean the forward aperture after urination or sexual activity involving creams or various discharges into and out of the vagina. Since this sluicing may be infinitely more pleasurable than the preceding sexual activity, a social time limit of two hours is placed on use, to allow enjoyment by others. Any soft tissue paper may be used to dab up any water remaining on sensitive parts; this is deposited, as per traditional toilet procedures but a lot cleaner, in the basket provided.

A further use is for the messy defecator whose waste cannot be adequately removed by a double flush. The hose may be directed at full force at any point of the toilet bowl, or the surrounding floor, walls or ceiling. And if it fails to dislodge a particularly unwelcome portion of limpet-like matter, its effects may be further enhanced by bringing into play the toilet brush. Should this be absent, you may with a certain feeling of justification take the most frayed of the toothbrushes stuck behind the water pipe. But do not use it to clean the teeth.

Bottom line:
There's nothing like a good hosing down. Unless it's a good hosing up. Many foreigners buy the toilet bowl hosepipe and take it home with them. Once try, always use. Enjoy.

34

On Going to the Toilet When There Isn't One

Expat's law says that when you are stricken with the mother of all diarrhoeas, it will be upcountry, where all you can do is stagger out to the wooden shack, lift out the makeshift door, and peer into the fly-infested triangular hole cut in the wooden planks. What, you are perhaps thinking, ever happened to the toilet?

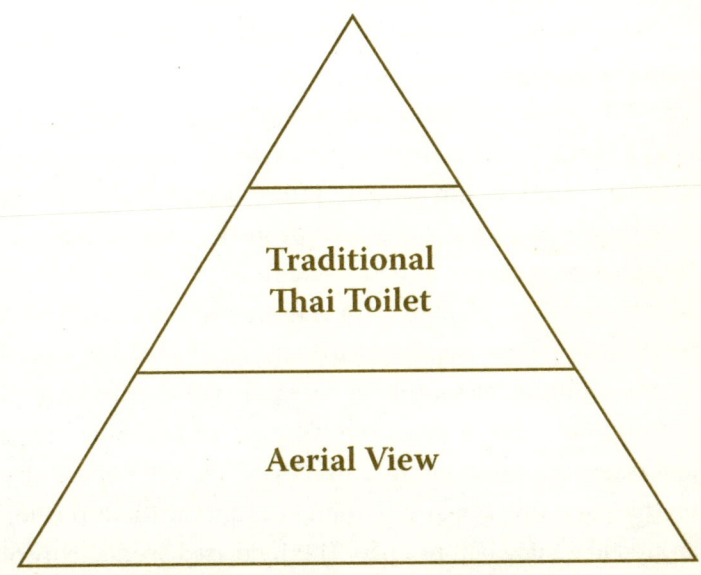

Traditional
Thai Toilet

Aerial View

The toilet is right there, on or in the boards in front of you. It is carefully crafted into a triangle, with the big side at the back and the point indicating the front. The original Thai toilet triangle was extremely small for humanitarian reasons. The small size saved, and continues to save, small children, dogs and chickens from a fate in the pit below that can only be imagined. However, it does require the precision of a smart bomb to use effectively. The less skilled will find the toilet affords a post-evacuation opportunity to examine in detail the 99 per cent of matter that did not go down the hole. This you will do partly to work out which particular culinary delicacy brought on the attack, partly in the hope of retrieving your car keys — although if these have an electronic fob attached they will certainly have guided themselves into the bombing triangle — and partly because you are wondering what to do about the mess that you have made, which the three small cut squares of newspaper on a nail will not begin to clean up.

Napoleon Bonaparte was faced with the same contemplations quite a few years back when his armies found their morning advances were not quite up to schedule. His attempts to bring civilisation to Europe finally succeeded when he invented the ceramic squat toilet, where the hole was barely any larger than its prototype but where the trough-like features assisted examination and cleaning, which could be affected with a minimum of water and a toothbrush. Napoleon's original design was further improved by the addition of footplates to raise slightly the level of the body and allow visual verification of bombing range and trajectory to target; importantly, it allowed his country recruits to know which way round to squat without turning around like a dog before a nap. This increased productivity of latrines by tenfold — that is to say ten soldiers could be in and out in the same time it took one to use the traditional toilet. His army was a whole lot cleaner too. With the new improved squat toilet firmly behind him, Napoleon had no problem conquering Europe, which was still at the wooden triangle stage of development. While not perceptibly a part of Europe, Thailand was quick to realise the merits of the Napoleon and before long, urban Thais were mostly practising the fashionable new squat. Disease rates fell, people smelt better and toilets were generally a nicer place to hang out in. Thus, if you find yourself contemplating a real traditional triangle, think yourself lucky, you have a unique opportunity to experience the pre-Napoleon world.

Napoleon never got round to issuing a set of user's instructions for his new, cleaner, faster toilet. For all its user-friendly practical superiority, the "new" squat shares some of the old squats problems, not least you have to squat. Thus, basic user instructions are overdue. An easy to follow 5-point plan is therefore given here. No guarantees. Break a leg and sue Napoleon, not me.

1. Since the basic toilet slab may face in any direction, do not presume you climb on board and face the door. You must overcome this cultural throwback to your home of origin. Should there be two slabs side by side, do not anguish or philosophise over this fact but take whichever one catches your fancy. And lock the door securely, making sure the piece of string is correctly hooked over the nail.

2. Place your feet on the two raised ceramic foot pads, undo trousers or raise skirts, etc., lower your body bending knees. It is recommended to retain footwear. If you can see a hole below you without looking through your legs, you are facing the wrong way. DO NOT SIT, DO NOT STAND.

3. Males should be prepared either to take off trousers completely and hang them for the duration of operations

on the nail thoughtfully provided (recommended) or to pull trousers etc. down more than the familiar distance required by the sit-down toilet. This is to avoid the inconvenience of recovering your wallet from a bottomless pit. You might wish to roll up your trouser cuffs before beginning then roll down the trousers to meet the cuffs, This makes a tight trouser wad around the calves on which you may rest your inner elbows should you be in for a long duration or feel inclined to read a broadsheet newspaper (not provided). Women have a definite advantage wearing skirts, and men who spend a lot of time squatting on toilets may consider transvestism.

4. For those who cannot go if they have nothing to read, small pieces of cut newspaper are stabbed onto another nail conveniently to hand when in squat position. Thai toilet owners who allow Westerners to use their toilets are obliged by the laws of hospitality to ensure a minimum of 50 per cent of newspaper squares include a Roger Crutchley column cut from an old *Bangkok Post*; the other 50 per cent may be made up of past pages from a child's English homework (the two

alternatives being of a single intellectual level). Unfortunately the cutting up has likely been done with little consideration for the reader of English and however much you try to put the pieces together, you are unlikely to get a complete picture of Crutch's dog. Having read the library provided, two courses of action are open to you. If you judge the paper sufficient and sufficiently porous for the purpose, wipe your arse, with due deference of course, to Crutch's column, and Bob's your Uncle, pop the paper in the basket to allow recycling, stretch those leg muscles and out the door — after having adjusted your dress. Alternatively, stash the reading and wiping matter in a convenient body fold and proceed to the washing. The backside should be as thoroughly cleaned as the water available will allow. Sometimes this is a challenge. If only a small tin of water is to hand, you must make every wipe count, and please wipe with the left hand, unless you have lost that hand or lost use of that hand, when the right may be reluctantly called into service. And please do recycle water by washing directly over the toilet hole, cleaning two orifices at a stroke. (On the toilet hole, use of the hand is optional but is not advised.) If, on the other hand you find a huge *ang* of water, or even a bath-sized trough of water, it is unbecoming to submerge the body in the water, even if you have completely divested yourself of clothing which now hangs precariously together on aforesaid nail. Custom requires that you use the scoop provided and patter the water from the scoop onto your sticky part or parts. If you find yourself engaged in a new enthusiasm and get carried away, you are likely to be a little too damp down below to dry off fully on Roger Crutchley. Your exertions and the watering might have prompted not a little profuse sweating; this and the lingering stimulations of Roger Crutchley's column, will suggest a thorough dousing is in order, particularly if your clothes are still on the nail and hospitable eyes are looking in at you from over the corrugated iron walls of the sweat box and offering, in their hospitable way, to help you out. Feel quite free to use the scoop provided to throw water all over yourself. While you are at it, a few scoops thrown in rapid succession at the smiling eyes above you helps to maintain the party atmosphere and definitely earn you social points for being a good sport. If you forgot your hankie, drying time in lowland Thailand is 40 seconds if standing to attention, half that if engaged in Thai classical dancing (recommended).

5. Exit to applause, but decline all calls for an encore.

Bottom line:
Always go to the toilet before leaving home.

35

On Good Girls and Bad Girls

The female population of Thailand is split into good girls and bad girls. The female population of farang-land is similarly split, but the split exists within a single individual.

A good girl heeds the spirit of the following advice, designed to boost her husband's ego and status — thereby boosting her own.

"Walk slowly. While walking, do not swing your arms too much... do not sway your breasts, do not run fingers through your hair, and do not talk.

Do not stare at anyone, particularly a man, to the point where he can tell what's going on in your mind. Do not run after men.

Love and be faithful to your husband.

Be humble in front of your husband.

When your husband goes to bed, wai him at his feet every night without fail. When he has aches and pains, massage him, then you may go to sleep.

Get up before your husband and prepare water for him to wash. While your husband is eating, sit and watch him nearby so that when he needs something he does not have to raise his voice. Wait until he finishes before you eat."

Sunthorn Phu
A Maxim for Ladies (Ovaht Krasattri), 1844

All Thai girls — and Thai men — learn this by heart at school. So, while Sunthorn Phu does not specifically advise against it, there is really no excuse for dancing naked on top of a bar or smoking cigarettes through the vagina. All girls who conform to the spirit of the Maxim are good girls. All others are not perfect.

Bottom line:
The ratio of good girls to bad girls is 99:1; or is it 1:99?

36

On Gratitude

How do you get a Thai to show gratitude? Well, you certainly won't get a "Thank You" for passing the *nam pla* at lunch; if you are lucky enough to get a brief smile, it will be the acknowledgement smile rather than the thank you smile. And don't expect to be verbally thanked anywhere unless you have just dragged somebody out of the path of a speeding train or sliced the head off a deadly poisonous snake about to strike a helpless baby left unattended while mother is negotiating the ingredients of her kwaytiaw nam.

It's all a question of habit. Large store management now instruct staff to go far beyond verbal thanks, which is why the girl or boy at the Tesco Lotus checkout gives you a beautiful *wai*, not just a token one, after you have parted with large amounts of cash. You will also get some sort of thanks in an upmarket restaurant. But don't expect a *wai* from a girl on Patpong; she's just as likely to spin the tray, throwing your tip to the ground and exposing the words, "Cheapskate Charlie" The *wai* is the traditional Thai way of expressing gratitude, it can accompany verbal expression to make a very big thank you.

The *farang*, particularly the oh so well-mannered English, will embarrass Thais by saying "Thank you" to the bus conductor for giving them a ticket, to the shopkeeper for taking the *farang's* money, and even to the policeman who has just accepted a 400 baht "fine" saving the deviant *farang* driver from a trip to the police station (actually, that one's worth a verbal thanks plus a *wai*). Thanking Thais when you don't have to do so kind of throws Thais onto the wrong foot. Give them a present and they will put it aside, only thanking you if they know that Westerners expect some sort of expression of appreciation. The *farang* who gets a present (it does happen), rips it open and expresses delight and gratitude is, to the Thai mind, making it known that he would like some more of the same.

Today, with the superficial Westernization of many Thais, and the fact that you might be entertaining Thais mostly using English, you might get expressions of gratitude that approximate more readily the patterns you are used to, plus some that Thais are used to. Thus, it is possible that instead of a gratitude-expression deficit, you find yourself in a situation of gratitude-expression over-abundance.

There is no logical reason for the *farang* to have his nose out of joint if people take without verbal thanks. You can take without thanking or you can thank without thinking. Giving something in order to get gratitude is perhaps a normal enough thing in all cultures, but nobody likes to say it is thus, so the Thais often say nothing at all, maybe they give a thank-you smile, maybe even a *wai*, but not necessarily anything. And it's basically the same however big or small a person you are and whatever the value of the object or service given.

Bottom line:

Is the gift you so nicely wrapped and handed over given from the heart because you wanted to give it? Or because you wanted gratitude and maybe something more? We all know it's the second of these. But we all pretend it's the first. If we did not pretend, a gift would not be a gift. Gifts must be free.

37

On Growing a Beard and Going Bald

It is recognised that growing a beard is a linguistic incongruity, describing as it does an inactivity as an activity. It is also quite true that if you grow a beard, you are in fact doing nothing, simply flowing with nature, which in Thai metaphysics comes close to the highest state of spiritual contemplation. It is also absolutely and unquestionably true that having a beard, whether you grew it or it grew itself on you, makes you perceptually older. And not older in the sense of *phi/nong*, where age is respected as the bringer of wisdom. A 30-year-old can make himself look 50+ in a week. Not bad if that's what you want. But the girls will avoid you, even if you use softener on your bristles, not because you look 50 but because they don't like beards and you look 50.

If you grow a beard as compensation for going bald, this does nothing to redress the balance — unless you grow a very long one, comb it up and over, and stay out of the wind. Having beard + baldness tends to create an image that aggravates the natural decline brought on by old age and a delinquent lifestyle. The fact is that Thais have been showing the utmost respect to those with nicely polished domes for over 2,500 years; on the other hand, beards, apart from a few lucky hairs growing out of a favoured chin walt, are generally not Thai. Apart from King Chulalongkorn's magnificent and

attractive moustache (not, notice, a full beard), which every Thai, even the men, would love to be capable of growing, facial hair is regarded as something of a turn-off.

So, if you want to appear attractive to the Thais, go for what the Thais find attractive. The traditional shaving of the head, currently enhanced by a fashion that started with football hooligans, suggests that the best way to disguise or deny creeping baldness is to get rid of the lot. Shave it all off and give your head a nice mahogany polish. And while you're at it, get rid of that beard.

Bottom line:
Put 20 years on, or shave 20 years off: up to you.

38

On Hair Cutting

On taking your regular trip to the hairdresser — once or twice a month in the case of gentlemen, once or twice a day in the case of young ladies — you have the right to expect both a haircut and pleasurable entertainment. Go only to such places that provide a stimulatingly vigorous or sensually gentle massage of head and shoulders — your decision, not that of the transvestite handling your body — and pamper you shamelessly with praise on your beautiful mousey hair. In Thailand, you want and expect and pay for, although not very much, to be treated in the manner to which you would like to become accustomed. Those on an upward mobility thing and those with a superiority complex need such ego-trips as the haircut. In Thailand, you are not old and balding. In Thailand, your beautifully clean head which, excuse me, is just too gorgeous to keep my hands from, is mature enough to have no dandruff problem.

Among the various characteristics you will go for, expect the latest in styles and technology combined with conformity to the honourable traditions of cutting hair from people's heads. These traditions are fading, so you may need to remind your young attendant of them. In Thailand, most public services seem to be staffed by the young; there is a good reason for this, apart from sexual stimulation, but I've forgotten what it is. But don't get the idea that girls and boys and, mostly, khatoeys, are simply whores with scissors: they are much more than that. Many have been trained in hairdressing schools in Bangkok, and even Manila and Singapore. So they know their stuff, even if they missed tutoring in the old traditions. So that you can sound really erudite re Thai culture, these are what those old traditions are.

Never get your hair cut on Wednesday, it is such bad luck hairdressers used to close on this day. Not any more; time is money. It is hardly done, however, to tutor your tonsorial artist on the traditions of his or her trade if you are relaxing in their fingers on a Wednesday afternoon.

One thing you can insist on is that your head and locks be treated with appropriate respect. Touching your sacred regions and cutting your phom must not be undertaken without the appropriate opening rituals to placate the spirits that buzz around just waiting to jump into your head. The phom used to be the only part of a commoner's body that could hope to address a noble (thus, by the way, the polite masculine pronoun "I" in Thai is *phom* or *kraphom*, which equals "my hair"). Unless you have already attained the ultimate ranks of status, these rites are today, with other customers waiting, contracted to a whispered "excuse me" before the scissors get to work. To avoid alerting rather than placating the spirits, this is often whispered into the ear of the customer. So if you wear a hearing aid, turn it on.

It may no longer be the norm to collect every hair trimmed from your sacred head in pure white sheets, parcel them up in satin bags and ceremoniously send them on their way with Brahmanic chantings down the regal Chao Phraya to the infinity of the sea. Such practices add enormous overheads to the cost of a trim, but since this is Thailand, anything can be arranged if you are prepared to pay.

Select your regular hairdresser on the basis of getting a good time, as well as a good haircut. While not wishing to doubly disadvantage the afflicted, it is as well, given the sharp nature of the instruments of the trade and their proximity to jugular veins, to select your hairdresser as you would your heart surgeon, and avoid any evident signs of advanced Parkinson's disease or alcoholic tremors. It is permissible to fall in love with your hairdresser, particularly when sleepily defenceless on your back and gazing up through the lather into the liquid eyes of the lady-boy of your dreams. If, however, your hairdresser falls in love with you, which, if awake, you might detect through your shroud as indicated by the rubbing of body parts soft and hard into your forearms and neck muscles, maintain a straight and unflinching gaze into the mirror, meeting there the vigilant eyes of your spouse sitting watchfully under the dryer.

This being Thailand, a hairdresser doesn't just dress hair on the head. Hairs curling up from the nose and out of the ears may also be clipped, if you are in the sad state of having nobody at home to do this job with tweezers. Nails on hands and feet can be fussed over if you want them fussed over, and you may ask re the blackhead removal services. However, unlike the situation in many Muslim countries, circumcision is not an optional extra.

It is your hair — at least it is while on the head — so you get to say how you would like it shortened, straightened or permed. If your Thai is limited, "short" may be interpreted as "military", so try to keep your eyes open. Keep your ears open as well, as a haircut entitles you to one free Thai language lesson. This is pretty much the same as the one you get with a taxi ride, but has functional terms like "sorry about the ear" thrown in. After a few haircuts, you will be able to say in passable Thai, your nationality, your age, how long you have been in Thailand, and how much you love everything about the country, and "Please be careful around the ears, if you don't mind too much".

A real hairdresser, one with a sense of tradition, will signal the end of the session by disappearing from your sight for a minute or two and returning with both palms rubbing together. Before you can say aray na, he will dump a litre of petroleum essence on the top-middle of your head and proceed animatedly to rub it into your tingling scalp and hair. This will set instantly into a rock solid crust while you are pushed abruptly forward over the washbasin, and hands and fists beat your backbone to its jelly. Finally, in triumph, the artisan will whip the shroud from your neck with a flourish that would do a toreador proud, and pirouette to the next seated customer.

Bottom line:
However sensually interesting you find a trip to the hairdresser's, do try to remember to have your hair cut while you are there.

39

On Honking the Dawn Chorus

When the mighty Mekong or the regal Chao Phraya or even the Mother Ping reflects the first hopeful rays of a rising sun and the sky is a halcyon mix of softly-lightening blues and teasingly-pleasing reds, your sleep of the wicked is punctuated by what sounds like the rasp of a 12" bastard file on the edge of a sheet of corrugated iron roofing. Time to get up and enjoy the view.

As you look out from your riverside balcony at the birth of time re-enacted daily just for you and a few billion other people, you will become aware of the resounding presence of humanity in nature's grand scheme of things. The old man of Chinese origins next door, a dozen or so monks in the *wat* across the water, the night guard stirred from his slumbers, and your cute little pyjama-clad maid, are all honking like a flock of geese running at an intruder across a rich man's lawn. Lungs bent double expectorate all overnight accumulations of chilli paste, garlic heads, frog livers, roasted dried squid, tobacco, alcohol, sweet soft things and sour-bitter things, all mixed up with the thick mucus secreted in abnormal quantities in the respiratory passages until a paste of sufficiently firm consistency is formulated that will, when expelled at full force and with practised competence, hit the inside rim of an enamelled spittoon at a hundred paces, giving off a resounding and rather pleasing ring, if the enamel is not too chipped. The rattling continues like a rusty machine gun or a corroded pneumatic drill an average of seven times per person. Sleep through that lot if you can.

And after the honking of the dawn chorus, the comparatively gentle but equally thorough cleansing of the nostrils tones down the decibel level to a cruising one-thirty.

These noises may be heard in isolated punctuation throughout the day, but only at dawn, when throats are fresh and full, is the absolute grandeur of the Asian grand clearance ensemble to be heard in chorus. And as you will know after reading this book, Thais, either spontaneously or by design, like to do things together. So, never mind the view, get honking.

Bottom line:

Before firing your accumulated overnight wads at a public target, it is strongly advised to practise in private. This avoids the loss of face involved in cleaning a gentleman's patent leather shoe cap with your silk pocket handkerchief, when you were aiming for the kerbside gutter next to it. Aim is improved quickly through practice. A good performance rises above the vulgar, but only practise with a mat-red well-enamelled spittoon of high resonance, not your 16th century Chinese black and white porcelain job. And preferably, practise alone and away from priceless oriental carpeting.

40

On Interrupting

The Thais, being essentially diplomats, have absolutely no problem in carrying on at least two conversations at the same time. They tend to attribute the same capacity to other peoples. Thus, when you are deep in meaningful dialogue with a friend, in Thai or English, they will not give interrupting you a second thought, or even a first thought — they just jump straight in. Similarly, if you are having a good chin wag with the Thais and their mobile phone rings, they will answer it and carry on another conversation, leaving you lost for words. When you call them on the same mobile, they may say hello then leave you hanging while talking to another.

Some Thais have learnt, through exposure to Western ways, to say "excuse me" before interrupting a *farang*, but this is almost always followed by the interruption anyway.

Interruptions don't seem to require polite hellos and goodbyes. Your presence, if the interrupter wants to talk to your partner, might barely be acknowledged, and when the interruption has run its course, the interloper is off with maybe a nod in your direction, maybe just a parting breeze as they flip out of your immediate world.

This behaviour is definitely not related to the language of the conversation, it is not that English is invisible to Thai ears. Precisely the same thing happens to Thais. Thais seem to be unaffected by such interruptions, but many foreigners, socialised from the earliest years *not* to interrupt people talking to each other, find this social habit decidedly lacking in social grace, and lacking in what the Thais pride themselves on: consideration for the feelings of other people. The reason for it *might* be that Thais are more used to group interaction rather than in-depth and intense one-to-one dialogue. If this is the reason, they should logically address both people being interrupted, but inevitably they address only one. But don't think too much in familiar terms of logic when interacting with Thais, or when being sidelined, if only temporarily.

What to do about this habit, which leaves you somewhat confused, since you like to think of Thais as polite, and possibly leaves you somewhat testy, as you see it as rude, even if no rudeness is intended? I can't think of a single thing. Every culture has negative and contradictory characteristics; some things you simply have to wince and bear.

Bottom line:
Please don't talk when I'm interrupting you.

41

On Inverted Nipples

Inverted nipples are considered luckier than a hunchback on a dwarf. But they are not exposed for public rubbing.

Inverted nipples, like so many things Thai, are not really Thai at all, but a genetic import from China. The incidence in Thailand is much lower than in contemporary China. The Lonely Peanut survey gives a total figure of 4.7 per cent of Chinese women in China having one or more inverted nipples. The same survey gives a total figure for Thailand of only 1.9 per cent of females — although it also gives a figure of 0.9 per cent males and 0.6 per cent for those of ambiguous gender.

Now, what, you may ask has this fascinating subject to do with your attempts to integrate into and raise your status in Thai society? There is, in fact, a direct correlation between inverted nipples and status. Inverted nipples tend to be more evident among the upper middle class and those on the move socially, but are hardly evident at all within the lower and upper echelons of society, those who have yet to begin to make it and those who have really made it. You are therefore unlikely to encounter them in the massage parlour, or on the naked dancer on a Pattaya bar top. You are, on the other hand, most *likely* to encounter them among the educated elite. If the Lonely Peanut is correct, some 5 per cent of female university students encompass within their surgically clean and starched white blouses a pair of inverted nipples.

While 50 per cent of university students go in for such things as eye and nose operations and breast and penis enlargements and virginity hymen replacement and permanent waves, those blessed with inverted nipples show a staggering zero per cent who wish in any way to change their bodies, not even by adding a cautious little tattoo or a colour rinse to their shampoo. All this means that if you land a pair of inverted nipples, consider yourself on to a whole parcel of original goodies.

The damnably difficult thing is to know which among all those clean white blouses, contain the inverted nipples. True invertees do not flaunt their treasures. Discovery is therefore something of an undercover quest.

It is certainly not on, and will lose you all your social points gained so far and even leave you in social debit, to request, even gently and tastefully, an opening of blouse and bra for a quick inspection. Instead, you have to rely on investigation of secondary characteristics associated with nipple inversion and add up your clues. It's a bit like looking for the reborn Dalai Lama, but you are not armed with bones, bells and trinkets. Do not baulk at this task. In itself, if handled with discretion, it can be a source of arousing pleasure.

Almost 99 per cent of inverted nipples are found on breasts of the smaller than averagely-small dimensions. The existence of falsies and various paddings need not unduly worry you, as a real invertee will avoid these as intrusion on natural body character. This refusal to tinker with natural attributes is quasi-sacred to the true invertee, who invariably has long, sleek, black, silky hair on her head and no hair on the other parts of the body. Small breasts on the fully clad are best perceived in a strong and direct sunlight; if the subject of examination is not wearing a bra you might resolve your quest without further ado. Unfortunately, things are unlikely to be that simple: while the bra tends to be functionally superfluous for the true invertee, the conservative character of the true specimen favours conformity to universal conventions re the wearing of undergarments. Nothing worthwhile is ever easy, but it remains a practicality that one of the best places to locate the small-breasted potential invertee is in the bus queues on a bright sunny day, when students make vain attempts to queue, books held above their heads, in the pencil-thin line of shade thrown by a street lamp post. Definitely, exclude any moustaches and D-cups from your quest.

A deceptively easy characteristic is the almost total absence of armpit hair on proprietors of genuine inverted nipples. This might appear a safe and easy comparison, given that young ladies, or gentlemen, are not likely to take the same degree of offence if you take a protracted look *up* their T-shirt sleeve as a protracted look *down* their T-shirt neckline. The armpit check, however, can be challenging because of the flowing silky hair, which tends to cover shoulders and upper arm parts. Armpit examination also places you in a difficult position for free-flow conversation, and perhaps more seriously gives you the humble aspect taken on by those of low-status. It is also, for the untrained eye, an unreliable guide to the true invertee. While the true specimen would never dream of shaving armpits or any other part of the body, and would have no functional need to do so, the sad fact is that many women, and a large proportion of men, shave their armpits regularly. It takes an experienced eye, as well as good eyesight, to spot fresh stubble. It is recommended that before embarking on your quest, you spend some lazy afternoons with telescope or binoculars studying Thais, or rather Thai armpits, at the more upmarket swimming places, where swimming costumes rather than sarongs and T-shirts are the norm. You should train yourself to spot, with the naked eye, any stubble within two seconds, which is about as long as you get before armpits close and backs are turned in your direction. When you do strike stubble during a quest, take your investigation no further — the subject probably has nipples the size and consistency of cow's udders. And cow's udders, while useful for hanging up your overcoat in the West, are unlikely to portend noble virtue in the East.

Other bodily characteristics of the true nipple invertee are less easily assessed than breast size and armpit hair. Inverted nipples tend to go along with very small vaginas, rivetingly-tight backsides and an absence of pubic hair so marked as to make any shaving superfluous. These characteristics are given here not so much to help you in your search as to boost morale and to confirm that the successful search can be infinitely rewarding in ways that might go even beyond status enhancement.

Very fortunately for those in search of the true invertee, there is also a tendency for invertees to fall within that part of the population without epicanthic folds. Since these are found on a part of the anatomy more readily studied, this may be considered a safe place to start your research.

Epicanthic folds, on males and females, are found above the eye. All *farang* have them, giving rise to the "round eye" look. Many Thais have a natural trace, and many have such traces put in, thinking themselves more attractive with than without. Those without are blessed with the beauty of "almond" or "slit" eyes, of whom a small proportion will be deified with inverted nipples and the accompanying attributes of eternal youth.

You might need to look closely to discern a complete absence of fold. Should these be pencilled in, or moulded by the surgeon's knife, eliminate the subject from your research. When closely examining an eye or eyes, it is advisable to put the subject at ease with such phrases as, "I hope you don't mind; I think I have never, ever, seen such an extraordinarily beautiful absence of epicanthic folds." Absence certainly can make the heart grow fonder. Only if the subject of scrutiny invites you back to her or his place may you proceed further with, "May I enquire as to the state of your nipples?"

One last word on inverted nipples. Some remain in an inverted state for life, or until a pregnancy, others may pop out when arousal takes place. Those pop-outs are, at least temporarily, known in scientific terms as *inverted* inverted nipples. This has led to some confusion among the less scientific and those who cannot handle double negatives. This confusion has led to adoption by the aficionado of the inverted nipple, of a popular term for such pop-outs; this is taken from the Oxford Inverted Dictionary, which specifies pop-outs as TV nipples — *temporarily verted* nipples. TV nipples have the added characteristic that they may, particularly if stimulated by a wet tongue, pop in and out at will. So, if your name is Will, there are even more treats in store.

Well then, now you have found your dream. Inverted nipples, nominal body hair, particularly in the pubic and armpit region, small firm breasts, tight little orifices, absence of epicanthic folds, almond eyes, long, lank, black, silky hair, all of it growing on the head and none on or between the legs or toes, essentially conservative, loyal, not readily aroused, and most unlikely to be part of bar-room life. What do you do with such a dream, be it M or F? Since the twin prime attributes of this rare and invaluable Thai are loyal aesthetic attachment to you and respectful admiration from a large segment of those well-placed to give you a leg up the ladder, a good thing to do is to pop her or him beside you in a British sports car and drive around to meet her or his friends, increasing your status with every kilometre.

Bottom line:
Inversion is innate, it cannot be acquired.

42

On Jenny Lover at Golobanhao

You turn left at Jenny Lover, go on until you come to Golobanhao and you'll see the surgery of Doctor Etakunpaiboon on your right. Can't miss it, everything's got huge signs up in English.

Well, sounded easy enough. Jenny Lover also sounded more interesting than the average landmark, and a name I was unlikely to forget. Must be a shop, I thought, maybe named after a *farang* woman selling silk and handicrafts. Names have that effect on me, make me wonder what goes on behind the name, behind the sign. But could I find the sign? Of course not. I trolled back and forth around where I thought it must be, driving slowly, people looking at me.

In the West, I thought, if an obvious foreigner kerb-crawled like this, the locals would be on the phone to the Homeland Security forces or the Morality Police. People certainly looked curious as I cased their street for the sixth time, finally stopping in front of a small café where a man in a clean shirt and shoes who I judged to be of schoolmaster ilk was drinking *nam dang*. "Hello," I said in my best Thai accent. Always a good start that. Funny, that word is the same in English and Thai. "I am looking for Jenny Lover. Know where she/it is?" I didn't actually say 'she/it'. Thai does not distinguish between she and it, or he and it for that matter, but in order to maintain my gender-correctness I opted for a common linguistic formula that simply omits the third person altogether. Very useful language is Thai, particularly when you don't have a clue what or who you are looking for.

He didn't know Jenny. So he called back into the small café. I heard "Jenny Lover" echo around the Chinese shop house, spiral up to the third floor, and come down again in the form of a plumpish girl with huge well-cushioned hips and a jiggling little child attached to one of them. "Who's looking for Jenny Lover?" she said, non-committally. The teacher-type headed her question in my direction and it came flying through the open car window. Could this be the mysterious Jenny Lover? I felt a little cheated.

"Me," I said, "I look for Jenny Lover."

"Over there," she said, changing hips and increasing the tempo of the juggling baby. "Right opposite."

I looked right opposite. All I could see was a factory gate with a large sign over it in English: General Wear. "Where?" I said. She pointed directly at the factory gate, no doubt wondering just how the foreign blind idiot managed to drive a car, but kind enough to keep her thoughts inside her plump round head.

I gazed at the sign, waiting for a revelation. It never came. I got out of the car, crossed the road, waved the gateman to me. "Jenny Lover. Where?" I said. He came out of the gates, pointed up to the General Wear sign arching over the entrance. "Jenny Lover," he said.

Revelation struck like a bolt of lightning. "G" as in gin the alcoholic drink, "en" as in en, "era" somehow as in y/I, "l" on end of "General" not pronounceable as *el* on the end of that word, so transferred to the next word, o to separate two consonants, wear as in ver. JENNY LOVER. The sign was screaming it at me now.

"Who do you want?" asked the friendly gateman.

"Actually, nobody." Bit sheepish now. "What I really want is the Golobanhao Company."

"Ah, Golobanhao. Just turn left here. Keep straight on. Can't miss it. Huge sign in English."

"And Chinese, I suppose," I added.

"Don't know. Can't read Chinese. Huge sign in English: Golobanhao."

So, I turned left and drove straight on. And there it was! A huge sign in English which this time I recognised immediately: GLOBAL HOUSE. Go-lo-ban-hao. I'll leave you to work that one out.

After that, finding Doctor Etakunpaiboon's clinic was child's play. There was the large sign in English: Eartrakulpaiboony.

Even when you can speak and read Thai, you will find some of the most troubling words in the Thai language are, in fact, not Thai at all; they are English. Apart from *bit-sii* (Big C) and just about every other supermarket in the country, some other little words that can throw you in a way Thais don't understand (especially if they know they are using an "English" word) are *sa-tem* (stamp), *san-wit* (sandwich), *bang* (bank), *lip* (lift), and *ap-a-men* (apartment). If you have difficulty writing Thai words using the European script, appreciate that the Thais have ten times the problem pronouncing European words in a way that is recognisable to people other than Thais.

"Can I see Doctor Etakunpaiboon please?"

"You mean Doctor Dang," said the receptionist.

"And what is the problem?" said Doctor Dang.

"It's my dog, doctor."

"I'm sorry, I don't treat dogs. There is a vet nearby, next to the Po-lit-sa-tay-shun."

"But I came to see you because you are a specialist," I persisted.

"If the problem is with your dog, I don't see how I can help you," said the good Doctor Dang patiently. "But tell me anyway if you like, what is the problem of the dog?"

"It bit me."

I threw that one in because there is a minimum quota of clean jokes required in a book like this. Now, where was I?

Bottom line:

If you can't find Bit-Chi-An supermarket, ask at Big Jean's.

43

On Just Joking

There is a *farang* point of view, one held popularly and one given some credit by (mostly *farang*) writers on Thai personality, that Thais tend to think, if at all, after pulling the trigger rather than before, and that the pulling of the trigger, or the running amok with a long knife, results from emotions pent-up to the point where they burst out almost independent of the will of the emotionally suppressed. This view generally considers that if Thais had a release mechanism, even if it disturbs the surface harmony, there might be a few less penises cut from sleeping males and tossed out the window to the ducks. The view is often held alongside the view that in Thai society anything goes.

To judge from the Thai papers, the penis-eating ducks must number in the thousands. Perhaps the frustrated wives might be less prone to such cutting revenge if they were taught to think first, but perhaps not. Perhaps the answer is to get rid of the ducks and hide the knives. Perhaps the answer is for philandering husbands to behave themselves. Perhaps it really is time for researchers to find a solution to pre-menstrual tension. Perhaps there needs to be other social constraints on action that might preclude the tendency to go for the knife-duck solution. A lot of "perhaps".

But is it really the case that Thais are so emotionally bottled-up that almost anything might happen if you say boo to them? Does Thai society really provide no release at all for pent-up feelings? Does it really fail to provide any boundaries to dissuade abuse and retribution? Of course they are not, it does not, and it does not again.

The same gregarious nature of Thais that seems to require not being alone, provides a natural restriction on anti-social behaviour. The slightest whiff of the anti-social and a Thai loses face among those he or she cares about, family, *puak*, village, neighbourhood. Thais keep themselves in line just by being around in reasonably large numbers, at least numbers larger than one. In these groups, emotional release activities may be present. Many Thai groups get together regularly for drinking sessions. These rarely reach village-wide African proportions and aim at mellowness rather than outright drunkenness. Often, in the countryside, a single glass is used and passed around a group, each person pouring a drink for another, whether it is home-brew or beer. The pace of drinking limits drunkenness and encourages chit-chat. As in other societies, the passing of alcohol allows a certain leeway in norms of polite behaviour and talk on these occasions might get quite risqué. Some individuals are cleverer than others, and the cleverest can almost criticise husband, wife or neighbour while making them laugh. This is done through the telling of stories slightly exaggerated, often as if they were quite true. A verbal parry-riposte may develop with some razor-sharp quick-fire repartee. The aim is to make people laugh — itself a release of tension for the "performer" and the audience. Laughter is a well-known healer.

When people are engaged in such tall story telling, or just throwing in an outrageous line or openly telling untruths, they are said to be engaged in *phuut len*. This is a favourite Thai activity, and you don't have to be drinking to do it. *Phuut len* can take place in a group, where it will be readily appreciated, or just between two people, where one may "send up" another. If one of the people is you, and even if your Thai is good, you might not recognise that you are having your leg pulled until your Thai partner says, "*Phuut len*". Just joking.

Phuut len goes beyond telling jokes, but often uses word play in a social context. Time for an example. Outspoken woman who suspects the young man sitting opposite her is not fully faithful to his new bride. Addressing the young man.

"*Chop mia maak, mai*?" "Do you like your wife a lot?" Pause.

"*Reu chop mia noy*?" "Or do you like your wife a little?"

The first sentence, given the ambiguities of Thai grammar can also mean, "Do you like a lot of wives?" And the second can also mean, "Or do you like your minor wife?"

Since there is no reply that does not get him into trouble, the young man has little choice but to laugh. Not to do so would mean that he, and not the outspoken woman, would lose face. In fact talk of losing face in such situations suggests there might be some tension in the air. There usually is not, and the laughter will be genuine, perhaps terminating in a spontaneous group "whoop', which may be seen as another release of tension, this time of the entire group.

Other opportunities for releasing tension and pent-up emotion may be further beyond the fringe of Thai culture and are mainly for men. These revolve around more persistent drinking bouts in bars and occasionally frequenting prostitutes in brothels, bars or massage parlours. Thai women do not have the same outlets for sexual release. On the other hand, the supportive nature of women towards each other, always stronger than that felt between men, is particularly strong among Thai women and some at least of the younger women enjoy homosexual love with a girl friend — in private of course.

Bottom line:

If you realise that you have made a terrible verbal gaff in a social setting, you can always try saying, "Phuut len". Just joking. You never know, it might even work.

44

On *Khatoey, Tom,* Man, Woman

Many peoples of the world manage to get by with a choice of two genders, M and F. In Thailand, official forms, documents and toilets also recognise only a limited range of two. Unofficially, there are a clear four genders and some vacillations in between. It must also be noted that some mild deviances, like cross-dressing, exist equally in the *khatoey, tom,* and what is often confusingly know as "straight" categories. Indeed, some of Thailand's greatest have been occasional cross-dressers, for one: Kukrit Pramoj, ex-Prime Minister, famous author, elder statesman and occasional wearer of women's clothing. So, if you are searching for a soul mate or sex partner, Thailand offers a fun choice of four major categories with a further choice of sub-categories.

If you are set on marrying a Thai, it is as well to be sure right from the start whether you want to marry a man, woman, *khatoey* or *tom.* This will save quite some surprises and possibly a disappointment or two later on.

Given the choice available for selection, you might be advised, rather than rely on such fatalistic decision as whoever is the first to walk through the door, to make out an Excel grid showing all your preferences and giving a weighting to each. Such a ready reference chart is exemplified here:

	male	female	khatoey	tom
$10,000+/mth	10,000	10,000	10,000	10,000
-21	1	4	6	4
99+	0	47	6	98
X-dresser	11	0	6	0
pubic shaver	1	20	6	98
inverted nips	0	230	6	45
under 5 ft	-50	50	56	60
big feet	-50	-30	-50	-30
gay	300	300	300	350
straight	400	-100	-400	200
spotty	450	450	500	600
red lips	390	10	590	590
univ ed.	0	0	0	0

The above preferences chart would suggest that the perfect partner for this particular normal person is a gay *tom*, who shaves pubic hair, has inverted nipples, is under 5 feet tall, spotty of complexion, with red lips. Second choice for this normal person is a straight male, cross-dresser, spotty with red lips. This individual also seems to have a penchant for older women, even those who think they are men, and a low regard for the educated. The monthly salary is a matter of total indifference. He should have no trouble at all finding what he wants in any supermarket.

Easy as this exercise is, the fact remains that very few people do it, or anything like it. The average man puts much more thought into buying a second-hand car, or even a second-hand book than he does a second-hand wife. Women tend to reverse priorities, go for a rich, straight man old enough to leave his fortune quickly; they spend much longer on coming to a decision, even longer than getting a perm in the *serm suay*.

Another way of making the difficult choice is not to make it at all, just wait until somebody selects you and go along with fate; that way you can at least deny responsibility later. If more than one selects you at the same time, choose the one who loses the contest, that way you have less chance of being bullied for the rest of your life.

Yet a third way is to go to a large bar with naked dancing, where you can at least see what you are getting. If you are a man, you pick out the naked body that most conforms to your fantasy and flick your thumb repeatedly over the edges of a tight wad of new 1,000 baht bills. If a woman, you completely undress, preferably slowly and in time with the music and take up a position on the stage, making your selection from the men who give the most money.

Having selected a possible, you might think to take him or her along to a well-known monk, who looks them up in his book and saves you the trouble of making a final decision, unless, as so often happens, it's a bit of this and a bit of that,

in which case you have to spend even more money going to a *mor duu*, fortune teller. Still, it is money well spent, since later nobody can blame you when the thing bottoms up. A good fortune teller should be able to warn you that you are steering course for a tempest.

Whatever your choice, you are advised to consider carefully pedigree and background. If he or she does not know his or her father, score a negative; if she does not know her mother, score a very strong positive.

Now that's all sorted out, on to the nuptials.

Bottom line:
When considering a partner for life, or until death do you part, always consider carefully pedigree. Does he or she come from a good bar?

45

On Knickers

Knickers of a normal persuasion, not the pearly thongs of Patpong's pubs and palaces, are the most private apparel known to man or woman. Private apparel that houses the most private parts. Outside of lingerie departments and market stalls, at which point the presumption is that they have yet to host privates, they have no public role in Thai society.

Because they exist in the private realm and because of the close association with genitalia, it used to be the norm that washer boys did not do ladies' knickers. Now they usually do, and another problem has arisen. Now there are washer boys and clothes line freaks with a fetish for ladies' knickers precisely because of that close association, and it is perhaps to be recommended for ladies to wash their own and hang them to dry indoors. Occasionally, maids will show the same reluctance to handle the knickers of men. In these days of washing machines, such quaint old habits are changing fast. But, should you encounter reluctance, it is not done to force the issue, unless that is you get a real kick out of imagining the maid or washer boy cuddling up to your personal garments; and if you do, what kind of deviant are you?

If hung to dry and air on a washing line in public — and many Thais do not like to do this — do make sure the line does not straddle a public way. And if you are walking in an

area criss-crossed by washing lines (although I cannot think why you should be), take care not to walk under any — an impossibility of course. This has about one hundred times the bad-luck effect of walking under a ladder, especially if there are knickers anywhere on the line.

Knickers may be seen as a very obvious symbolic representation of the private and public dichotomy. The two do not readily mix in the Thai world. Wander the privacy of your house and your dreams as you will, but wear something on top as you walk the streets.

Bottom line:
Don't wash your dirty knickers in public. And only hang them to dry in the guests' toilet if you have absolutely nothing else for the guests to play with.

46

On Lines of Marriage

A foreigner wishing to marry a Thai needs to arm his application with a few marriage lines. These are not difficult to obtain and compared to many countries, are no great problem. Maybe this is why so many couples don't bother, and why so many odd couples do.

The first lines you will need will come from your embassy in Bangkok, or the embassy that handles things on behalf of your country if there is no direct representation. This involves you going to the embassy and completing an internal document or answering a few questions like, "Are you married already?". Answer yes to that one and you have to produce the divorce certificate. The embassy, not knowing you from Adam, will then empty your wallet and provide a signed letter which states, diplomatically, lines to the effect that: "Joe Lawless says he wants to marry Pornstar Phonsavan. We don't actually believe a word the lying bastard says but we have no evidence to prove the contrary. We therefore know of no impediment to the marriage, if Joe Lawless is to be believed, which we don't but never mind."

This letter is written in English, or maybe your national language. This is in spite of the fact that the "letter of no impediment" has been a requirement for decades and it must be in Thai. The embassy will not give you a letter in Thai, but will give you a list of approved translators who will "translate" the letter into Thai for a fee (going to one is quicker, as they have the format set out already on their computers and may do it while you wait — for a fee).

Just occasionally a consulate might decide to interview both parties (embassies differ on this point and it rather depends how bored the staff are). As long as you both stick to the same story, and don't take along your children, this is a formality.

You will also need to get a letter from a doctor proving you are alive. It is supposed to say that you have no communicable diseases, but if you go to an overworked Thai hospital, rather than a high-tech hospital or clinic providing coffee and ice-cream service, the doctor, always under pressure and often with three patients at a time in his examination room, will simply ask if you are okay and somebody will type a letter saying you are in good health. This is enough. No X-rays or blood tests, they only raise questions and clog things up.

With these lines of authenticity, off you go to the Amphur to sign your name and get a certificate each, nicely bordered by sea shells. If it doesn't work out, back you both go to the same place and sign your names again for a fairly painless divorce.

Bottom line:
As long as the Lines are officially signed and stamped, they must be true, mustn't they?

47

On Loving

The Thai objects of love, as measured in the time spent in company of a being, the respect shown, the amount of money spent on the love-object, the regret shown when the individual is sick or dies or disappears, and the extent of communication when separated by distance, fall into a set order, as follows. The order is the same for male and female.

1. Self
2. Mother
3. Younger siblings
4. Older siblings
5. Nieces and nephews
6. Grandmother
7. Grandfather
8. Father
9. Family dog
10. Family buffalo
11. Friends
12. Children
13. Spouse

Bottom line:
Recognise that family and friends come first. If your spouse or partner doesn't love the family, he or she cannot love you.

48

On Marriage as a Hazardous Undertaking

For a Thai man marrying a Thai woman, marriage might appear to be the most hazardous undertaking of his life, and quite possibly the last undertaking of his life.

This statement is based on a totally unbiased sample of over 9,999 *farang* husbands of Thai women. The evidence was gathered from these *farang* husbands, none of whom spoke Thai, but all of whom were 100 per cent convinced their wives had told them 100 per cent of the truth 100 per cent of the time. Over 100 per cent of these women had been previously married to Thais (some more than once). Of this 100 per cent, 100 per cent of Thai husbands mercilessly beat their wives every day, and beat and sexually molested the average of 1.7 children each wife had by that husband. Not one of these husbands ever gave his wife a baht to help towards housekeeping. Instead, the wife in every case was forced to pay everything for her husband, even for his minor wives. Of that 100 per cent of Thai husbands, 87 per cent **died** within weeks of the birth of the second child. Stone dead. They died just to spite their wives. Each wife was left to bring up 1.7 small children, which was all hubby left behind. The other 13 per cent continued to beat their wives and molest their own children until a *farang* knight in shining armour came along and rescued her. All in all, it is a constant source of surprise that any Thai woman marries a Thai man instead of going straight for the *farang*, and that any Thai man marries a Thai woman, when it is obviously tantamount to a death sentence.

Those few Thai men who survive the gauntlet of marriage to a Thai wife and the cuckolding by the *farang* knight in shining armour usually manage to hop into middle or old age and do quite nicely, ending up with enough in the bank to take another wife. The wealthy and wily old Thai picks his new wife from the masses of poor in an attempt to make amends for his past transgressions in life. He will always pick some poor little gorgeous virgin of 17 years still living with her parents, whom he will honour with a goodly sum.

The *farang* knight in shining armour, having rescued a damsel in distress and her brood, is responsible for them for life. He therefore marries her, adopts her children as his own, provides the means to pay for the cures and operations of the wife's family, every member of which is about to die

within two weeks unless help is forthcoming, and finally, in his last humanitarian gesture in life, gives his new wife all that remains of all his money. Pure *nam jai.* The new wife, in appreciation of her knight in shining armour, continues to care for her new husband whenever the proprietorship of her new bar will allow her the time. When he finally snuffs it ten years before the time allocated for the final act in his home country, the wife mourns his parting all the way to the funeral pyre and beyond, sometimes even as far as the bank. Selling off her children for a good price to Thai men who have previously been married to her friends, she settles down to enjoy plump middle age, a serial widow with a nice capital investment, with the husband's pension now paid to her, full of the social status that only real money can bring in, and with the added value her children will bring in regularly and lay at her feet. So you see, the trials and tribulations of life aside, there is a happy ending for some if not for all.

Bottom line:
Farang knights in shining armour will find plenty of Thai windmills at which to tilt and plenty of Thai damsels in distress awaiting salvation. Who could ask for anything more?

49

On Massage Parlours

You might have noticed that Thais either seem to be in constant need of a massage or to be employed in the provision of massage to others. Perhaps all the conflict avoidance and remaining cool in spite of the traffic, heat, pollution and matriarchal demands take their toll and make Thai people, or at least Thai men, particularly prone to muscular stress and the need for comforting hands to provide relief to pent-up tensions in the body and mind. Perhaps. Whatever the reason, the string of huge buildings, each employing hundreds of people in Petburi Road (Petchaburi Road) and similar establishments elsewhere in Bangkok and in each major town in Thailand, and the myriad of smaller establishments suggests that the institution of massage is as quintessentially Thai as Thai boxing; other people do it, but nobody does it better than Thais.

It is important before embarking on a trip to the massage parlour that you determine in broad measure if you require services of the traditional or the modern. The first of these genres is usually signposted as such, invariably adding the magic words *Wat Po* somewhere on the sign. (This Bangkok *wat* is said to be the home of original Thai massage and the temple grounds continue to provide training in the art and a flourishing and *non-sexual* service to tourists and locals.)

The second is modern by default, although modernity involves a comfortable — and legal — adaptation of the oldest profession. You may frequent either or both places with no fear of being labelled a deviant, or of a heavy policeman crashing through the door to arrest you (prostitution is a crime in Thailand, believe it or not). But if in a traditional venue, where the community spirit takes over and lines of starched white sheets and ranks of mattresses (and the low price) suggest that you should desist from gropes and gooses even if you and the masseuse are the only ones around. You are in a public domain and rules on public behaviour apply. You will be given a light pyjama and a curtain is drawn around you; when the masseuse or masseur opens the curtain, she or he expects to find you meekly stretched out on the mattress wearing both parts of the pyjama. It is *not* acceptable for you to be naked on your back, manhood errant in the air and urging the laying on of hands with the words, "Come on baby, fly my kite". The laying on of hands in the flying-of-kites sense is not part of the *Wat Po* training. You have made the mistake of confusing tradition and modern. And if you want modern in a traditional place, you have to cough up the extra for the VIP room.

Modern massage parlours come with a choice of masseuse, and occasionally masseurs. Indeed the choice is often overwhelming. But whether there are three or three hundred, all will usually be safely behind glass, displayed on tiered, carpeted steps in clothing designed to allow selection by the window shopper without the need of trying on to ensure a good fit, their eyes fixed on the Thai-drama unfolding on the TV screen with its back to you. While modern in methodology, the basic norms of Thai society are maintained and each girl or old woman (all tastes are catered for) wears a large red number to remove the need to point out your choice with a finger to the man on the microphone — pointing at people being considered among the worst of *farang* manners by Thais. Norms are fully maintained in the public arena and no feeling up or removal of clothing should take place until you have navigated the corridors and stairs, entered the room accorded you, and the door is locked behind you and your 90 minutes officially starts. Then you either fix with the masseuse as to precisely what depths of decadence she or he will go in your pursuit of complete stress removal and how much it will cost you in addition to the basic massage fee you paid downstairs. If you have paid in advance for the "full service", you need utter not one word, although an occasional groan is permitted and expected as you enter into the spirit of the session and serves to relieve the silence.

You will be given an assisted bath, and it is not well thought of to expend your wad into the bath waters; this is unthinking of the next occupant, will involve the masseuse in menial labour beyond her job-description... and what would you do for the remaining 89 minutes?

Both genres, like most services in Thailand, include a Thai lesson. The traditional tends to be traditional, while the modern introduces terms you may not have heard before, inevitably flattering the considerable dimensions of your engorged appurtenance. If you fail miserably to understand the delicate beauty of the Thai employed on this occasion, most masseurs are able to render their practised astonishment in advanced special English, massage dialect, as "You big boy, wow". If you are looking for something a little more on the intellectual side, the traditional will serve up, probably in comprehensible Thai, "Now, where does it hurt?" On this question being posed, you may feel free to point to any part of your anatomy except the private. Should, as sometimes happens, the traditional cutting off of the blood supply to and from the groin cause an involuntary concentration of humours in the very part to which you have not pointed, it is proper to raise one knee to accommodate this potential source of embarrassment.

Having gotten what you wanted, leaving a tip is optional. Too large a tip given in the traditional encounter might promote a taking of your hand and a leading into a private VIP room that you didn't know existed — and she seemed such a nice girl that you had already planned the marriage and the next 20 years. Too small a tip in a modern setting may result in an accidental raising of your zip on tender extremities.

Don't ever get angry in a modern establishment. Should you be for any reason unsatisfied with the service, you may if you wish mention it to either of the two man mountains in the ogle gallery. They will gladly listen to your complaint as they assist you to the exit.

Bottom line:
The coexistence of tradition and modern is evident throughout Thailand's institutions. You pay your money and you take your choice.

50

On Masturbating Alone

On masturbating alone, it is appropriate to seek a private environment. This might appear to fly in the face of the gregarious nature of the Thais, and so it does. One gets no social points for solitary masturbation, even if it is undertaken as a form of meditation. In fact, one is also unlikely to get any points for bipartisan play, or even the group pulling of plonkers, although it does very much depend on who you are pulling with and the assumption of correct physical attitudes of deference.

Buddhism has little or nothing to say on the matter and is neither for nor against the practice of flying one's own kite; but it does hold celibacy in significantly higher regard than coveting thy neighbour's wife, even if you are only looking around the curtains as she takes a bath in her back garden, and that only to direct your thoughts for correct meditation as you activate your flow of consciousness.

Should you find yourself in a social environment of significant numbers when an involuntary but physically all too obvious manifestation of your stimulated cerebral state threatens to assuage consideration for the feelings of others, it is acceptable to seek relief at your own hand. The primary concern must always be to avert embarrassment to others. In Thailand, one must always remain first and foremost considerate of the feelings of others.

A rapid adjournment to the nearest toilet or bushily-shrubbed landscape could present an easy escape from the public domain. Unfortunately, this is not always possible. The sky train, the funeral, the discotheque, the Bangkok traffic jam, the golf and rugby fields. All examples of locations where privacy, when most required, may evade you.

Thailand's tropical heat means that penile erections cannot be easily hidden under an outsized mackintosh without making you even more an object of public focus. As in all matters, prevention is better, and safer, than seeking a cure or a cover-up. By far the best prophylactic is to direct your mind to the statue of Queen Victoria at the British Embassy in Bangkok. If, in spite of this proven safeguard, an erection threatens to protrude into the public world, hang your hat on it and take it home with you.

Bottom line:
First and foremost one must remain considerate of the feelings of others. Bonk yourself crazy in private. Show no unsightly bulges in public. Refrain from groans unless performing at a funeral, when you should try to throw in a wail. Grief affects us all in different ways.

51

On Matchstick Men and Women

Bangkok is the centre of the Thai world. The Thai people there are never referred to as *luuk-krung* (half-child, referring to Thais of 50 per cent *farang* parentage), but almost all have a Chinese element above 25 per cent. In addition are those who have absolutely no problem in being 100 per cent Thai and 100 per cent Chinese. The Chinese are among the thinnest people in the world, although by no means as thin as they used to be. The thinnest Thais are young female office workers, almost all of whom appear to be training to be fashion models. They are to be found in large numbers on the sky train, although it is doubtful their slender physical attributes result from the steep climb to get up there. Next in line for perfect figure awards are traffic police, men clothed in high anxiety and uniforms so skintight they have to be painted on. As one leaves the centre of Bangkok, the matchstick men and women disappear and people become increasingly fuller figured. This trend continues until Norway, where people burst.

Bottom line:
Thais with really beautiful figures all live within a comparatively small circle regularly registering the highest pollution index of Bangkok.

52

On Matriarchy, Mothers and Money

In the good old days, when everybody knew their place and everybody had a place to know, and that place was publicly identified by reference to a man's *sakti na*, all Thais were ranked, from King Paramatrailokanatha downwards, according to the amount of land they had (*sakti na* = power of the fields). A man's position could be raised or lowered at the wish of King P by the giving and taking away of land. A man could also have as many minor wives as he could afford. Wives were ranked from major wife down to slave wife. As a man rose in the system, so his wives all went up a rank. A slave wife would become a minor wife, and free, if she bore a man a son. That was the system that was. The poorest man could — through effort, the support of his wife or wives, a large slice of luck, and a lot of ingratiation — rise through the system, even if he had a provincial accent and working class parents, to be a Big Man. All Thais adjusted their behaviour naturally depending on the social status of the man or the man's wife he was interacting with. Women were recognised as "the hind legs of the elephant"; their role was at the back, supporting their men. That was the way it used to be, and in large measure still is when it comes to questions of social status. But the role of women has changed dramatically. What on earth went wrong?

Today, the matriarch rules the domestic roost, is often active in the local market economy, and controls the land, passing it on to a daughter who stays in the family home to care for Mum in old age, incidentally also caring for Papa. This might be the youngest daughter, but maybe another who did not marry or, as so often seems to happen, was widowed early. If everybody is in Bangkok, sewing or selling, one daughter will have to come back as soon as Mother requires it, and not temporarily, but to take over the matriarchal role as soon as Mother abdicates. Her husband can tag along and live in the house and do little, but he can't own it — so a Thai husband is in something of a similar position to those *farang* who buy land, property and businesses through Thai wives; both can live-in, but (more often than not) neither is the customary or legal owner.

But don't despair. If you really want to get your hands on mother-in-law's land, there is a way. It is called money. You keep throwing money at the property and expanding whatever brings in more money, and consistently paying all taxes due, and pay somebody else to look after Mum in her dotage, then your wife will be Mum's favourite and inherit. Then you can go and put your feet up on the farm and wait for the time when your own daughter cuts your toenails, if she is not too busy looking after her Mum.

Such is the solidarity of the women in the family there is no competition for land ownership. And if it should happen that two daughters live on in the house caring for *Mae* equally, the land may be divided equally between the two. This solidarity is, and you *farang* men had better note this, extended to taboos on sex partners within the family unit. So, you can by all means be friends with your wife's sister, but hands off. Even if your wife divorces you, you can't marry her little sister. This is not a legal restriction but a far more important social one. Just as European literature is full of stories of men who marry their mothers, so Thai drama has plenty of stories where a man by design (if a nasty guy) or unintentionally (if basically a nice chap) marries or has sex with a sister of his deceased wife, who always comes back in some form to cause the man grief, rarely hurting or blaming her sister. The special relationship between sisters extends to sexual partners outside of marriage. Even a whore who sells her body without much thought for the buyer will not knowingly sleep with a man who has slept with her sister — *unless the price is right.*

The value of sexual integrity within the family extends to those marrying into that family, which in Thailand means both men and women. Some anthropologists suggest there is a high incidence of incest, most often by fathers or half-fathers who are often absent working outside the community much of the time, and under-aged girls. It is impossible to verify this as the shame and loss of face involved in public disclosure encourages a quiet solution — the man goes away to work outside and simply never comes back. Even if incest does exist, it is not acceptable. The concept extends to in-laws, of which you may be one, and it is no defence to say that in your society incest involves only blood relatives. If you are in a decent Thai family, or even a half-decent family, you are strongly advised to look upon everybody in it as out of bounds.

The solidarity of sisters helps to ensure the matriarchy of their shared *mae.* If sisters have different fathers, never mind. Brothers/sons come in here somewhere. Pregnant mothers always want their children to be boys. This is not so much an economic factor, although the daughters bring in most of the money and provide the most care in old age. It is rather a social factor. Women, even mothers, cannot ordain as monks. Thus Mother cannot directly get her hands on the great deal of merit ordination manufactures. No matter how much they feed the monks in the morning and how religiously they attend *wat* every *wan phra*, they can never be sure of accumulating enough *boon* or merit to ensure a good rebirth — and somewhat surprisingly they want to come back as a *man*. They need at least one son to get this merit for them. All sons *should* enter the monkhood for a spell, and before not after they get married; this means the monk-son transfers the merit he makes to his mother, not, heaven forbid, to his wife or mother-in-law. At this time, many young men do not become monks but there will always be one at least who goes in, even if for a short, almost token, stay at the *wat*.

So, here the cunning plot thickens. Want the super fast track to establishing a real relationship with your wife's *mae*? Unless you happen to have a Buddhist mother or ancestors who also wants the merit: ordain. Make it clear that you will transfer all the merit accumulated to your mother-in-law (you anyway cannot keep it for yourself — that would be contrary to the whole idea of being a monk). During your time in

robes, both your wife and her mother will have to treat you with the utmost respect, and you can sit immobile while they crawl before your feet. Perhaps this is not the perfect reason for entering the monkhood, but *mae* for one will think it is, and after all there must be worse reasons than to contemplate your mother-in-law. Perhaps you'll never want to come out. Nobody will insist you do. And like interest in the bank, merit will keep accumulating.

If you don't want to ordain — and nobody will suggest you should, although everybody will be delighted if you do — you can take an easier path and sponsor (i.e. pay for) one of your wife's younger brothers to ordain and make merit for Mother. If it comes to it — for example let's say Mother is sick or dying — you can even pay somebody from outside the family to ordain and transfer the merit to Mother. Even a young girl ordaining as a nun creates some merit, even if the ordination only lasts 24 hours, and even if the girl is no relative at all and only doing it for the small amount of money you offer. So, don't overlook the traditional way to your mother-in-law's heart and soul when seeking to consolidate your place in the family. And it won't cost you a fortune.

The mother-daughter bond and the mother-son bond are the strongest relationships for Thais, with sibling bonds following from them. Believe it: a Thai family that does not place the utmost value on these relationships is a bad family. There are mothers who sell their daughters (less so in these days of affluence, but wants are infinite…), there are even mothers who sell their daughters to their old *farang* lovers, there are even daughters who sell on their younger siblings to the same *farang*. This is certainly keeping things in the family, but in the worst possible sense. Such families are universally seen as *bad* by normal Thais, and the daughter of a bad Thai mother will be bad in turn, not bad to her mother but to just about everybody else, including her own siblings. Normal Thais will not be at all happy with anything that allies a bad family with their good family, and will try hard to discourage marriage into such a family. Since you probably have no family to influence your actions (until you marry into one), nobody will bother to discourage you. But why give yourself a tremendous disadvantage in making your way in Thailand? You really do not want to belong to such a family. Such a family is certainly the easiest to get into, and might even be fun for a time as all taboos are out the window and almost anything goes, but your status in normal Thai society will be among the lowest, in spite of your comparative wealth, and in the end such a family will bleed you dry and leave you in grief. Enough *farang* have been there. And plenty more will go there.

In the end, the fact that so many foreign husbands have great difficulty adapting to life with their Thai family is due to a contradiction of systems. The foreign husband is most likely to come from a domestic society organised on patrilineal lines with bilineal aspects, the Thai wife is likely to come from a society with strong traditions of domestic matriliny/matriarchy. Taken to the extreme, this places the foreign man as family head and decision maker whereas in Thailand the Thai woman expects to control the purse strings and be a senior or equal partner in decision making. Therein lies the rub.

Bottom line:
Love your mother-in-law and your wife will love you. And should your wife ever get out of line, you can fall back on those immortal words against which there can be no argument: "I'll tell Mummy."

53

On *May Pen Rai*

May pen rai not so long ago was the leitmotif of Thai life; some, Thais and non-Thais, even thought it the quintessence of being Thai. Well, if it ever was, it's not any more. Or is it? The term means "never mind" or "doesn't matter" and sometimes "I couldn't care less".

Stressed-out foreigners, visiting Thailand for its therapeutic effects, used to like to think of the Thais as very laid-back people, easy-going, easy-coming. When something was too much trouble, *may pen rai* was the perennial answer. Put off whatever is causing you anguish until tomorrow and maybe it will solve itself or go away. Not so long ago, foreigners learnt the expression *may pen rai* immediately after *sawatdii*. Now the term is not heard that much, and when you do hear it, it is often in response to saying thank you, which is said much more than it used to be.

In *economic* life, Thais are now Asian Tigers. Pretty clever, well enough educated, technologically aware and more or less disciplined to weather the difficult bits of modern times without falling asleep. In other words, just about the opposite of *may pen rai*.

In *social* life, a large measure of *may pen rai* continues. Thai society remains "loosely structured" with — if we compare the structure to more rigid forms of social organisation like those in India, Japan and the UK — a reasonably high degree of movement up and down and sideways. Jig-jig boom-boom; Thai society still accommodates a large element of fun for the 63 million people who make it up. Try to clamp Thais down too firmly to set social roles and they stop playing. There remains a large degree of "Asian fatalism" about things that will not be changed overnight. And while a person may think, or half-think, that he or she has been born in the social gutter because of bad *ka'ma* in past lives, the fact is that some Thais *do*, as individuals, move out of the gutter, or whatever socio-economic drawer they are born into — and when they do manage to get out, they do not carry with them a debilitating stigma of low caste or class or nouveau riche/new money, and they don't have to shun former friends and family. Perhaps the demands of the family can be just as debilitating, but the security net of family to fall back on can also be seen as an important factor allowing an individual to reach for the stars. Well, maybe not for the stars, but for the next rung on the ladder towards the stars.

May pen rai is evident in the habit of slipping in and out of social relationships. This was always part of traditional life back in the days when a woman gave birth to 6 or 7 children. Men would often work away from home, perhaps out of the country, and as the Thais say only half in jest: one day away you miss your wife, two days away and you are looking at the girls, three days away and you have a new wife. The taking of a minor wife is an age-old Thai tradition, which in the very old days was nicely crafted into the system. Just a generation ago the majority of marriages in the rural area (which was 75–80 per cent of the population) were traditional village marriages without any legal basis outside of village public opinion; children were born and rather than looking for child-support from their parents, were expected to respect and support those parents. Men and women moved out of one marriage into another and raised children without too much concern over who the genitor was. Today, most marriages are eventually registered (although divorce before remarriage is often not) and children receive birth certificates which at 18 will give them ID cards, passports and so on. But slipping in and out of relationships continues to be normal enough behaviour that raises few eyebrows. (A little note here to say this is *not* the same as promiscuity.)

How do we square the apparent flippancy of many social relationships with the strength of the family, which this book indicates is an essential part of Thai life and personality? Perhaps, with an average birth rate of just 1.7 children, such squaring will become increasingly difficult to do in the future, but for the moment, as in the past, families seem capable of surviving over time and space, and weathering — perhaps shrugging off — many of the events that are seen as traumatic in the West. The extension of kinship terms to friends and neighbours certainly helps maintain much of the appearance of the extended family. Thais know, of course, who their real parents are, and their real brothers and sisters — although many a *farang* gives up on working out who is real and who is not, and Thais do not often make the distinction. Indeed some unreal relationships seem to become real over time.

Of vital importance to the continued strength of the family is the matriarchal aspect of the home of origin. Traditional inheritance patterns (land and fields and animals) involve mother and one or more daughters. If one man slips out of the loop for a few years or forever and another man slips in, the disruption is less significant than it would be if the father and husband is the sole breadwinner and plays a full authority-decision role. For this inheritance pattern to continue through time, at least one girl child is required.

A figure of 1.7 children per mother cannot guarantee this. But there is always a mother's granddaughter or a niece to take over the job of caring for the mother and father and maintaining the traditional home — if the traditional home has not been sold off for the value of its wood content.

Paradoxical as it may sound, the principle holding the modern Thai family together while allowing lots of movement of individuals might be seen as *may pen rai*. Of course there are plenty of examples of jealousy and individual attitude change which are decidedly *pen array* (one is included in this book), but these frequent exceptions can grow into monstrous contradictions of the *may pen rai* principle precisely *because* the structure is loose enough to allow them to do that — problems untreated either go away or grow until resolved by violent confrontation. Either way, they do not appear to result in terminal damage to the fabric and structure of Thai society.

Perhaps as long as people continue to treat all small children as their own and do not get too possessive, a sudden disintegration of the basic structure of Thai society might be avoided. On the other hand, it might not. If the *may pen rai* principle allows movement up and down the social strata, and in and out of overlapping social groups, it can be seen as a very important part of modern life, facilitating development and change.

Thus, it is suggested that *may pen rai* — not really bothering too much and not really thinking too deeply about things — provides an explanation for the changes that have been absorbed into Thai society without substantively changing society's structure and value system. The corollary is made that if Thais start to become overly definitional and protective of their "Thai-ness", a rigidity could be introduced into what is still a flexible and easy-going system. Should that happen, foreigners, be they Chinese, other Asian or *farang*, might find it a lot more difficult than they do to integrate into Thai ways and structures.

Bottom line:
Most things don't matter much and some things don't matter at all.
Never mind.

54

On Menstruation

This natural phenomenon is universal. Well, some 50 per cent universal once most men are discounted. Well, some 25 per cent when pre-pubescents and post-menos are taken into account. So, on the subject of menstruation we are into minority rights. Less people menstruate than masturbate.

Thais take a tolerant attitude to menstruation. Women during their menstrual cycle are not regarded as any more impure than at other times of the month. Unlike the situation in the sub-continent, women in Thailand can even enter temples and make merit while menstruating. The particular Thai-ness of this universal is that women in Thailand, used to doing things together, ALL start their period on the same day. And NONE know this. Even more extraordinary, not a single woman has a single sanitary pad in her handbag at the time it is needed.

The coincidence of menstruation is shared by all within the greater Thai world. Thus Thai communities in Laos, where they call themselves Lao, in Vietnam, Myanmar, China, Malaysia and San Francisco, ALL come at once — like the shrill of cicadas in tropical treetops.

Male Thais also like to do things together and therefore at precisely one week before mass menstruation of their dear loved ones, ALL go missing or stay locked safely away behind the closed doors of bars and clubs. They come out only when the cute Channel 7 newscaster is again seen wearing a relaxed smile.

Bottom line:

Women can feel free to menstruate at will. But only if Will doesn't mind.

55

On Miniskirted Buttocks Backing Into You on a Public Conveyance

On receiving unexpected caresses from a miniskirted bottom in a crowded carriage of the metro, bus, sky train, or lift, first ascertain the gender of the owner. Your view will inevitability be limited to the back and top, unless you are passing through a tunnel and the window opposite becomes a mirror, or unless you are a rather small dwarf. Chances are that if the lady has the following characteristics, she is no lady at all, but a lady-boy:

- Extremely short gold-lame miniskirt
- Large feet in gold shoes
- Large hands that will not be kept to themselves
- Matching gold handbag
- Blouse transparent and buttoned at upholstered cleavage
- Exposed midriff
- Visible red or black plastic bra
- Hair long, well-ironed and detachable
- Overdose of fake Channel No. 5
- Blood-red lips
- Gross exaggeration of rouge and powder on the cheekbones

You will have very little time to evaluate each of these qualities. The best test of all is to do nothing and see what transpires. If the buttocks in question do not rapidly and reproachfully rebound to their former position, presume you are under a backside advance by a *khatoey* well-skilled in her art. Note: it is politically correct and also gentlemanly to refer to *khatoeys* as "she" — particularly when in the Ladies Powder Room or a dark corner of a car park — unless you are in the company of pseudo-macho *khatoey*-haters, in which case the pronoun is 'it'.

Of course, doing nothing, even for a split second, indicates to some perverted little minds an acceptance of the status quo, even a conspiracy to subvert. This will certainly be the mindset of your *khatoey* molester who will indeed be highly flattered by the attention you are literally obliged to thrust upon her and inclined to increase the pressure, particularly if, in spite of yourself, you find you sport the best erection you've had for months.

If you do object to being pressed like a sardine against the happy hindquarters of a *khatoey*, you will have precious little time to make that objection clear. During the brief encounter — save some of the normal people in your conveyance think you are enjoying yourself — maintain an expressionless demeanour and look everywhere except down below. This is easiest in a lift, where everyone is looking at the number display or the roof. Your bearing should throughout the brief encounter be that of the pained citizen who does not like to cause a fuss. This is not a good time to ogle the full lips or prominently nippled T-shirts of your fellow passengers or even to look them in the eye. And under no circumstances moan and sigh.

Submitting, with good grace, to the inevitable, is a good Thai reaction and one that certainly loses you no social points. Just pretend it isn't happening, although keep one hand on your wallet and watch out for any lurches on sharp bends in the road or rail, or unexpected jolts to a stop before the lift reaches your floor. These might leave you exposed to the public eye, which is definitely a face-loser, even if you never started it. Thais *know* what *farang* and *khatoey* get up to.

Believe it or not, there are things worse than being backed into by a *khatoey*. You could be backed into by two *khatoeys*. They might be working together, one going for your zip, one for your pockets. If they both go for the zip, the indication is they are in competition rather than cooperation and you are really in trouble. Serious counteraction is required.

On feeling a second set of buttocks pressing firmly into you, do not weaken or hesitate. Reach around to the front of *both* sets of buttocks and rummage among the padding and straps until you find the hidden appendages. Then, taking each situation firmly in hand, give each one an agonizing twist. The disturbing noises that follow will create a space around you, even in the most crowded conveyance, but will also lead your assailants to waddle to the door and descend at the next stop.

As the *khatoeys*, in pain, leave the transport of delight, your victory may be short-lived. You might be approached by a fellow *farang* passenger, probably a Norwegian, who, in spite of all your efforts at discretion, has witnessed most of what happened and says, "Really! How dare you treat a lady that way?" If this happens to you, shoot back a sincere but firm, "I really don't know what you are talking about." Either that, or, "Why those filthy little varmints. I think they were trying to pick my pocket. God, how embarrassing." And if that doesn't enlist sympathy rather than hostility, you should be able to regain your privacy with a concerned and plaintive, "Do you think I have caught any disease?" If that doesn't work, take solace in the thought that Norwegians don't really matter much when it comes to your comfortable integration in Thailand, unless they clock you on the jaw and break your backbone as you go down.

Bottom line:

As soon as you feel the intrusion of unfamiliar buttocks and certainly before reaching round the backed-up buttocks to take matters into your own hands, make absolutely sure that the khatoey really is a lady-boy. The cheap perfume, the detachable hair, and the upholstered chest are, in Thailand, not always 100 per cent indication of gender-bending.

56

On Mites and Men

On your first encounter with arachnids in the private region, be aware that these are creatures of no compromise. No space at all for *may pen rai*. You must act fast and exterminate fully before you are yourself exterminated socially.

These particular little mites, the ones with the most instructive of names, have an instinct apparent at the first scratch — to dig into the flesh like crabs into sand and there to hang on, occasionally loosening their hold only for breeding or migratory purposes. They have a fondness for pubic hair; in fact, they wouldn't live anywhere else. So, for the survival of their species they have at the same time to dig in and to be constantly on the move. The digging in is the bit you, as host, will find particularly unpleasant. Each of the little buggers will pick a hair to make its base, burrow and wait, taking an occasional bite of flesh, while their colony grows at an alarming speed. They are in no way gender sensitive and treat male and female exactly alike. In Thailand, however, where in general the oriental female has a lot fewer pubes than the occidental male or female visitor, they go for the foreigner by preference.

While crabs are visible to the naked or bespectacled eye, this may not be the case if you are lying on your back with a large belly blocking the view. Should this be your situation, and your partner remains beside you, DO NOT ask him or her to take a look at what's troubling you. If that partner is within screaming earshot, immediately on feeling the first bite, and before you are even sure you are under attack, make the full-volume accusation.

Words you think: "You filthy whore, you've given me the crabs, you bitch!"

Words you say: "You filthy tart, you've given me the crabs, you bitch!"

The response is unlikely to be apologetic, especially if your partner is freshly shaven in the X-zone. Never mind, you got in first. Should a civilised discussion develop — unlikely but possible — you can both agree that you must have both caught crabs from the dirty bed sheets. This argument might not be tenable if talking to your wife or boyfriend in the marital bed — but it just might, after all this is Thailand and you can always blame the maid (but not if you have just slept with her).

However, while it is *possible* that your partner is within voice range when the crabs begin to bite, it is more than likely that he or she is long gone and you are standing to attention raising your glass on the occasion of the official birthday of the Queen of England, Scotland, North Ireland and associated Antipodean territories. Surrounded as you are by Thai and foreign crème de la crème, this is not the time to thrust both hands down the top of your skirt, kilt or trousers for a boisterous scratch. By all means *walk* to the toilet, as normally as you can, where in the solitude of a cubicle you may verify that you are being fed upon. Upon confirmation of your fears, do not tarry in vain hope of remedying the situation. No matter how many you prise lose — and they are tenacious little beggars once they have decided you owe them a living — you will never dislodge and pop them as quickly as they multiply. But these are not Thai in-laws; they are diminutive parasites with an intelligence quotient equal to one millionth that of a retarded flea. Were it not for their numbers, and their choice of location, even the feeblest foreign body should be able to outwit them. And you can too.

In Thailand, disappearing tricks are more readily tolerated than in many other countries. This has nothing at all to do with the incidence of crabs. So resist, if you can, the temptation to flee the scene, carrying your scourge with you, and say your proper goodbyes to your hosts just as soon as you have confirmed your source of discomfort. If you are the best man (but not the groom) at the wedding of the girl you have just spent the night with, or if a pallbearer at your father-in-law's funeral, you must balance the social negative of physical absence against the social negative of being found out. And it is one of those extraordinary imponderables that people who would be sympathetic if you had a terminal illness will avoid you like the plague if they know you harbour the crab lice, even if you are fully dressed and they are aware that crab lice can only migrate with the assistance of a hairy pubic region in direct and close proximity. All in all it is perhaps best to stick it out and try not to flinch under the bride's withering stare, and of course, not to falter as a couple of hefty bites cause the coffin to jiggle on your shoulder — a fact that onlookers will attribute to your emotional sensitivity and award you extra social points.

Whether the discovery is made in your own bed or at the event of the year, the remedy is the same. DO NOT reach for the bug spray and give yourself a liberal dose. This could indeed kill anything down there. It would also engender a suffering in the region of a scale halfway between napalm and Hiroshima. Shampoos which might work on head lice will have no lasting affect on these little buggers. DO reach immediately for the Jacutin Gel and rub this well into all hair bases. Oh, blessed relief. But you have to keep up the applications, as eggs will hatch and a new little army will be on the march before you know it. Having plastered yourself with Jacutin, you will realise the little bugs are dead but not gone, and getting them and their eggs out of the hair base is a *magnum opus*. You have a choice, continue with the gel and wait for them to grow out — which is fine, but sticky and you will have to live with the fact that a close examination will show crab lice sticking to your pubics, even dead ones, which is not going to enhance your sex or love life. *Or*, shave everything off... well, all the hair that is, you can keep the organs responsible for the trouble.

How to explain your total lack of pubic hair? Chances are, nobody will ask... this is Thailand, where people ask about all kinds of totally inconsequential things but avoid seeing

anything a bit odd. If somebody does ask, you can mumble about just coming back from having your appendix out. And if they are unsympathetic enough as to ask after the absence of a scar, you look at your partner as if he or she has just crawled in from *ban nok* and ask incredulously if they have never heard of keyhole surgery.

Never admit to having crabs, since there is a universal and unreasonable fear and loathing of people infested with the crab louse. Condoms and the pill will provide no protection against crabs. A minute inspection of your partner before activity is more effective: take your time and keep the lights on. This may be most tastefully and discreetly accomplished through treating your partner to a session of exploratory cunnilingus or fellatio. Of course you have to keep your specs on. Don't forget to scrutinise any backside hairs also. And while you're at it, a quick inspection of the nasal passages and armpits can do no harm. Of course if you are lucky enough to have drawn a partner with inverted nipples, the possibility of crabs is reduced to less than slipping over a discarded banana skin. Should you not be so lucky and your inspection notices little movements on white skin or sheets (always have white sheets), you suddenly jump out of bed. To the toilet with you, for a close inspection; and if free of the crab louse praise the Lord Buddha and request that your partner take his or her menagerie to beds other than yours. Then boil the sheets and pillow cases and hang them full in the hot Thai sun for three days. To boil yourself and hang yourself in the sun for three days would also preclude any problem you might have overlooked, but other means are more convenient. Watch carefully during these three days and if nothing much stirs in the nether region, consider your precautions successful.

Almost needless to say, catching crabs does nothing to enhance your social status — and it doesn't matter if you catch them from a *khun ying* or a kitchen girl, the manifestation is precisely the same, as is your accusation and bitter denial: "*I* haven't been near a sexual organ for six months before you". But if this is countered with, "And just before I met you, *I* came out of a year in a nunnery", then do the noble thing and present her with a large tube of Jacutin and offer to shave personally her pubic region.

Bottom line:

However much or little you trust your partner, never admit to the likely origins of your infestation. Blame your partner for going to a dirty noodle shop where he or she picked up the little monsters and brought them home. And should you get the response that crabs are not caught in dirty noodle shops unless one is screwing there, immediately riposte: "And how do you know that!?"

57

On Mites and Women

Should you happen to be a foreign woman married to, or in a strong relationship with, a Thai man, you might have special problems in coping with a migratory army of crab lice *and* maintaining your innocence.

If you don't have a good reason for staying and your man has not chained you to the bed and put your passport in a safe deposit, this is probably a good time to practise conflict avoidance and flee the scene, taking with you everything you can get your hands on and leaving the swine with only his mites for company, and a large character message, written in bright red lipstick across the bed sheet in capitals (don't try for italics). This should be something that is ambiguous, just in case he is *not* hosting crabs. You, of course, accuse him, as women do, of doing something so despicable you can't even mention it: NOW I KNOW WHAT AN ABSOLUTE BASTARD YOU ARE, is enough to set him thinking as to what he did wrong. If you can write that in Thai, the maid should carry your message throughout the community without any need to bribe or threaten her. You'll be gone, but it's always safer to be the innocent party, even when you are not there.

If you love him, this may be a good time to stop doing so. On the other hand, if you have three of his children and don't want to leave forever, you will just have to be prepared to forgive the bastard. But only if you are absolutely sure that yesterday you didn't sort of accidentally come into very close proximity with the gardener.

Do you risk calling his mummy? Mummies are really not very skilled at objective assessment and your husband's mum is more likely to believe her little boy than you. And even if she doesn't, she will blame you for failing as a wife and driving him to it. You didn't, did you? If there is a 1 per cent chance that maybe you did, then it really *is* all your fault. After all, if you hadn't come to Thailand and insisted he marry you, the poor boy would never have caught the crabs.

If you did, just for five minutes, have a close nozzle with your husband's boss, who has been promising him promotion, and you only did it for your beloved's sake, which is not really your fault since you wouldn't have had to do it at all if your husband was just a bit better at his job, then you do have a leg to stand on, just one. Thais are much the same as anybody else when it comes to a wife's infidelity, but they feel somewhat differently about same-sex relationships. So, you tell him you had a fling with a girl you think he fancies — or better still with his boss's wife. Just a cuddle between girls. He'll forgive that. You might even both laugh at it as you take turns shaving each other and gossiping about how the boss's wife, or the boss, could have caught the crabs.

Bottom line:
If you are going to make a habit of this, it might be best to stay well shaved. That way there is much less chance of picking up a few unwanted guests and less of a need for explanations. Come clean.

58

On No Longer Being a Dirty Old Geezer

On making the transition from *nong*, younger one, through *phi*, elder one, to *lung*, "uncle" (elder brother of father) or *pa* (elder sister of mother/father), you step up in the age hierarchy, and this automatically doubles the status points awarded for anything good or clever. In fact by the time you get to an advanced *lung/pa* stage, it is often difficult to do anything really wrong. Thais, particularly those a bit *baan nok* (upcountry), will often throw in a *phor/mae* (father/mother) category. It's all part of flattery and respect. But it does mean you are getting older. There are a few consolations: no dandruff problem, you can be crotchety without offending Thais all that much, and you can (if a man, and a well-off man) marry or partner an 18-year-old to pander to your whims and cut the toenails you can no longer reach.

Should you begin to doubt the wisdom of growing old in Thailand, return to your native land for a brief sojourn. Should that native land be England or the USA and you hang around in it long enough, you will be granted a senior citizen's substantial reduction on transport, bringing the cost down to only twenty times that of an equivalent journey in Thailand. And at certain times and places, like between 4.00 and 5.00 am on a Thursday morning in a 24-hour supermarket café — deserted except for old codgers who think Phuket is pronounced with an initial "f" followed by a short "u" — you will get a special old fart's price for your beans on toast which is only twice what you would have paid for barbecued prawns back in that great big retirement play-land called Thailand. And if your gaze happens to linger on the bit of rough slopping out the beans, you will be called a *dirty old geezer* (UK; US equivalent: dirty old hot water heater). And god help you if you smile at a child. And if you explain that the beautiful 18-year-old Thai with you is not your grandchild but your bride or boyfriend, keeping you company during the visit to the fatherland, you will hear the quaint expression, "Well, I never did!" The only answer to which is, "Well, perhaps you should have, madam!" The gerontological barney that follows will be persuasion enough that you and your beloved belong back in the Land of Smiles, where teenage spots can mingle more or less happily with age spots.

We do not stop playing because we grow old; we grow old because we stop playing.

Bottom line:
If, when astride your Harley-Davidson, your T-shirt flowing in Thailand's tropical breeze, the consolations of old age appear small compared to the impairments and frustrations of getting ever older, at least take solace that your situation will not last forever.

59

On Not Attending Newborn Babes, Weddings and Funerals

Tick off one indicator of success if you receive an average of one formally printed invitation every three days. These must be delivered or handed to you in an envelope addressed to you personally ("To Whom it May Concern" doesn't count). You will receive rather more wedding invitations shortly before Buddhist Lent, and a great deal more once the young monks have disrobed after three lunar months of sexual abstinence and, having somehow proved their manhood by not exercising it, are ready for the marriage bed.

Wedding invitations that come during Buddhist Lent can happily be discarded. For three months good people don't get married, and if the Chinese medicine did not work, you don't want their bad luck rubbing off on you. Unless of course this involves the child of a top man, who's daughter could only come back from Washington at this time; then you make absolutely sure you attend.

If the names on the cards mean nothing to you, do not throw it away. Is it nicely embossed? Where is the reception? What are the two family names? If a really big man is involved, you might request to attend also the traditional Thai ceremony, which is very early in the morning. This request will always be met. However do this only rarely, as it does mean getting up and dressed very early, and for once the Thais are always on time. It is also rather tedious to attend a string of such events in close proximity; evening receptions are more easily handled, although if you have no clue what the couple look like or how to pronounce their names, get a Thai to tell you. It can be a salutary experience to wait in the meeting line at the start of such events, knock back the whisky offered, pop your 1,000 baht in the heart-shaped money box, and congratulate warmly... the wrong couple.

It simply does not do to go to every invitation. To do so devalues your presence and suggests you have nothing better to do, or no events of higher status to attend. If you should find that you are the guest of honour, arrive at the normal time for the reception, i.e. 45 minutes after the time on the card. Inform your hosts that you have three weddings to attend at the same time, but have made this the first. Indicate that you can stay no longer than half-hour. They will then rush to get you photographed with the couple and in the family picture and with as many people of indifferent status as they can. Having said half-hour, eat little but drink a lot if the whisky is good, and leave after one hour, making sure everybody sees you off. Go straight home without stopping at McDonalds on the way.

The 80 per cent of declined invitations deserve the return of their envelope but not your presence. Inside each envelope, you have to put an amount of money. This will be noted by the recipient family. For those families with money to burn, who have no need of your charity, a large amount, perhaps 1,000 baht or even, for those really oozing, $50. For such receptions, you will of course stay until they scrape you off the dance floor. For those who are not worthy of your presence, three 100 baht notes, folded not stirred, is more than bountiful.

Babies are comparatively easy to visit and no invitation cards are sent out. You can give a present for the baby and/or flowers or fruit and, if the new parents are poor, a few red notes given to the mother. A boring event, unless you like newborn babies, and ten minutes is enough — unless the new mother is following traditional practice and being roasted over a fire. Try to get the gender of the baby right and say a girl looks like the father and a boy looks like the mother. In those cases where genitor is uncertain, better say the baby looks like the father (no need to state who it is). It saves time during the baby season to accumulate such visits over a few weeks, drop into the supermarket on the way and get an appropriate number of packets of Pampers, and do the whole lot in one circle.

Funerals are far more important than anything else and a big man will have a lot of guests, the more the better, to see him off. Of course, you won't be spending much time with the big man himself, but do make it clear to his survivors that you are there. Send a tastefully lavish wreath, the second biggest they have in a real flower shop, not a market stall, with your name clearly marked, to arrive either extremely early on the morning of cremation (close relatives don't really sleep that night) or the night before. You wear your best black and if you want to make a point of your attendance, arrive early at the house and eat a simple breakfast before accompanying the corpse on its last journey. You will find people especially receptive to your attendance, so funerals are a good occasion to get to know people. Don't be shy of taking photos and giving copies later to the close survivors, many people really want as many photos as possible and not everybody is as thoughtful as you; in fact a lot of folks think taking pictures at a funeral rather tacky. But what do they know?

Bottom line:

Babies and weddings can be combined, but not funerals. Don't go anywhere, except possibly to another funeral, until you have shed your black.

60

On Not Thinking All That Much

To feel at home in Thailand and with the Thais, it doesn't do to think too much. If you did well at school and university in the West, you are carrying lots of excess baggage and have quite a disadvantage to overcome. You can keep all the superficial attributes you picked up on the way: the fancy degree certificates that your Mum insisted on framing, the pictures of you in gowns surrounded by important people, such magic titles as Dr, and any entertaining little tricks that you picked up along with learning how to think, like jumping the cue ball over the yellow to pot black, playing the guitar, and turning water into wine. The rest doesn't have a lot of purpose and can be happily relegated to inactive posts in the back of the mind. Take a deep breath, let it out with your thoughts, and let your mind start anew as a virgin.

Thinking too much leads to unhappiness. If you have a pain in the neck right now, that's enough to cope with, rub it with yaa mong or go to the doctor and let him think about it. Don't compound the present pain with last night's pain and the possible pain you might feel tomorrow. And don't ruin today's relationship with your sweet little wife by thinking about her boyfriends before you and her boyfriends of the future that currently exist only in your mind. If the noise from the temple microphone is too loud and too long, don't waste your time thinking of ways to educate the monks — they are trying to educate you. And if the guy at the next table is talking at only two decibels below that of a Thai disco, either turn off or change table or restaurant. Back before progressive education took hold in the West, there was a wise man called William Shakespeare, who taught that there is no love, sorrow or hate but man's thinking makes it so.

Thailand is an almost developed country but the teachers and philosophy of its education system are very much products of underdevelopment and tradition. This is not bad in itself. The Thai system produces Thais, and you like them don't you? What, only some of the time?

Step back 400 years or so, to when Ayudhya was a larger city than London and certainly a much cleaner one. The literacy rate in Ayudhya at that time was several times that of London. And literate people did not just read religious texts in Sanskrit, they read in Thai and in Arabic-Melayu and even in Persian. They used their skills practically: the capital was a prosperous centre of international diplomacy and trade. Thais certainly learnt a lot of things apart from reading. They learnt how to survive and prosper in a deference system that still exists today. Persians, Dutch, British, Malays, Chinese, and so on, all had their areas of town allocated to them and had their own deference systems within those areas, but in dealings with Thais, they fitted into the Thai system. After all, this was Thailand, even if it wasn't called that.

As centres of production, trade and diplomacy, countries like Britain and France took over from places like Ayudhya because of historical accident. People in control-freak colonising countries might have invented steamships and power mills, but only because they had coal and other places did not, or couldn't get at it. At the height of colonial expansion, education in the West was reserved for a small elite. The cannon-fodder did its job best without minds cluttered by too much thinking and with zero-democracy. Today, Thailand has an economic base and a growing pool of technical expertise that could equip it to overtake many Western countries within a generation or two — and it will certainly not require the kind of thought that Western universities consider innovative to do this. Students still go through school in Thailand with a good measure of learning by rote. Higher levels of schooling continue something of this tradition. Students learn to function within the kind of corporate culture in which they will be required to work; and they all want to get a good job, and the jobs are there — so why approach such good jobs with a questioning mind? Thais learn from the first day of life to follow their elders and betters and to avoid conflict, not to enter dialectical dialogue in search of a non-antagonistic solution. The Thai way may

not always be terribly democratic, but there is plenty of scope for social mobility — for those who move within the system. The foreigner is not necessarily excluded, but he might, with the best intentions in the world, exclude himself unless he cuts back on his thinking, and particularly controls an urge to tell other people how to think. The question "Why?" exists in Thai, but overuse would devalue its meaning. Anyway, thinking too much makes your head ache.

Thai intellectuals do exist, but the situation is more like that in England rather than France and Norway. Ask a hall full of Englishmen for the intellectuals to raise their hands and no hands will be raised. Ask the same question of the French and 70 per cent will raise their hands. Ask the same question of the Norwegians and 150 per cent will raise their hands.

Bottom line:
The cut and thrust of intellectual debate and dialectical dialogue is not part of Thai tradition. Widespread literacy has for centuries been geared to reading and ingesting religious texts and truths; the education system has been largely built on that tradition, in much the way that mass education was organised in Europe in Victorian days. The foreigner in Thailand might find opportunities for the exercise of his intellectual capacities limited and unappreciated by most Thais. So why bother? Beats me. Take it easy and you'll be liked all the more.

61

On Nuptials, the Costs and Benefits

The various bits of activity and documentation that together form a marriage can be done in any order. Some people do the paperwork first and stop at that point of legal marriage. Others go through a more traditional wedding in the home of the bride and never get round to the legal marriage: this is useful if you have an impediment to legal marriage or if you want to give this marriage thing a trial, keeping the little woman's family happy and keeping the little woman herself under reserve, without official commitment. Official commitment, by the way, is more than the stroke of a pen; it makes the marriage legally binding in your home country, with all the problems and expense of the divorce settlement. Of course you won't be thinking of that when you get married, will you? But given the failure rate of around 50 per cent of marriages between Thais, and a very similar percentage in European countries between *farang*, there is no reason to believe Thai-*farang* marriages have any greater chance of durability.

So, the wedding nuptials can be as complicated and protracted as you care to make them — or your partner's family makes them. Or they can be non-existent.

Usually, mother-in-law is not going to forego the bride price, although today even that is not always insisted upon. If you are one of the rare *farang* females marrying a Thai man, nobody will discuss what bride price should be paid to *your* mother, even if she flies out to attend the wedding, and sometimes the *farang* female ends up footing the bill.

Traditionally, the amount of bride price is settled at the *mun*, often translated as "engagement", although this can be little more than a meeting of the two families or their representatives, and it can be dispensed with altogether — any negotiations is simply a matter between the groom and the bride's parents. How much you agree to pay depends on several factors — pay a lot and your status and that of the bride and her family goes up (sometimes the bride's mother privately gives a poor Thai groom some more money so he can give it back publicly). Traditionally the groom will move into the house of the bride, or build his own house in her compound. Land and house generally pass from mother to daughter(s). So much for the supposed male domination of Thai society.

How much is a reasonable bride price? Between Thais of average status, around $1,000, plus at least 2 baht (weight) of gold in the form of necklace and/or bracelet, worth some $500 more. A "wedding ring" can also be part of the gold package, but be aware that this is not really a symbol of marriage, a 10-year-old child might have one and a married mother of three might not. An uneducated girl of poor family and unattractive to boot is not likely to hold out for the $1,000. A Thai who cannot pay can defer in the hope of paying later (if he does not pay, nobody will take back the wife and, probably, child). During this time, the indebted son-in-law would traditionally work a lot of the time on his wife's parents' land without pay or much of a share in produce. The bride's parents host the wedding at the house and should host (and pay for) an evening reception either at the house or in a restaurant. Even if it is pretend, it is normal for the groom to give — publicly — somewhat more than the amount agreed with the bride's parents.

Over one generation, the rural population has dropped from 70 per cent to less than 50 per cent. However, the majority of brides are rural, even if their husband is urban. This often results in a Thai groom not taking up his right of residence in the bride's compound; instead he takes the girl away to an urban environment, where they may both work. The bride's parents are equivocal about such a move: they would prefer the couple to stay near at hand, but appreciate the regular sums of money that come in to them.

A *farang* marrying a Thai is most unlikely to want to live in her parents' house and gets no obvious benefits from his new support group. Economic rationality says he should pay less, social realities require him to pay more. The Thai logic is that he will take the girl away, not only from the parents but also from the country. Unspoken is a distrust: the girl might be stranded overseas and the extra money needed to bring her back. This fear is the reverse of almost all realities — the formally married Thai woman overseas can always get money from her husband, even well after a formal divorce, and even when she is entirely responsible for the divorce. But this kind of argument when negotiating bride price would certainly not be appreciated.

Should you want out of the relationship, here is your chance. Refuse to pay any bride price because your respect for women does not allow you to think of them as chattel to be bought and sold. This is safer than offering $10, knowing it will be refused. And while it will result in accusations that you don't know Thai society, perhaps some Thais will understand that you know it only too well. The same goes for the Thai woman or her mother. If they want to kill the thing dead, they insist on $50,000. Pay at your peril.

Some rich Thais will pay a high price partly for status and partly because they expect to get a beautiful young girl who is still living with parents or a close relative and has little if any sexual experience. How much then should *you* pay? Well, are you getting a fresh 17-year-old who has been under good parental control? Probably not. If the bride has had a dispute with her parents (it happens less often than in the West, but does happen) and has in many ways left the Thai world to live with foreign lovers or play the game, and has not been supporting parents or siblings, you might get her for nothing; indeed that might be the value placed on her by her parents, whom you may never meet. For all other girls, paying double the normal seems to be acceptable and to show a very small margin of generosity, particularly if other gifts are made to the family (big TV, new fridge. etc.). Compare this to the great mark-up on the entrance price foreigners pay to go into Thailand's major attractions and it is not a bad deal. Bride price negotiations should *never* become unpleasant. In the end, maybe you get what you pay for, and to agree to $5,000 for a virgin who has been to university and comes from a good family would be a good settlement. On average, for a pretty-enough girl, 100,000 baht should keep everybody happy. Of course, if you want any beer on hand for your *farang* guests, you will also meet all or most of the reception costs.

Of course, the payments made at the wedding are only the beginning. And here you may console yourself with the thought that never will anybody be able to say that you married your little precious for her money.

The bride might help her husband in his work or business, or she might be a perpetual drain on his resources. She might, as is traditional, handle all household expenses frugally, or she might greatly inflate them, insisting on two maids and a gardener-driver, daily trips to the beauty salon, quantities of shoes and clothing that remain unworn until given to the constantly visiting siblings. You should have a good idea what kind of wife your bride will make by her behaviour before the marriage. If she was constantly asking for money before the wedding, for herself and family, you can be 100 per cent sure she will continue to ask, with increased persistence, once you are married.

What do you get for your money? Many of the benefits you will not want. You can always farm out your children to the family, but will they go and do you want them to go? More likely is that members of your new family will gravitate to you and your nice cool home. Your new brothers, sisters, nieces and nephews, and people you had no idea were part of the family, will turn up unannounced. Unless you enjoy filling your days and evenings hosting beer parties and watching Channel 7, you will be part of the furniture, the ATM machine that allows your wife to fawn on her relatives, heal the sick, educate the underprivileged, provide succour to the needy and put braces on their children's teeth. There is nothing you can do to control this; your wife can, but will she?

On the other hand, and there *is* another hand, although many *farang* in Thailand deny it. You might meet the family halfway — speak to them for a start, preferably in Thai and not always through the marital mouthpiece. You will find some you like, some you don't. Spend your time with those you like, while not saying anything bad about any of your in-laws. If your new wife has any sense, she will have grasped before the marriage the real extent of your disposable income and will tailor activities accordingly. *If she has any sense.* When friends and family visit, unless on special occasions, the beery seafood dinners at an expensive restaurant will be replaced by home cooking village-style — lots of leaves, lots of bits and pieces to pick on, nothing expensive, groups of women sitting around spending hours preparing what seems to you to be a simple dinner, hours of social interaction before the eating starts, and the remainders put in the fridge for breakfast. If she has any sense, she will say "not necessary" when you propose paying for braces for her 12-year-old niece, beautiful except for a terrible mouthful of criss-cross teeth, and "not necessary" when you propose a hearing aid for her grandmother. If she has no sense at all, she will be insisting on these things and much more. If you are trapped in a no-sense situation, sorry, you should have been more careful at the selection stage. Sometimes, letting your concerns out to your wife's mother, if you have yourself had the sense to ally her on your side, and if she is not simply the origin of your wife's demands, can produce temporary results. However, if your wife is addicted to the new status of life that marriage to you has given her, maybe a turn in your home country, with nobody to clean the house or cook dinner but her, and your father's toenails to clip and his underpants to wash, might sort her out. Then again, it might not.

One surprising thing that you might find yourself getting out of the marriage is the warm holier-than-thou feeling of the altruist. This must of course be broadcast from the rooftops. People will definitely like you. You might even begin to like yourself. It is, after all, a great feeling to give a wheelchair to somebody who is, until your largesse, restricted to those places he can drag himself to. Even building an extension to mother's little fiefdom, with running water and a toilet that even you can use without risk to life and limb, will swell your status where it most matters, where the home fires burn. And feeling your status swell, your heart might just swell with it. And before you know it, you have insisted on paying for the niece's dental treatment and braces — around $1,000 for a two-year mouth refurbishment — and she owes her stunning looks all to you, as she will tell everybody. Truly, if you have a wife that doesn't vacuum all your money into her gambling sessions and endless face-jobs, you have the opportunity to use your wealth to assist those less fortunate than yourself, which can bring its own rewards *and* greatly improve your standing in Thai society at a greater level than the wife's family.

Having a beautiful, young wife will only add to your status if she is faithful to you. Having an older, educated, wife will only really add to your status if she comes from an important family, in which case that family will be looking for a useful marriage alliance and the bride price payment might be secondary, although high because of the need to maintain status.

Where does love fit into all this? You might well ask. It is nowhere in any documentation. The embassy declares only that it knows of no impediment to the marriage, the doctor is concerned with your heart only if it stops beating, the wedding has no mention of it. At the reception, guests put the envelope containing their money gift, clearly marked with their names, in a heart-shaped box — that's probably as near as the public world comes to symbols of love.

Bottom line:
One must not think that Thai nuptials are without consideration of love. They very much are. Love of a bride for her mother.

62

On Ordaining as a Monk for the Wrong Reasons

You might look real cool with your head shaved and mahogany-oiled, and dressed all in saffron with the blackest of shades, beaming soft rays of loving kindness to all the adoring boys and girls that hang around your *kuti*, telling them all in flawless Thai your ultimate cop-out of all conversation: *om, those who speak do not know; those who know do not speak.* You could, as a monk, dine out on those lines every day of your days in the robes. People would say, "Very deep this *farang* monk", and that would be enough to make your reputation. Thais would have bus trips from distant towns to see the enlightened *farang* monk give a few thoughtful sweeps with the broom around the Bo tree. Your picture would appear on the cover of monkish reviews. Thai big shots and *farang* film stars and musicians would seek you out just to have you gaze into their souls and say a silent mantra and spit holy water over their head.

Ordination does offer a short-cut to the highest status in the land. One minute you are just an ordinary Joe Soap, resigning yourself to a slow integration into Thai society, the next you have a bowl, robes, and off you go barefoot, women queuing up on their knees to feed you. Everybody, however high, *wais* a monk; the monk *wais* nobody but the Buddha.

When travelling by train the monk travels first class because first class is at the front of the train; not only that, he gets put in the front-most cabin of first class. In public, in the all important Thai public, whatever the monk does, even sitting down quietly, is one great step in front of what any ordinary mortal can do. Thai monks have walked through murderous gunfire coming at them from all sides, bringing their superior message of peace to warring factions: not one monk killed because nobody dared fire on a monk, or, as many Thais thought at the time, the bullets could not hit the monks. Well, that sounds like a nice position doesn't it? Who needs an army? But there is more. The monk gets to sit at the front of just about all shows and meetings where there might possibly be monks attending: the first row of seats is for monks, the second is for really important people. And while the monk is supposed to eat with distraction anything in his begging bowl, even a leper's thumb, women always give him the very best, and happily eat his leftovers. Sounds pretty good doesn't it? There's more. Once a monk has shown his mettle, he'll be exorcising young ladies full of the urge to procreate or not procreate, and standing between the dangerous spirit world and a material world full of beautiful people that the spirits want to inhabit, protecting these people with just a look or a sacred word. All this *and* refuge from the wife and kids; all this *and* no more hassles about who pays the bills. All this *and* people think you're the best thing since rice cookers.

But things don't come that easy, do they? The twist in the tail is that should you be foolish enough and deceitful enough to ordain for anything other than the right reasons, you get absolutely no merit at all. Indeed, even if you are the best motivated monk in the world, all your fasting, meditations and learning of the scriptures bring *you* no merit; it all goes to your mother or, heaven-forbid, your Thai mother in-law.

This might not be quite what you had in mind, but what you had in mind probably has as much relevance to *karma* as what goes on inside a cockroach's brain when it climbs happily into the trap that he meets on his *karmic* path. You cannot escape *karma* and whatever you do as a (false) monk will be *bad karma*, which is not only deadly for your future rebirth but through *karmic* workings in this life, a death blow to your social ambitions. Somehow — and you'd better believe this — your social ranking will be dragged down to minus figures, probably settling somewhere between that cockroach and the *took-ger* that will one day crunch it up.

There are things you can do to make retribution for just about anything, very public things that have people quickly once again saying what a grand fellow you are. But becoming a monk for the wrong reasons is the most difficult of Thailand's invisible transgressions to overcome.

Bottom line:

If you are caught out as a false monk, you might as well pack your bags and leave the country. Keep the shades on as you leave.

63

On Paying for Life-saving Operations

In spite of the rapid and substantial increase in real GDP, which means, or should mean, that more people have more to spend on more things, and in spite of the praise lauded on many Thai hospitals and doctors as among the best in the world, an amazing proportion of the population seems to be within two weeks of death if it does not receive a life-saving operation for which there is no money. Particularly, but not uniquely affected are girls working in bars and keeping the company of *farang*. Obviously, since this occupational hazard is aggravated by the constant presence of *farang*, so *farang* should help pay for the required operations. The cost of these operations is negotiable, but generally falls between two and five thousand dollars. Some of these girls are so strapped for cash, they don't even have any clothes on their backs and are obliged to shower in the cubicle on the bar, with everyone watching. Poor kids. Beaten up by sadistic Thai husbands, abandoned, forced to do whatever in order to put some food in the mouths of the starving children that bastard of a husband left her with. Worst of all, such operations create complications that lead to the need for further operations.

"But, Lek, I gave you $2,000 to have the cancerous growths in your uterus removed only last month."

"Yes, my honey. But these new cancerous growths are in the uterus of my mother."

You are such a nice guy and while, as a full-time teacher of English, you earn, if lucky, about half what an attractive bar girl makes in Patpong, you want to help the underprivileged of the world in a country which has yet to be officially classified as developed but which no longer receives much non-military aid from those mean and insensitive Western countries. And when a nice sweet girl like Lek, who has had such a hard life, and who has just undergone an operation herself, finds out her mother has the exact same thing, and of course she has no money to help her because she has to work in a bar and sell her body just to get enough to keep all the children in the family fed and at school, well, what can you do? Makes you feel guilty just sleeping with her, doesn't it?

Hey, if you feel you really must do something, why not pay the bus fare for the mother to come from Nakorn Nowhere to a really good hospital in Bangkok, where you will act as guarantor for her uterus operation.

"You don't think she might interpret that as an indication of distrust. I don't want to hurt her feelings in addition to all the other problems she has."

I thought her mother was dying?

"Right. No time to lose. I'll tell her right now. Hey, where'd she go? Guess she had to go back to hassling johns for enough short times to pay her mother's operation. Jesus, poor kid. Maybe she's gone home to be with her mother."

Well, never mind. You met Noy from Isaan, didn't you? She needs the same operation and is looking for someone to pay. Her mother also needs the operation. And her elder sisters, two of them.

"Uterus? Must be the way their Thai ex-husbands treated them. Poor kids."

> *Bottom line:*
>
> *There is certainly an operation required. The farang needs his wallet removed. While the surgeon's at it, a full frontal lobotomy might help the patient distinguish fact from fantasy.*

64

On Paying Through the Nose

If you find yourself frequently paying through the nose, always carry with you an outsized handkerchief or a pair of nose plugs tailored to release only so much within 24 hours — a bit like an ATM machine, but adjust the limit down as far as it will go. Learn to say with conviction, "I'd just love to help you, but I only have 10 baht in the world until my right nostril comes into play at midnight, at which time I will have the happy sum of 350 baht to spend for the day. So, catch me tomorrow after breakfast". In the unlikely event that you are understood in any language, you will probably get the request for money repeated with a lower threshold — but not 10 baht. Why don't they catch on that you are not going to pay up forever? It could be because sometimes you pay. Or it could be that you are very polite, in a Thai way, and never say No, but never quite say Yes. If you ever do say Yes, say Yes as in No. Could you give me 500 baht? Yes, next month after I come out of hospital.

There are times when it is productive and reasonable to pay with alacrity and magnitude. Imagine, for example, the tragic scenario of your Thai mother-in-law *together* with your father-in-law passing into the great space between births. You can happily contribute an amount appropriately huge to allow a funeral grand enough to ensure rebirth of both as

Channel 7 TV idols. By doing so, you get the greatest respect from all relatives and neighbours. Your fame will spread as fast as Thais can gossip. And you get to keep a bit of merit for your own rebirth, when the happy day comes. And you certainly won't be hearing from those two any more re the roof and bird flu.

Other occasions are less expensive but as immediately rewarding. When the community comes together for just about anything, it is always a chance to show how generous you are. Hire a table at a *wat* fair for the night, ensure the beer keeps coming and rove far and wide within the community of tables, filling glasses with *your* beer. Instant popularity from a bottle.

If you want to be a big man within your new community, it can't be done on the cheap. But spend on those items which are most publicly altruistic in the Thai sense of altruism, which ranks money spent on building or repairing *wat* right up there with sponsoring funerals. You can even ensure your name goes into posterity with a well-directed dispersal of funds. You won't be alone in contributing funds to a building activity within your local *wat.* And you don't want to be. What you want is to see your name, in Thai, at the very top of the contributions list on the huge concrete slab erected to show who gave what, or even on a marbled plaque set into the temple walls. You want to see, and you want everybody else to see, your name with 100,000 baht beside it, and you want to see, humbly grouped below, all the other contributors, with full public details of their voluntary contributions, their few thousand baht, their few hundred baht, or their few baht. You are certainly spending through the nose. That's one-seventh the price of a new Honda sedan! But wise and public giving to others is about the best all-round social investment you are likely to find.

Another way of courting popularity (and poverty) is by being magnanimous on a one-to-one level with those you judge need it most. One can fritter away on such small benefactions quite a small fortune. Example: What to do when somebody invites you to eat at his or her parent's home? You take along some flowers and sweets and while there call for and pay for a crate of beer. On leaving, your friend's father shows you a wedding invitation he has just received. "That's nice," you say. "Yes," he says. "Can you give me 300 baht or I can't go?" Now do you care if he goes to this wedding of people you don't even know? Probably not. Then why should you pay for him to go?

The 300 baht is not an attendance charge. The man received an invitation card. If he had just been told about the wedding on the morning or the day before, and if it were a village setting, he could just turn up whether he contributed or not. But the invitation card formalises things. He would be expected to put the envelope the card came in, clearly marked with his name, in the box at the entrance. Even if he doesn't go, sending a formal card is like asking for money, so he would still be expected to send back the card with at least something in it. To go and put an empty envelope in the box would be a real loss of his face. Do you care?

In this real example, your friend's father is afraid of loss of face among people he knows, be they relatives or a distant community. Yet he asks *you* for help to prevent that loss of face. Where does this guy get off? Doesn't he have any pride? What about loss of face related to begging? Why on earth should *you* help him, if he needs help, let him ask a relative.

Well, yes, almost right. If you are not particularly interested in his son or daughter and your relationship with them is not one you particularly want to take off for heaven, getting father out of his little fix is none of your business. It's awfully tempting to tell him this to his face. But the guy has a face-loss problem already, and you did just eat in his house, so you at least have to be polite (or *you* lose face). It may be only 300 baht and we are not talking about any principle here. Well, you were leaving anyway, so put on your shoes, wish your friend goodbye, hand out the small change to small children, and make your goodbye to the father short.

On the other hand, if you want for whatever reason to continue the relationship with this family, here is a cheap entrée. So give the man the 300 baht.

If there is a principle here, it is that money opens doors and creates or maintains relationships. Even a Thai groom arriving with his relatives at the bride's house has to pay her relatives to let them enter. All very symbolic. In Thailand, symbolism is everywhere, but the foreigner often doesn't see beyond the money.

Another principle is that any significant money (apart from that invested in the *wat*) passes hands between kin only, or classificatory kin — those who seem to be relatives and are in and out of the house all the time. If your girlfriend's father asks you for $2,000 to buy a second-hand truck, he is really asking if you want his daughter. If you do, better switch terminology to bride price quickly. If he wants to buy a truck with the money, that's up to him — or to his wife. If money changes hands between non-kin, it is most likely to be on a very businesslike basis, involving loans and calculation of interest. Such interpersonal loans are frequent in Thai society, where banks are not always happy to lend to small holder agriculturists or shopkeepers. They always involve interest and pay-back dates. In short, they are the opposite to the passage of money between real kin or people who are so close they might as well be kin.

So, the next time somebody you barely know asks you for 50 baht for the taxi fare, you could draw up a contract and say sign here with two witnesses, terms 10 per cent per month maximum six months. But that smacks of sarcasm rather than *phuut len*, so just smile as you go on your way.

Bottom line:

Try to look beyond the money to the symbolism. Give it to relatives, or people with whom you would like a close relationship with no thought of return (nam jai). Lend it to those outside the kinship/ close friends circle. Use money wisely; it oils Thai society in just about all activities at all levels.

65

On Paying Your Share

Almost unbelievable, but unfortunately true. I have seen and had to explain — *farang* who went for dinner with Thais and paid their share of the bill, leaving their Thai companions to pick up the rest. Chief offenders are the Dutch, all Nordics, and Germans, with some English. In their countries, this is an acceptable and reasonable cultural norm. Not so in Thailand.

Certainly, you will find some young Thais out for a good time on the night of the monthly pay day putting together an amount of money and eating and drinking their way through it. Sometimes this is done at the place of work, but usually in a restaurant. Sometimes they each give a certain amount of their salary to a different member of the group each month, and this person, temporarily a much bigger person, treats them all. And sometimes, you will see Thais dividing up the bill. This is perhaps because on such occasions they spend much more than they usually would and are in a large group. But if the bill is thus divided, which is already an exception to the way things should be done (but *sin deuan*, month's end, is a rather exceptional time), no individual is going to work out what he ate or drank and pay for that alone, the total is simply split by the number of people — and this is agreed beforehand, or is an established procedure for a regular event involving more or less the same people each time.

If you are called to join such a group, you are unlikely to get stung with the bill if you sit down. However, there is a difference between a mixed group of young people on a trip out from the office or factory, and an all male group of hardened drinkers. The first can be fun, the second can be fun but at a point the fun element can click over into aggression — that point often comes when the beer runs out, so make sure you run out before the beer. If you join a nice group and are enjoying yourself, stay. It would be normal enough for you as an outsider to order a few extra bottles of beer and pay for them. You can do this by going to the toilet and speaking to the staff. Be clear and precise (otherwise the beer might keep on coming): you want six bottles for that group there and I will pay now. Similarly, if you do want to pay for everybody, it makes a very nice impression if you do this during a toilet trip. Don't tell anybody at the table, let somebody call for the bill only to find the *farang* has paid. It might happen that you try the toilet trick only to find another person has already paid using the same method. I have never found a shop where the staff take double payments; you can trust some people sometimes, but *sin deuan* is a very busy time.

Those foreigners who make a point of insisting a Thai pay his or her share — yes, plenty of foreign men seem to think female liberation has stretched to Thai girls paying their way; nothing is further from reality — find they are changing their Thai compa°nions rather too frequently. It's the quickest way to develop a reputation as *farang khi niao*.

> *Bottom line:*
> *If you invite somebody to eat, pick up the bill, unless that person pays "behind your back". In situations where the inviter is uncertain, the person of higher status pays — probably you. Men pay for women, unless a businesswoman is on expenses and does the inviting.*

66

On Peeing in a Thai Country House at Night

On being invited to spend the night in a traditional Thai house upcountry, you will of course accept — at least, you will on the first occasion such an invitation comes your way. Your chance to experience real Thai family and village life. Jolly good. Even the well-placed Thai has country cousins that he or she cannot ignore. Marry a Thai and chances are you just have to get used to some quality time in the village. Complaints are not in order; precautions are.

You will be prepared for the unsophisticated toilet arrangements and a lot of heat, and you would do well to be so prepared. When visiting upcountry, one should always go to the toilet first.

Some foreigners in the know cheat a little on the toilet rite of passage and dose up with Imodium before leaving home. This will limit their visits to the sweat-box at the bottom of the garden to those required for passing water, which some folk manage within the space of one very deep breath (taken before, not after, entry).

There is not much to be done against the heat. Casting aside any ideas of dress and decency prescribed by cultural guides, and ignoring your own observations that those really in the hothouse frontline and up to their knees in rice paddies are wrapped around from head to toe to keep the heat out, you expose a maximum amount of skin, train the fan (if there is one) fully upon you and sweat within the charming old hardwood planks and beams, which, in combination with a corrugated iron roof conspire to create a charming atmosphere of a sauna. Finally, you will give in to the heat and (dare it be said?) boredom, and order a couple of crates of beer and a bathtub full of ice. One thing can be said with certainty about Thailand. However remote your upcountry is, there will always be a shop within two minutes selling beer and ice. Another certainty is that unless you brought one with you, there will be no bottle opener in the entire village. Thais are born with a natural opener where other people just have teeth. Don't try it. Although you may, if you don't mind losing half a bottle of beer, emulate the other method used by Thais to open beer. This requires upending one bottle and opening it with the top of another bottle. Done dexterously, this is movement art at its best. Done less confidently, things get awfully sticky.

With all that beer inside, you will be creeping happily under a mosquito net and nestling your head into the hard roll of pillow. You might even slumber. When you wake, it is pitch black and you desperately need a pee. No hand basin to go in. Absolutely taboo to pee through any cracks in the woodwork, you never know who may have stretched a hammock down below. Nothing for it but to get out of the net, make your way to where you think the door is, on hands and knees in case you step on a sleeping body, locate the door bolts, draw them open, push the door open on complaining hinges, make it down the house ladder and either try for the box, best avoided in the dark, or let flow in the vegetable patch. Well, there is another way.

You might have noticed some spittoons dotted around inside the house. These are used by betel nut chewers, now almost entirely the senior citizens of the family. These oldies have the same problem as you with a pee that won't wait 'til morning. They take their spittoons to bed with them. It's quite in order for you to borrow a spittoon for the night. Given the beer and the capacity of the average spittoon, better make that two. Problem solved. Your inclination as a good guest will be to carry your full spittoon(s) down to the thunder-box and empty them. No real need. If you invite a couple of younger members of the family to show you the early morning market, which may be the highlight of your day — and buy them a nice blood and noodles breakfast there — all spittoons and mosquito nets will be cleared away by the time you return.

Bottom line:

So, that's how to get through the night in your charming old wooden Thai house. Or, if that sounds too much trouble, you can just pop your night bag under the net, making sure it contains the great Bangkok reliever, a Comfort 400, and a packet of tissues.

67

On Playing Cards

At funerals, children are given packs of cards and small sums of money with which they gamble in imitation of their elders. The game of chance is symbolic of the world of fate entered into by the deceased. An individual is dealt his or her cards in life and plays them with varying degrees of skill and luck, and this play determines what the future brings in this life and the next — rebirth as a homeless puppy or as a child of a Bangkok property developer.

Thais believe in fate, but if the cards of life predict something they would rather not experience, there is always a way out. It might take payment to an astrologer to find it, or perhaps a wise monk can help out with advice, but, however bad things sound, there is always a way to make them better. The way is likely to involve religious activity — building up merit. It could also involve behavioural change — wearing certain colours, foregoing alcohol and even avoiding gambling.

Fortune-telling and card-playing go together, so does playing the lottery and betting on cock fights, Thai boxing and a hundred other chances to improve one's lot in life. Women are particularly vulnerable, and they hold the domestic purse. Some, by no means all, become quite addicted to gambling, which is against the law (unless sanctioned by the state), and such mothers usually pass the vice onto their children, with the result that the family is almost always in debt and resorts to prostitution or crime to make ends meet.

As a foreigner, you will play your cards rather differently. You will be aware of the importance of the business or visiting card. As long as you look reasonably like the man or woman who should be behind the card, it can give you instant status. And if you don't have an important position with an established company or organisation, you can at least have a nice visiting card, and in a very little way perhaps, you can be a big frog in a small and probably unknown pond. A nice coat of arms helps, preferably embossed and colourful. Card makers can take it from your passport or a letterhead from your embassy. A well-thought out card will not by itself change your fortunes, but it can hopefully serve to stop you being rejected at the first meeting.

Do not rush to hand over your card, and only do it once, on first acquaintance. Preferably, you do it after introduction by one reasonably important person to another even more important person, and in response to a card that has been handed to you. There is something of the deference system even in the handover of cards — as with the wai, and even the smile, the lesser individual should play his card first. And the really big man might not give his card in return. But, never mind, he has taken yours.

Be aware that many, perhaps most, Thais will consult a fortune-teller when there is something important in their life. This is not so much an act of accepting their fate, but trying to change it, at least whatever they don't like about it. Your entry into their lives and business, if it involves money or love, might indeed be something to consult a fortune-teller about. And professional confidentiality is not built into the system. So you can follow somebody's fortune through their friends and perhaps even their fortune-teller. You can also hold a semi-public session for yourself, and make sure you do all that is required of you to ensure good luck. If your future looks bright, people will know. And Thailand is certainly a place for the self-fulfilling prophecy.

Bottom line:

People with a bright future tend to hang together. So do those on the way down and out. The first choose to do so, the second have no choice.

68

On Popping Pimples

Who has not felt the thrill of squeezing mature pimples until they explode onto the bathroom mirror? In the farang world that particular pleasure is confined to an individual's private existence, something to do behind closed doors. In the Thai world, the same taboo does not exist in the public world, although it certainly does not do to pop pimples when sitting tightly alert in a big person's presence, with your upper body held at a 30 degree angle of respect, your knees trying not to cross and your hands down and under control. You should really have popped them before coming. Similarly for nose hair tweaking and scrotum scratching. Of course, there is nothing stopping the big person from popping his own pimples; but even he or she should not start on yours, at least not without an "excuse me". And if he or she should invite you to have a squeeze of one of theirs, it looks like you are getting on extremely well indeed.

Now that modern shampoos and gels have limited the comforting closeness of picking nits from each other's hair, monkey-style, a couple may still enjoy that special togetherness that comes from popping each other's spots. Should you have no wish to participate, there is no need to do so actively, but to deny your Thai partner the pleasure and expression of affection that popping your pimples and weeding your nose would give them, is a bit selfish, especially if you then go into the bathroom and selfishly do it to yourself. Passive acceptance is recommended, along with a supply of tissues.

Bottom line:

You scratch my back and I'll pop your pimples.

69

On Pretending to Speak Thai

Really speaking Thai is, of course, the preferred state and learning to do so is strongly advised. However, you will hopefully find yourself from the beginning of your stay interacting in Thai circles, where everybody is speaking Thai; and for them to turn to you and speak English would cut you out, just at the time when you want to integrate and are most motivated to learn Thai. Also, nowadays, many Thais speak English, and a lot many more like to think they do. Once you establish English as your common language, even with a Thai who speaks quite poorly, there is a strong tendency to continue to use that language. This means that speaking English all the time is wasted in terms of your learning Thai, and slows your rate of integration. It might help your Thai interlocutors improve their English, but this is not your objective. Establish Thai as your common language and you will be learning right from the start, even if you don't understand a word said. For this reason, at the beginning of your quest get your hair cut often, take taxis everywhere, stroll through temples, and frequent simple Thai establishments rather than places where waiters will address you in English. Hair cuts and taxi rides should come complete with a free Thai lesson, monks will want to practise their limited English but five minutes will exhaust it and exhaust you. You will rapidly learn that having a conversation in Thai is not that difficult, although you may understand next to nothing at first. Essentially, all you have to do is wind up your conversational partner by saying hello in Thai and punctuate any pauses with one of the three magic words that follow.

The three words that will get you through whatever follows "hello" are these: *cap* (man talking), *kha* (woman talking), *ker* and *ler*.

Cap, often transcribed *khrap*, is an affirmative. The nearest translation would be something like, "O Respected One". When somebody says whatever and looks at you, you say cap or *kha*. It means you agree with the speaker, who will then continue. The agreement is only a courtesy one, simply acknowledging what was said, so don't worry that you might be taken to task over it later. You will find that *cap* will get you through most conversations; use the occasional nod of the head for emphasis, but only smile in return. If your companion pauses unreasonably after one of your perfect *cap*, a hearty cough is a good conversational gambit. If necessary, a series of coughs and an "excuse me" look as you make for the toilet.

Ker (*keu*) is used surprisingly little by foreigners. It is used all the time by Thais to fill in gaps in a sentence, much as "... er..." is used in English, although unlike "er", *ker* actually has a meaning. When in the compound *ker wa*, it means "it means" or "that's to say". *Ker...* is a short form of *ker wa*. The verbal row of dots can trail on until you find the word you are looking for or drop dead in the process. Don't be afraid to let your *ker...* trail. If said during an awkward silence, it shows you are thinking; and if it trails on long enough, somebody is bound to step in and finish your sentence for you. The trailing *ker* record is said to be 49 minutes, set during a UN reception at a conference to discuss Bangkok's traffic problems.

Ler (*leu*) is another little helper underused by foreigners learning Thai. By itself, it means "really, is that so?". Together with a word or phrase you have just heard, it asks for confirmation, either that you heard correctly or that the speaker actually meant to say that. It may not be terribly intellectual, but ler can actually sound rather refined. Thus:

Speaker: "*Ron!*" "Hot!"

Listener: "*Ler?*" "Is that so?" or advanced use: "*Ron ler? Cap.*" "Hot? Is it really? O respected one."

This is the basic tennis gambit, the ball is back in your companion's court, and your companion must lob it back or retire defeated by your extraordinary grasp of the Thai language.

As you advance in your use of *cap, ker* and *ler*, you will find other words creeping in. You are learning Thai! But don't discard these three little helpers.

Pretending to speak Thai at cocktail parties is easiest of all since everybody is really interested only in hearing himself speak, not in listening to others. So as an eager listener, you will be sought after. The important thing is to get people started in Thai. You can probably manage a reasonable *sa-wat-dii-cap/kha*. Except in the most formal of circumstances, this can be shortened to *wat-dii* with the *cap/kha* dropped when talking to people you know well or when talking to a member of the lower classes — such contractions suggest familiarity and fluency with the language. If starting out, always use the *cap/kha* respect words on the end of everything you say, although you won't be saying much at first. *Hong nam yuu thi nai, cap* — "Where is the toilet, O respected one?"

Meeting a Thai for the first time, and getting in the hello bit in Thai, you will often be asked if you speak Thai. Never say *nit-noy*. It sounds like you are in a bar and that these are your only two words of Thai — which they might well be, but don't broadcast the fact or after ten years, they might still be your only two words. If you don't like to lie with a simple ambiguous *cap*, then smile broadly and say in Thai *may-day-lok-cap* (contrary to what you seem to think, I cannot, O respected one). Practise this until it is perfect. You score on speaking Thai well and on opening with a sort of joke — since only a good speaker is likely to use the particle *lok*.

> *Bottom line:*
>
> *Who knows does not speak. Who speaks does not know.*

70

On Quintessence Quotidian

Nitty-gritty time. What is the daily quintessence of Thai society that makes it specifically Thai and not Lao, not Burmese or Chinese or Vietnamese or Malay? Is there a single thing, or a combination of things that we think of as Thai that really is or are Thai in essence? Is anything so much a part of being Thai that if we took it away Thais would stop being Thai?

Let's brainstorm for a moment. Freewheel and see what we come up with. No particular order. As they pop into the mind. Hands up when you think of something and I'll write it on the whiteboard. After all, if we don't know who we are talking about, why are we here?

Inhabitant of Thailand. So are you and I, but we are not Thai, are we?

Citizen of Thailand. Fine as a political definition. But it's rather tautologous. A Thai is a Thai. So are all the minority groups who also inhabit Thailand and are citizens. And Thais living overseas, where perhaps they have given up their Thai nationality in order to take on another, yet still see themselves as Thai, where do they fit in?

People who speak Thai as their mother tongue. Well, at least we are into a cultural definition now. It rules out you and I. However beautifully we speak Thai, we cannot in this life change our mothers and our mother tongue. That's fine. But it also rules out all those Thai citizens who speak Chinese or a minority language as their mother tongue. And what do we mean by the "Thai" language. If it is the national language of Central Thai, the definition probably excludes the majority of the population of Thailand, who can speak Central Thai but have a regional dialect or minority language as mother tongue. At a pinch, we could include Thai dialects in "mother tongue" as Thai-family languages. But that might mean also including Lao in Laos and Thai-family speakers in Vietnam, China, Myanmar and elsewhere. So language alone, even if writ large, perhaps confuses as much as it illuminates.

People of the Buddhist religion. I think the problem here is obvious, even if we specify Theravada Buddhism, we are talking about a religion which, while undoubtedly central to Thai society, is a universal, shared to some extent in all neighbouring countries, and in Sri Lanka, India, Bhutan, Nepal and just about all countries where there are Buddhists, which is most countries in the world.

People who share a common history. Depends how we define history. All the neighbours and some peoples from a long way off share parts of the history of Thailand and the Thais. Practically no Thai fully shares a common history with another, although they may recognise a common history.

People who share a common gene pool. This would be an objective scientific measure but could never be accurate because of intermarriage. There are plenty of Thais who share the genes of Malays, hill tribes found throughout much of the region, Chinese, even farang.

People who share a common structure and outlook. We may be getting somewhere here. Almost all Thais — at least Thais in the cultural sense — are born into a structure that is bilineal (i.e. the father and the mother are principal figures in life) with significant matriarchal elements. Outside of this loosely structured family, a child is expected to show similar deference to that shown to parents and elder siblings, to strangers above him or her on the social ladder. The outlook towards elders and betters is predictable and socialised from an early age, but the outlook towards marital partners and friends is characterised by a may pen rai attitude, which allows significant movement of individuals, by this means protecting rather than destroying the basic structure. This structural definition appears to hold good for Thais in the wider sense, in Vietnam, China and elsewhere.

People who consider themselves Thai. Perhaps in the end, this is the nearest we can get. But how do they see themselves?

Probably they do not see themselves in a nutshell! However, we have to try to fit the Thai way of seeing themselves into just that amount of space if it is to become manageable. So, here I quote from my own book CultureShock! Thailand, which in turn cites a Thai folk tale in which a Thai king meets a Thai peasant. This tells us at least the way one Thai sees himself, and since the folk tale is itself part of Thai culture, transmitted over time, maybe it is in some way representative.

In this tale a king asks a peasant rice farmer what he does with his surplus rice. The peasant replies: "Your Majesty. All the money I am able to save, after paying the expenses of our frugal household, I divide into four parts. The first I bury in the ground; the second I use to pay my creditors; the third I fling into the river; and the fourth and last part I give to my enemy."

Well, on the face of it, that sounds like pretty strange behaviour. At the king's request, the peasant explains.

"The money I bury in the ground is the money I spend on building up merit (*boon*) which will serve me after I leave this life. The money I give to my creditors is what it costs me to keep my father and mother, to whom I owe everything I have. The money I fling into the river is the money I spend on gambling and drink and opium; and the money I give to my enemy is the money I give to my wife."

The peasant spends his money on four things: religion, parents, enjoyment and wife. That he divides the money equally suggests he places the same value on each. Thus his wife, and by extension her mother and father, gets the same as his own parents, although perhaps the peasant is not altogether happy with giving money to his "enemy".

This is the way the folk-tale Thai sees life. It is very much a structural-functionalist view, with the wife's family figuring as much as the man's own parents and his enjoyment being balanced by commitment to religion. Most Thais today would probably agree with the essence of what the peasant says. We could therefore say that the daily quintessence of being "Thai" involves a balancing act between the four major components of his character and of his society.

As a foreigner living in Thailand, you might come closer than you think to the views of a Thai peasant. You may not spend much if anything on religion, but you are likely to invest something for your future and the future of those you leave behind; your parents may be gone but there may be family or other "creditors" requiring you to send money "back home"; you will certainly want to enjoy yourself in Thailand; and if you are a man and you marry a Thai, there will be expectations that you will help to support your wife's parents. The proportions might seem a little exaggerated: why should you give a quarter of your money to your wife and her family, after all she is not a peasant's wife and doesn't work in the fields all day? But if you can work out what is left over after meeting the needs of your less than frugal household, and where it goes, you probably do just that, maybe more. As long as you have the same amount to spend on enjoying yourself as goes to your wife and her parents, isn't that all right by you?

Bottom line:

The quintessence of being Thai is placing an approximately equal value on family, including in-laws, religion, and enjoyment. While, of course, fully complying with the deference system and avoiding conflict. By behaving in this way, a Thai feels comfortable in his social structure, which allows him plenty of room to move. If you feel comfortable in this way, speak Thai and conform to Thai ways and values, are you Thai? Maybe you are. Almost.

71

On Receiving an Unsolicited Proposition

When walking alone at certain times and in certain places, you will attract the attention of undesirables who offer or request sex. This goes for women or men, although the offer is for some reason always made to men and the request is made of women. Many men feel flattered by the attention, or at least not too bothered by it, whereas women feel at best insulted, at worst afraid. Why this should be the case, when any man taking up the offer stands to pay, and any woman accepting the request stands to profit, defies any economic law and goes directly to the defenceless nature of a woman alone and the social role of the man as protector and predator. If you are a man, you should, however, think at least twice before going with a girl (or a boy) from the streets into an unknown guest house, particularly if the bulge in your trousers is caused by a wad of banknotes.

While white-skinned foreigners are particularly prone to such propositions, the important factor is not so much gender or race but temporary social position. Alone. Alone is unprotected and unconstrained. The individual in a group will not be propositioned — although occasionally a khatoey will try her luck with a group of men, often offering a free sample of goods for hire, a sample that should never be tasted in public. The foreigner, particularly a woman, will feel that they are targeted precisely because they are not Thais; this is absolutely not the case. A Thai girl walking alone in a sparsely populated area or after dark will be propositioned in exactly the same way. It happens less to Thais only because they are so rarely alone.

What to do? Prevention always being better than cure, don't walk the streets alone, particularly if you have been drinking and it's late. Easy to say, but on occasion everybody finds him- or herself alone, with the shops around shuttered and no escape from the two guys on a motorbike who seem quite persistent. There is no sensible advice to give, and once you have survived a scary situation, you will make special efforts to plan your evening so you do not end up on the streets alone and on foot.

Do not attempt any communication, even if it is to say No! Walk fast and know where you are going. If you come to a restaurant, go in and ask to call a taxi. It's worth the expense. In fact, you should have a mobile phone with you at all times and the number on it of a reliable taxi service. The very best service will take time to arrive, particularly if you cannot say precisely where you are, so call before you get into such a situation. Put a number on your phone now and try it. And never put your phone down on a disco table — it will disappear before your eyes.

Bottom line:
When there is no cure, preventive action is a must.

72

On Receiving More *Crap* Than You Give Out

On receiving more crap than you give out, rejoice. You have passed the halfway mark and are now in the upper half of Thai society, even if you still look distinctly foreign in the mirror. You absolutely do not load crap on those beneath you. You step back and let them crap upwards on you.

The word *crap/cap (khrap)* is men only. Women have to say *ka (kha)*. It is usually said at the end of a sentence, although the really deferential can pop it in almost any pause there is. The term oozes subservience, but is today used between strangers who don't know each other, who may be almost equals or who may have a social divide as wide as the Gulf of Thailand between them. So you would say it to any shop assistant, although not as much as they would say it to you. The inferior might also say *craphom* which is simply more of the same. There isn't a really good translation for these particles of respect. Historically, they meant something like slave or "my hair under your feet", but such references have long ceased to have any meaning. Omitting them when they should be used sounds very rude and uncultured, and using them when you really shouldn't sounds sarcastic or overly formal or just plain foreign. You can stay a month in an upcountry Thai village and hardly hear *crap* or *kha* — everybody knows each other, they are all farmers, so why walk around greeting people as if they are "O Respected One"?

Another word you won't hear much in the upcountry village is *khun* meaning you, he, she or Mr or Mrs. Quite a useful little word and definitely to be used in respectable society, attached to somebody's first name if you know it (with *crap/kha* after the name if calling). But in the village, you won't hear it much outside of the school. In the *wat*, it is too low a term — for monks the word becomes *than* (rhymes with gun). In the village generally, as in the family and between close friends anywhere, people just use first names without any prefix or suffix. There is a social line to cross here. We are not just talking about friendliness: it is equally friendly to say, "*khun Noy crap*" as "*Noy*", only the respect and familiarity changes. Use *khun, crap, kha,* whatever and you are playing safe. But don't believe too much those cultural guides that tell you these words must *always* be used. Most of the time, Thais do not use them among themselves.

Thais addressing you, of course, should use these terms, even if talking English. If they are omitted inappropriately, a steady but not over-prolonged stare may send the inferior tumbling into an excess of polite particles. You will never give up using these terms entirely, but overuse might tend to suggest you are less of a big fart than you really are.

Bottom line:
To get a feel for manipulation of particles, you must listen to Thais speaking to each other. This is sometimes evident in TV dramas as scriptwriters have a duty to educate the public, so they tend to over-formalise. Learning to use them is easy. Learning not to overuse them is harder. Bide your time and it will come naturally enough.

73

On Reciprocity and Redistribution

However much or little you give out of your wallet, don't ever think about getting anything back in return. Give without thinking of reward and you won't be disappointed.

That's fine in terms of nam jai philosophy. And you as a foreigner will definitely accumulate more social points the more you give away. But these social points can't be cashed in like green stamps, and if you need economic help, those you have been generous to will not recognise any obligation to "repay". This bothers many foreigners, who may give to a charity with no expectation of direct or indirect reciprocity, but who see very little return on their "social investment" in Thailand. Indeed, generosity is in one direction only. Westerners are brought up to think of social investment in terms of economic rationality — by all means scratch somebody's back when he or she has an itch he or she can't reach, but the expectation that backs will be scratched in return does not always work in Thailand, at least not in the way many farang think it should. So expect nothing. If your generosity results in only your disappointment and bitterness, you have completely wasted your "investment" and completely misunderstood the Thai system. If, on the other hand, you have given with only thoughts of kindness, you might get something back, if not in terms of economic credit at least in terms of accumulated merit and reputation.

Fine, but do Thais really think this way, or is it just a justification for milking anybody who may have two pennies to rub together? Well, the answer is that many Thais do think this way, but when it comes to putting their money where their thoughts are, some do and some don't. The well-off Thai might be generous with everybody, not only his own kin and not only with those who some day might be in a position to return help financially or physically. This is usually in the public arena, although not always, which means he or she cannot escape the "credit" of a "patron-client" relationship. Not that the recipient has unthinkingly to do everything the patron suggests (although this is a possibility), but that he or she will certainly speak well of a person who is generous, and this is the cornerstone of building a good reputation. The reverse is also true: the person who has the means but is not generous will get a reputation as khi nio. Such a reputation will not help you integrate into Thai society.

Like all cultures, that of the Thai developed over centuries. Thai culture is changing, but not in one-to-one conformity with economic development. In its village origins, the nam jai system perhaps had more of a reciprocity element. Gaps

between rich and poor would be reduced by the generosity of the comparatively well-off, both within their kinship group and within the wider society of village neighbours. The generous man or woman would not necessarily benefit from direct or indirect economic reciprocity, but would be accorded social status in return. On the base of this social status, the big person in the group would emerge as the village headman or be in other ways influential. Such socio-political positions as village representatives would involve decision-making and interaction with a larger society and economy. This could involve economic advantage, even if this were not the motive for the generosity which led to representative office. This is still the system within many a village setting. The foreigner is most unlikely to be part of that system, as indeed many urban Thais are no longer part of the system, at least not when it comes to meaningful influence and decision-making in their villages of origin. Thai culture continues to place a very high value on generosity, and that is all you really need to know.

Real wealth (and poverty) stays within the family. For the Thais, as for anybody else, real charity begins at home. It is simply the definition of home that is different. For Thais, the family continues to be writ as large as possible; for many foreigners, the family of their concern is as small as possible. All that may change and is perhaps already changing. But the foreigner who really wishes to get on in Thai society as it is now will not get far if he avoids all opportunities to be generous. This is why the bill for the food and drink more often than not comes to you.

Bottom line:
The only redistribution of wealth you are likely to be involved in is the redistribution of your wealth.

74

On Second Thoughts

This is absolutely the most beautiful girl in the world. No doubt about it. I'm madly in love with her. She's everything I've always wanted.. On second thoughts, maybe I'll marry the niece.

Thailand is truly amazing. I can hardly believe the freedom I feel. Everything and everybody is so beautiful and friendly and I have all the sex partners I could want. *And* the beer's good. I wouldn't live anywhere else. On second thoughts, maybe I'll move to Laos.

In Thailand, expect to change your opinions, and even to live with contradictory opinions. No country could be as great as you imagine Thailand to be. No girls could be as beautiful. No people as easy-going.

The big man who welcomed you last week can't remember you this week. The fantastic house you moved into, with the most spectacular river views, floods in the rainy season and is full of rats and *tookgers*. The incredibly tasty Thai food you loved in California just sends you to the toilet in Thailand. That most beautiful girl in the world has fat thighs and can't even peel a banana. The peace and tranquility of the temple next door is broken, along with your sleep, by the drumming at 4.40 am and the interminable loud speakers blasting out the sermons on *wan phra*.

In Thailand, first impressions are important. Social life is most often on the public surface and if people have a bad first impression of you, why come back for a second look? So be beautiful, good-mannered, and as generous as you can reasonably afford. That should take care of Thai views of you. As for your view of Thais, enjoy your first impressions, but don't trust them. And don't blame the Thais for failing to live up to them. A flashing smile can beautify the most homely features and draw your attention away from fat thighs. Give yourself time for second thoughts. And maybe third thoughts come closer to reality. If, that is, you want reality. If you are happy with your illusions, that's fine too, but you will probably need to change your Thais often.

> *Bottom line:*
> *Row, row, row your boat, gently down the stream, merrily, merrily, merrily, merrily, life is but a dream.*

75

On Sensitivity and Tolerance

Dear Uncle Robert,

After five years in Thailand, two failed marriages to avaricious Thais, a hundred superficial affairs and years wasted learning the language, I have belatedly come to the conclusion that I don't like Thais very much.

Thais will interrupt you when you are trying to say something important, they will disturb your sleep with their noise, they say they love you and miss you then disappear for days or weeks without a word, they will agree to meet for dinner then not show up, they will let you pay for everything then ask you for money, they will turn their TV on full as soon as you enter their restaurant then ignore it and talk at full volume on their mobile phones. This, to me demonstrates, at best, insensitivity to the *farang* guests in the country, and at worst is bloody rude.

If they were just thick-skinned and insensitive, perhaps I could take it. But if you patiently explain that you are talking to somebody privately and their interruption isn't helping you, *they* get offended. If you don't tell them every five minutes that they are the most beautiful person in the world, they ask you what's wrong with them — maybe just fishing for compliments, but if you so much as hint that you have things to do other than pamper their inflated ego, they get offended.

If you say you'd rather not invite their friend or relative, who cross-dresses and hustles in a bar, they get offended. If they keep you waiting two hours and you greet them with a sarcastic remark to break the tension, they get offended.

These people show incredible sensitivity when their rudeness is pointed out to them, yet absolutely no sensitivity when it comes to all the many things that offend the *farang*.

Bitter in Bangkok

*   *   *   *   *   *   *

Dear Bitter,

The Thai are indeed very sensitive, but if you know the cause of their sensitivity or insensitivity, and your letter suggests you do, perhaps you should try a little harder to look at these things from the viewpoint of those Thais you know. Sensitivity goes hand-in-hand with tolerance. Most Thais will tolerate the things you mentioned — interruptions, broken social appointments, coming late, false flattery, cross-dressing, requests for money.

If you cannot approach such matters with the same spirit of genuine tolerance, you might try the muzzle technique — you don't actually have to wear a muzzle, but imagine you are doing so whenever you have an urge to tell the Thais what's wrong with them. In English, we might advise counting up to ten. In your case, counting up to twenty could be more appropriate.

Thais are tolerant of many things — but they have a low tolerance threshold for sarcasm. Sarcasm may be the soul of wit to you, but it is criticism to Thai ears and far from breaking any ice, it will freeze social interaction solid. And whatever you say is not going to change the Thai world, or those bits of it that you don't like, so why bother? Perhaps by

placing an imaginary button in your lip, you will be able to continue enjoying whatever you enjoy in Thailand. You might also find that if you stick to one main partner, the requests for money (which you are not obliged to meet) will disappear (since you are already "owned") or that such requests will at least stay within the realm of giving you the chance to demonstrate your *nam jai*.

You are a *farang* who speaks Thai. Imagine if you did not speak a word, perhaps your case five years ago, would you have the same problems? It is often during the early part of the stay in Thailand, when you don't know enough Thai to disagree with anybody, that illusions are constructed. When the Thais fail to live up to the image of what *farang* want them to be, the *farang gets offended and disappointed and finally bitter.* Tolerance and sensitivity cuts both ways. If a Thai is living in Europe, I would advise him or her to adjust their behaviour, even if it means adjusting their tolerance level and sensitivities; if a *farang* is living in Thailand, the same advice goes. You have been here long enough to overcome the illusions of first impressions. If, on balance, you consider that things are better back home, why not give it a trial run? Return home for as long as you can. I bet it doesn't take you long to miss Thailand — and miss the Thais. Then you can come back and start again with the benefit of what you know about the Thais, their culture and language. But next time, really take it easy on expectations. Good luck!

Uncle Robert

> *Bottom line:*
> *Tolerance always has limits. Thailand might teach you yours. Or the Thais may cause you to adjust your tolerance levels. Either way, you have learnt a lot about the Thais and a lot about yourself.*

76

On Sharing the Bathroom with
a Jurassic Monster

On waddling into your state-of-the-art bathroom, naked as nature intended, cup of morning coffee in hand, today's Bangkok Post under the arm, your mind in the passive neutrality born of routine... you find you are not alone. Two large limpid eyes stare up at you from inside the toilet bowl. This has never happened before. Attached to the bulging eyes is a bulging head with a wide mouth showing a line of sharp teeth on top of a body the size of a demi-baguette, covered in lumpy red spots. Yes, you are awake. No, your coffee has not been doctored.

You will either flee the scene or stare in disbelief at your prehistoric reptilian bathroom companion, a small crocodile with the addition of Spider Man's suction pads on its large splayed toes. These help it climb up tall buildings and also attach it to your toilet bowl, to the ceiling above your head, to the wall behind your fridge, to the drawer of your dressing table and even to your nice rosewood bedhead; in fact, they hold it firm to just about anywhere it wants to be. Jurassic Park has come home. DON'T SIT DOWN.

You are having a close encounter with a creature that has been around long before Man built the first bathroom, and for that matter, long before Man. Toilets, it must be said, have never really been designed for two; particularly for two species separated by the Great Flood. Wherever and whenever you meet your Jurassic monster, you will find all of the advice on coping with culture shock helps not one jot more than a Steven Spielberg movie on the Jurassic era. You will have an irresistible and perfectly understandable urge to be alone.

Enter the tookger. Before the encounter you might have heard it "crying" (as the Thai says) on a hot night. Took... ger... took... ger. If it does seven it's supposed to be lucky — at least that's what you can tell the children to keep their minds off what now has you in an eye lock. Typically, tookger cry, or cry most, in the March–April hot time. And as long as they stay out of your kitchen, they are part of the tropical symphony of frogs and crickets, adding an exotic background soundtrack to your life in Thailand.

Don't be taken in by the initial docility of the stranger in your toilet. Like many upcountry Thais, tookger can lie around for hours or days in a cool place with little sign of life. Then they might spring into action, or they might not. Admittedly, even when dormant, it takes a lot to love a tookger. They have been called the ugliest creatures in Thailand because they never, ever smile. If you want to make a point about the poor aesthetic qualities of your teacher or boss, words like "Face like a tookger" come close enough to being superlative. Avoid making such comparisons — in public. In fact, avoid tookgers if you possibly can.

Tookger, being Thai, don't like being alone. One tookger usually makes two, and two tookgers can make a whole lot more. You're a reasonable person, but you did not invite them in to enjoy free bed and board, and facilities to raise a family of lots of little tookgers, that place themselves on the hinges of doors, windows and refrigerators, waiting to be crushed to an eye-popping death when you swing a door shut, that crash onto your plate during a dog-fight to the death with a flying pterodactyl, that have the inhuman capacity to poo while hanging upside-down above your dining table, and, of course, that hog the bathroom whenever you want to go to the toilet.

Getting a house with two bathrooms is strongly advised, and if both are occupied by primordial creatures, then a third comes in handy. While contemplating what to do in this your first encounter, a sharp learning curve is recommended (together with a sharp pointed instrument). These are the attributes and myths of tookger lore. Learn fast.

• Tookger are not related to *jinjoks*.
Different tribe, no intermarriage. *Jinjoks* are little house lizards which practise formation dancing around a light source and eat up some of the unwanted insect life, including mosquitoes and, if they can manage it, a termite or two. *Jinjoks* never grow up, at least they never grow up to become tookgers. Size does matter. Few *farang* are afraid of the sweet little jinjok. Even when it falls into your soup it will be spooned out and sent on its way with a hearty, "There you go, little fella". But almost all *farang*, and — if they were not so economical with the truth — most Thais, would admit they prefer not to share their house with tookie and friends. Tookgers have been in Thai houses for as long as the Thais have been building houses, and looking at Ban Chiang and such, Thais were the first human beings to do anything much, and along with pottery and permanent fields, were among the first people anywhere to build permanent houses for themselves. That's a long time sharing domestic life with the tookger. And, amazingly perhaps, after four thousand years or so, the Thais have never really found a neat way to keep

tookgers out of the house, or to get them out when already in. Instead, they have developed a Thai rationale for never minding. Believe it or not, it is this: it is good luck to have a tookger in your house, especially if your wife is pregnant or you are in business; lots of children and lots of money coming your way. (Lots of tookger too.)

• Tookger are good parents.
This has never really been tested but no tookie has ever been seen spanking its youngsters and many feel protective enough towards their young to take on your family cat when it begins playing with their children — all in the name of maternal instinct. The tookger only resorts to violence when cornered and attacked. Of course, being cornered and attacked are rather subjective states of mind, and the tookger, if it thinks at all before it acts, is likely to be on a wavelength separated from yours by a few million years. This makes reasoning with the tookger more than a tad difficult. "Look here. You take your kids outside in the garden and I'll bring you breakfast every day." This can work with unwanted spirits, but not with a tookger. Tookger think they own your home and that they put up with you.

• Tookger lock their jaws after biting into your flesh.
This is one I haven't tested personally, preferring to keep a long, sharp object between those wide jaws and my fleshy parts. I advise you to do the same.

• Tookger are not poisonous.
So if, in your mucho attempts to impress the maid by grabbing your tookger by the tail (detachable) and swinging it round your head, you get bitten, and have not been bitten on a vital part, and have been able to unlock those locked

jaws, you will not die of venom thereafter; and a bottle of Thai whisky poured over the wound and down your throat, should assist regeneration of the bitten part. Tookger are not known to carry any obvious diseases, but lying around for a million years is a long time, so best pop off to the pharmacy or clinic — giving the maid the chance to get the tookger quietly out of the house or in between your bed sheets.

• Tookgers will stay in their place if you just leave them alone.
True, but they think their place is your house — all of it.

• Killing a tookger in the house will bring bad luck.
Okay, you have decided that, much as you respect the environment and its species, and the general principle of live and let live, you would much prefer to live without the company of tookgers. Willing to take a chance on the bad luck aspect, you peruse your instruments of death. Plastic waste shovel for doggy poop, several brooms of the grass variety, hammer with 12-inch handle and a handful of nails, kitchen knife and chopper, mosquito spray, box of tennis balls, two plastic handled umbrellas. The following methods are by no means guaranteed.

1. Lock the tookger in the bathroom and spray flying insect killer through the door crack. This will immediately deprive tookie of its food source. Death by slow starvation, as long as the insect repellent spray holds out, is assured in a few weeks or months. Can you really wait that long to use the toilet?

2. Crucifixion. Much as this might give you temporary pleasure as well as a use for those stainless steel nails waiting to hang yet more pictures for yet more tookgers to hide behind, it is the most impractical of solutions. The little monsters just won't stay still

unless you land them a lucky or well-practised blow on the head with a blunt instrument. Are you an expert with a hammer? Do the police know? More importantly, does the tookger know? Well, go ahead anyway if it will release the disgust you feel at looking at a creature which, through no fault of its own, you deem just too ugly to live. Zap it with the hammer, chopper, or garden spade. Face your foe, raise the instrument of death, and strike the death blow. Then you will discover that tookgers, who can, like crocodiles, stay immobile for hours, can also move surprisingly quickly. And not just in a straight line. Quicker than any Ninja. Up the walls. Over your head. You have already knocked a chunk out of the toilet bowl. A few more wild swings and there goes your floor tiling and there's a hole in the ceiling board. With luck, your tookger might disappear through the hole in the ceiling. Of course what goes up will probably come down. And come down where it can find a way down. And, unseen, come down again into a room of your house, a room that has far more places to hide beneath and behind than the bathroom.

3. Deportation. Open all the doors leading to an outside one, gather all the people you can and arm them with brooms of the grass variety and the plastic umbrellas. Ignore any suggestion that you might be kicking luck out of your house or counter that your neighbour can offer asylum and thereby bring all the benefits of tookger permanent residency to his own hearth. Go in and hassle that tookie; sweep it off its feet and, with a lot of help from the neighbours, out the front door. Easy to say. You will find that not only is tookie difficult to sweep off its suction-padded feet, but it is

also a plucky little fighter when it has its back to the wall. Certainly you will get lots of jaws-wide-open drama, maybe even a hiss and a lunge or two. Finally, when all objects to scuttle behind have been removed or destroyed, tookie will run out of the bathroom. Your helpers will scream and get in each other's way — the tookger is a master at creating such panic and disorder. Through the legs it goes, a few feints at disappearing up the insides of trouser legs or into the folds of flowing skirts, and, almost before you know it, the tookger is outside your open door onto your welcome mat. On the other hand, he may have run the gauntlet of brooms and now be nicely tucked up in a part of the house that you will not know about until he once more rears his ugly head. Why, he might finally have left your house and even now be wiggling up the back of your car's driving seat, waiting to pop out and sit on your shoulder.

Tookger have been successfully caught by men wearing thick and rigid gloves, such as fire-fighters wear. Such tookger-proof gloves are not available in any supermarket. If, using something thick and protective (not the bed quilt), you can catch it — both hands — and put it into a sack (not plastic bag) and put the sack into a sturdy box — or into a bucket of water if you are into final solutions (or into a large bottle of rice liquor if you are into Asian aphrodisiacs). It can then be carried away from the house and released. But take it as far away as you can; tookies home.

Lacking fire-fighting gear — which is not too popular in Thailand's heat — and lacking sprayable asphyxiates, for some reason unavailable on Tesco-Lotus shelves, your best attempt at a solution might be the one enlisting the help of the neighbours. Whether or not the door is finally closed on tookie's back, it could be fun shared — the essential ingredient of any activity worth doing in Thailand. Whatever the result, you can always claim a victory as you break out the whisky. You can even credit yourself with having turned an unpleasant situation into an occasion for social activity and common-cause, and clock up a few social points. But don't gloat, and for heaven's sake don't brag "that was easy". Like all little nightmares… tookie will be back….

> *Bottom line:*
>
> *A tookger will never lie to you, be unfaithful, ask for money or give you the clap, but the chances are that, with a tookger being as different from you as you can imagine (and, possibly, as the tookger can imagine), any love affair will not last long; so adopting one as a family pet is not a good idea.*

77

On Sinking into Shame

It is extremely difficult, probably impossible, to sink into shame with any grace, so resign yourself to having a humiliating experience. It will be one where all your grovelling so far is but a prelude to the remedial action required if you are ever to raise your head again.

One thing is for sure: you are innocent. That goes without saying. Others have blackened your name. And therein lies the only element of grace left to you. Accept, with your chin hanging low, all the dishonourable accusations that others heap on you. Do not attempt a counter-attack. Go quietly and meekly into your fate. Others have got you into this mess. Others can jolly well get you out. Confine yourself to the Thai defence.

The Thai defence in its milder exposition is more likely to be seen in a government office than in a Thai-boxing stadium or in a Thai chess championship. It requires self-recognition as the underdog. This concept of the "underdog" means subtly different things in Europe and in Thailand. The English make a cult of supporting the underdog — the individual or the team least likely to win. This is probably because England so rarely wins anything, but the reason is irrelevant; in England and some ex-colonies, it's how the underdog plays the game that matters. If you find yourself in an underdog position in Thailand, don't expect large sections of the Thai audience to be cheering for you. It is largely because of them, and whatever minor contraventions of obtuse Thai norms you might, unknowingly and unintentionally of course, have committed, and which have so unjustly been exaggerated out of all proportion by those same people, that you now find yourself sinking into the hole of shame.

In much of Europe, the term underdog is used figuratively. The underdog as hero is not expected to boast or strut. He or she should maintain a quiet dignity while never saying die, a pose which prompts public admiration for his or her courage, particularly if the much stronger or more skilful opponent is prancing around with a swagger of gloating expectation of victory and open scorn at his opponent's pathetic attempts to strike only above the belt while taking everything on the chin.

The Thai underdog, unfortunately for you, has more reality about him. If you are that underdog, forget about quiet dignity; get on your back immediately, with your paws in the air, your tail a blur of self-lashing movement. Place yourself at the complete mercy of anybody who feels like giving you a good booting. Whine, cringe, cry softly, never growl, and never even hint at anything that could be construed as fighting back. Only when you have quite convinced everyone, including yourself, that you pose no threat at all and are sincere in your begging for punishment, might the great Thai public, united as it is against the vile and shameful, pass up this heaven-sent opportunity to give the *farang* a good hammering and realise that you are genuinely trying to make amends. If you are obliged to be seen at all in public during this indeterminate period, a pair of wooden crutches or even a wheelchair, together with a deathly pale expression, will enhance your vulnerability and offer some protection.

Nobody is likely to reach in a hand and help you out of your hole, but once convinced of your impotence, a lingering cultural apathy, tinged just a tad with the Buddhist concept of mercy, will help the abused or insulted quietly forget about you in time. Then and only then can you slink out and very quietly but publicly start making amends through at first small, then somewhat larger, public benefactions, finally sponsoring the building of a whole new *wat*, a mass-ordination of 500 juvenile delinquents, and the release of all animals slated for the chop in the nearest slaughter house — although this should be done judiciously since nobody will thank you for introducing a running of the bulls to their back *sois*.

What was your crime that everyone turned against you? Caught masturbating on the sky train? Suddenly illuminated by security lights while having an early morning pee on the doorstep of the general next door? Believing the *Khunying*'s daughter or son when she or he said she or he was 18, not 12? Taking a dozen scantily-clad *khatoeys* to the *Kamnan*'s birthday party? Or something really serious like putting into your own pocket change passed by a female shopkeeper to hand on to the monk paying for his ice cream, or even, heaven forbid, helping yourself to the food in a monk's bowl. The details are almost irrelevant; the *fact* is you got caught. Your public guard was down. No excuse that you were drunk at the time, or that with all that make up on she looked 18 when *she* propositioned *you*, or that you honestly thought the money offered in change was yours because you were first in line, or that you had just put the food in the bowl without tasting it and wanted to be sure it was as good as the market-stall seller had said it was. As for the *khatoeys*, were it an isolated incident, you might escape, but compound it with all the rest and it just emphasises publicly what a shameful piece of lowlife you are. The fact is, you got caught. *You* made perfectly nice people feel awkward and offended. You have only yourself to blame.

And if you can't climb out, whatever you do, but sink farther into shame, what then? Well, there is always suicide. This is a private action, but you are permitted, on this final occasion only, to leave an epitaph mildly criticising those who drove you to it. If you are really peeved, the more conventional note, carefully penned in correct Thai and suitable for publication and distribution, may be replaced with a 10-metre neon sign surrounded by cluster bombs proclaiming: *You made me do it, you bunch of no-account cock-fighters who can't see further than your mother's arse.* Just make sure that the illuminations appear after you really have gone for good.

Bottom line:
It takes much more to climb out of a shameful situation than to sink into one.

78

On Sniff Kissing

The Thai sniff kiss – *jup hom* – is made by rubbing the nose just once rapidly up one cheek while sniffing in. The literal translation is "nice smell kiss". And if you have yet to experience a sniff kiss, maybe it's time to think about how nice you smell.

Sniff kissing is a bit like the French kiss on both cheeks — the lips may barely or not at all touch the face. It is a mark of affection, and need not be a prelude to something more.

But unlike the French cheek-kiss, it is not passed around between strangers. In fact it is only used between people already closely allied.

Whether we can say this is peculiarly Thai is debatable. Certainly it is common among Lao, but they are of the greater Thai family and share most cultural attributes. Somewhat surprising is that many foreign men with Thai spouses can go their entire married life without a sniff-kiss; indeed, many can live in Thailand for years and never hear of this little Thai secret, which is given in the private rather than public arena.

The sniff kiss does not require any reply or response. Whether it's the same with long-nosed *farang* as initiators rather than passive recipients is a matter of opinion. It's a rather nice way of reminding someone you are there without using words and without disturbing very much whatever the partner is doing. Great when the husband is hard at work at the computer and doesn't want to be disturbed. Great when the wife is into the ironing or TV drama.

Bottom line:
If you get a sniff kiss, don't try to respond. Just enjoy the brief warm glow that comes from the expression of affection.

79

On Sons and Mothers

That primary bond between mothers and daughters seems indestructible. Even girls treated badly and sent away at an early age to make money in the city will remain devoted to Mother and pass on to Mother much of any money made. Boys may also go to work outside the family economy and community, but they have a much easier time of it. From the first days of life, a boy is pampered and spoilt — by his mother, sisters and every female in the family. He does not grow up to be a spoilt brat; perhaps surprisingly, he grows up to be polite and, usually, gentle. But all that mothering does have an effect. The son feels most comfortable when with his own mother and family. He will be looking for a wife to provide the same sort of treatment he receives from his mother. Sometimes he will find it, often he will not. On marriage he has all the pressures of a son-in-law trying to please his mother-in-law, and in this area he can rarely turn to his mother for help.

This is perhaps one reason many men prefer to "marry down", taking a pretty girl from a family that is poor but honest, one who maybe doesn't add much to his status, although any honest wife capable of having children avoids the negative status of being alone in life and any pretty wife serves as a status symbol. A poor and comparatively uneducated girl, the perception goes, is less likely to make great demands on her husband to prove his economic worth, since she has already risen above the level of her friendship group. Of course a son's primary love relationship will remain with his mother and sisters. The relationship with his mother-in-law will be one of respect tinged with *krengjai*, the feeling a Thai has when faced with an authority he or she must please, respect with just a tad of fear. He may speak little to his wife's mother, but when he does, it will always be polite and if asked to help out financially, his reply will always be, "I will try", even if he knows there is no possibility.

The "loosely-structured" Thai social system has been seen as responsible for marital distance between husband and wife, and dissatisfaction of each with the other. Nobody can compete with Mum. When the need is felt, the boy returns to his mother and family for support, the girl to her mother and family. It is only well into marriage that a couple think of themselves as forming an integral family unit, and it has been suggested that some men never do.

So, in the extreme stereotype, the system produces men who are "mummy's boys", perhaps to the point of wearing women's clothing, painting their faces, or having sisters paint their faces, tripping around in platforms or high heels, and wanting to be women in the kind of support groups that only women have. Mother love is something that has to be overcome in the West; in Thailand it can continue throughout life. This not only gives Freudian psychologists something to think about, it supports the matriarchal role of the mother in domestic matters, including the family economy. Mother will always be there, and when marriage collapses, or a man has a hard time in life, it is to his mum that he looks for comfort.

The foreigner in Thai society will often stand in fairly stark contrast with the average Thai man, who never quite manages to cut the umbilical cord. Many foreigners appear confident and independent to the point of barely having a family or community, strong to the point of dominance, caring for those they shouldn't and failing to care for those they should, clever and educated but unable to understand, decisive and dictatorial. The Thai son and brother may be none of those things. But he is not afraid to cry on a female shoulder. You cannot become like him, and no doubt you are relieved to hear that. But don't make his life difficult by expecting too much of him — he has or will have a mother-in-law to do that.

Bottom line:
Mothers cannot prepare their sons for a truly independent life.
Mothers-in-law can never replace Mother.

80

On Suicide as a Social Activity

In contemplating suicide, as with so many mentally-stimulated images, be aware that anticipation is often far more satisfying, and a lot cleaner, than actuality. The reality of suicide is extremely difficult to reconcile with enhancement of status. It therefore poses an interesting challenge to those among you intent on a controlled maximisation of status to the very end. Notice, I do not write to the *bitter* end. You must take all care to avoid any hint of bitterness. If you are to stand any chance of suicide increasing your status, it must be 100 per cent clear to all and sundry that you are topping yourself purely for motives of the noblest kind. Being in a Thai social system places you at a disadvantage here. If you are a noble philosopher in Greece, the *democracia* will remember your act of voluntarily drinking the poison and write epic poems about you and teach your name in school for thousands of years. If you are a Japanese traditionalist, committing seppuku *is* a great public attention getter and sales of your books will soar in Japan. If you are among the first Irish or Indians to starve yourself to death, memorials will go up in your name and plaques will be placed on your house. But to find a Thai revered for committing suicide is an uphill task.

Thus, faced with the especially difficult circumstances for would-be suicides in Thailand, contemplation should perhaps centre on the practicality of your final action within the realm. It is as culturally determined as any other social action. Maybe, after all, you might prefer to turn out the lights permanently back where you started off. Only if fully determined to end it all in Thailand need you read on to the following *modus operandi* requirements.

Wear your very best bib and tucker. You do not want to be taken for a foreign vagrant down on his luck or a junkie overdoser. A few 1,000 baht notes distributed around your body will garnish this image.

Going out smartly will be appreciated by the Thais a lot more than hanging yourself naked. Comfort should not be a consideration. So no shorts and flip-flops. Neckties are optional, especially if you are going for a hanging; but hanging in itself is likely to distort the facial expression and therefore, like throwing yourself in front of a ten-wheeler, is not really on in Thailand, where the highly thought of go out cleanly shaven and best bedecked. Imagine yourself dead before you go and remember that the Thais have a fine sense of the aesthetic when applied to people. So have your hair done, cut your nails, clean your teeth and change your undergarments. The more attractive you look, the more people will admire you: in life as in death.

There are, however, some dangers in looking overly-attractive on your way out. Should you have a fear of unwanted attentions by unknown necrophiliacs, always contact, prior to the act, those necrophiles you know and the like. The time to do this is just before you leave the world, unless you think they can be trusted with a key and a schedule that will find you well and truly gone, but still sensuously warm to the touch. Obviously, giving your last pleasures after your death is a real token of friendship and should not be spoiled by any carelessness. Your friend or friends should find you waiting patiently in bed for them, or perhaps stretched out on the leather couch in your best red undergarments, with boxes of scented tissues very handy and the TV definitely off — although some light romantic background music is permissible, as is a smart box of chocolate liquors.

In the event that you do not know a single necrophiliac in Thailand, you must be especially considerate of the location for your departure.

The bus station is out. There is nothing status-enhancing in the environment; poor dishevelled people with skin diseases and worse often live on or under the benches and you certainly don't want to be taken for one of them. And the 1,000 baht notes you have distributed so thoughtfully around your fine clothing will disappear before you are cold, and probably most of your impeccable garments will follow at an alarming rate. Any poignant last message to set the world crying or praising your selfless act that you have pinned to your shirt before taking the entire bottle of one hundred

SAD'S "GOODBYE CRUEL WORLD" PARTY

sleeping pills washed down with a bottle of San Miguel beer (or Leo, if the bus station café doesn't run to classy foreign alcohol) will be made by exploited child labour into little paper bags to hold fried bananas.

You might feel inclined by pangs of jealousy, hate or even love, to make some kind of statement at the bar where your girlfriend or boyfriend or equivocal friend or spouse, much to your continued chagrin, seems intent on destroying your attempt at status enhancement by publicly dancing naked up and down a chromium pole set in the middle of the bar and receiving 100 baht notes placed in various body clefts by probing fingers. Some sort of statement is certainly called for, although this might be a case for assassination rather than suicide. Non-violence, at least towards others, being the only acceptable form of suicide, it is especially difficult to make any point at all in a bar full of drunks and whores. Certainly don't even consider poison or sleeping pills, you would simply fall off your stall and at some point be swept out with the rest of the garbage. Perhaps the *Leaving Las Vegas* solution, in which you drink yourself to death, is appropriate. This costs a lot of money at girly-bar prices, but if you have no further use for it, that matters not one jot. By all means treat all in the bar at regular intervals. This is the easiest way of encouraging sympathy for your predicament, and to an extent will, in an inverted kind of way, earn you points, particularly if you are very nice to the locals, most of whom will be naked, with destitute mothers, with younger siblings unable to go to school because of lack of funds, and every single one of them, and their mothers, and their children, in desperate need of somebody to pay for their operation. By paying through the nose, you will introduce a *sanuk* element into your suicide, which might endear you to some Thais at least and might even start a trend.

The time it takes to drink yourself to death depends on various factors, but you should pass the point of no return after two or three weeks. Tailor your funding and set aside a nice amount for the funeral. While still *compos mentis* and before the final calling of "Time", oversee the brass plaque that will go over the bar to immortalise your leaving of the world, and get the spelling right. Without moving from your chosen seat of extinction, which with your departure will assume magical properties, spread kindness not hate. Give your money away. Bequeath your eyes to the blind. But please don't leave your liver to people who already have enough problems. You will live on, at least for a time, as some kind of legend. This is a kind of status within a subculture, even if the Thai population at large is unlikely to be impressed, unless you leave behind the means to fund a temple renovation or two and ordain a hundred bar girls as nuns for a day.

Bottom line:

Suicide is not recommended as a solution to your problems, but if you think it is, try to make it fun for those who might remember you and introduce a nam jai element so Thais will think of your last action as social rather than selfish and conclude that you were, after all, not such a bad bloke.

81

On Taking a Girl Out of a Bar
to a Cultural Show

Revamping a tart as a lady has been a literary and media theme for centuries. It did not start with Suzie Wong, but was perhaps first realistically treated by William Wordsworth in his, "Lines Written Above Urinal 7, Patpong 2".

> You can take a horse to water
> But you can't make it drink.
> You can take a whore to culture
> But you can't make her think.

Bottom line:
On taking a girl out of a bar, always remember you cannot take the bar out of the girl.

On Taking and Viewing Photographs

Don't forget your camera. A small digital model is highly recommended as this facilitates the deletion of many unwanted pictures and the snipping out of the berk standing next to the beauty of your interest. Most important, it allows you ready-editing of the big man or big woman, or their son or daughter, whose image you will enlarge and present to the target of your interest in a grotesquely ornate frame, earning a big leg-up social ladder.

In Thailand, when taking the obligatory group photo, always wait for the hand with the V-sign to appear above a person's head. This V stands for Virgin. The spirits, like many men, are struck powerless when faced with virginity. Spirits always appear and hover over a group when a picture is being taken and the V is the signal that the spirits may inhabit the picture but cannot inhabit any member of the group, protected as it is by the V sign. Never make this sign yourself. You will do it wrongly and end up being inhabited by the spirits you are trying to avoid. Strictly speaking, this sign can only be made perfectly by a virgin girl or boy of 14 summers. But do not hold your breath waiting for the perfect V.

Should you be so vain as to put yourself in the group picture, or if this is insisted upon you against your modest declines, you will not be available to press the shutter.

Be aware that, contrary to the preconceptions of many visitors, the serving staff at restaurants and resort hotels have not all had extensive training in photography and the taking of pictures is not written into their job description.

The combination of spirit activity, conscripted photographers and changing social values regarding virginity, means you are likely to find yourself with a magnificent set of pictures of feet or torsos with the heads cut off, particularly the head of the tall *farang*. If correct V-sign procedures have not been followed, then the entire group, including you, is infected by spirit-virus. The only real remedy for this is to take a whole lot more pictures and to replace the 14-year-old V-maker with a real virgin. If one cannot be found, the headless and feet pictures must be shown on the camera's small screen viewer to all in the group at the same time. When a spontaneous whoop of *whee-ee* leaves every mouth at the same time, the spirits have been exorcised.

Upon viewing photographs taken by Thais, take your time. These will be brought out for your inspection in a family album, or, if you are particularly unlucky, in a large stack of family albums. Often the main target of your visit to a Thai home will be engaged in curling hair, selecting an appropriate dress in which to meet you, occupied in various activities in the toilet, or watching the final episode of a six-month-long Thai drama. These all take time and it is not done to say to whoever has been sent to keep you company and make sure you look at the family pictures, "Jesus! How much longer she going to be?" Instead, relish this heaven-sent opportunity to know the family better by informing yourself on their photographic expeditions. Be lavish in your praise and when it is pointed out to you that you have just inadvertently turned over three pages at once, say, "Oh silly me." Whether the target of your visit is obvious or not, pay that person special attention, which will be reported back at a suitable time.

Avoid the dull silence of disbelief at the documented display of a whole family's photographic ineptitude by making comments such as, "And this must be Noy as a little girl? How cute she looks in knickerbockers and plaits." The answer will come, "No, that's father in drag." Never mind. Saying anything flattering is better than saying nothing. Even if you sound a bit strained to yourself when you begin the sixth volume as you ended the other five with "lovely, beautiful", remember that one can never get or give too much flattery, and appreciation of the family album is appreciation of the family. It is quite possible that the person keeping you company is Mother herself. Do not simply *pause* at any pictures of Her, positively *linger*, only dragging your eyes away with difficulty, as you sip the glass of tendered water like it were the nectar of the gods.

Bottom line:
Never take a photograph of a Thai before the V-sign goes up. Never yawn when viewing the sacred family album.

83

On Telephone Manners

Hello. The standard answer when picking up the phone in Thailand. The caller repeats "Hello" perhaps adding a *Sawatdii*, but *never* telling the called who he or she is. If the caller recognises your distinct *farang* accent and realises he or she has called the wrong number, the phone is usually clunked back down on your inner ear, or clicked off with rarely an "excuse me". Thai norms of polite face-to-face encounters are reversed on the telephone. So if somebody, name ungiven, asks to speak to Nit, and you have no Nit that you know of in your house (always a good idea by the way to check on the various names by which your Thai partner is known in other circles), you may simply say *toh pit* (wrong call) and hang up.

This of course doesn't improve your Thai conversation skills very much. So, if you wish, you can practise saying, "Who do you want". If the answer comes that the caller wants the noodle shop, you can, if you don't want to hang up immediately, explain that this is the private residence of Lord Home-Pronounced-Hume. Almost certainly the caller will not have listened to a word you said, so much for conversation practice, and will ask, "Can I speak to Noy, then?" There are a million possible answers to this, but since the caller is not a listener, you might as well practise, "Wrong call", and hang up.

Callers on the telephone abhor a vacuum, so if there is a millisecond's silence, one person says "Hello" and if there is no immediate Hello in return, proceeds to "Hello, hello, hello". Note that this is nothing like the aggressive French equivalent; Thais pronounce the H and place a rising inflection on the O. Also if your partner to the call has been talking some time without getting any periodic confirmation you are still there (you should say *crap* or *ca-ca* every 2 seconds), they will suspect you have placed the phone in the fridge and therefore go into the "Hello, hello" routine. Believe it or not, but in one out of ten telephone conversations, the only word spoken is "Hello".

Telephone manners are not rude, but they are much truncated. The caller can at any time decide he or she has got all they are going to get out of the cost of their call, say *thao ni* or *thao nan* (that's it) and down goes the telephone or the button, sometimes leaving you in mid-sentence. In spite of — or perhaps because of — the shorthand form of many calls, phone call talk remains, like that in face-to-face communiqué, full of *crap*.

Crap, in a language lacking any single word for "yes", is the shortest way of saying "yes", which it does except when it means "no", as in *may chay crap*. Of course if you are female and you say *crap*, it will be presumed you are a man and people will speak as to a man — you know, macho stuff, sex talk and quaintly robust expressions like "buffalo's penis", "you smelly cunt" and "son of a whore". As a foreign female, this may be your only chance to hear this aspect of the Thai language. *Crap* is a high-tone men-only word; but if you are female and want to play this game, try to deepen your whole speaking range. If you are a man, or think you might be, you can have similar fun on the phone by saying the girls-only *kha*. In girly talk only, giggling is permitted. If you (man) need some guidelines on getting your *kha-kha* right, just listen to a *khatoey,* who is full of it. Since nobody ever gives their names on a Thai telephone, you are reasonably safe. It is advisable however, when playing phone, to use a landline rather than an easily traceable mobile phone.

Such is the power of *crap* (even in it's shortened form as *cap*) and so much do people like to hear it said — since the only literal translation is "I agree with what you say and respect you deeply for having said it" — that you can safely let the simple word monopolise your side of the conversation, even if you don't have a clue what the call's about. Here, for example, is an actual transcription of an entire phone call heard from one side only, that of the callee.

Hello

Crap

Cap

Cap

Cap phom

Cap

Cap

Wat dii Cap

After the above conversation, the callee was asked who was on the phone. "Don't know," he replied. "He didn't say."

A few last words on the use of the ubiquitous *meu teu,* the mobile telephone. This has the advantage of showing the caller's name in the window if you have keyed it in, so unless the phone has been borrowed or stolen, you have a good idea even before you begin, as to whom you are speaking. If there is no name and you don't recognise the number or the voice — all Thais sound the same — be careful about saying, "Who are you?" Even in tele-talk this sounds a bit brusque, and therefore should be preceded by a short statement asking if the caller is speaking from the back of a motorcycle or in a Chinese noodle shop. Before you get the name you will receive declarations of disbelief that you cannot remember somebody who served you ice cream six months ago. Then the name will be Noy, which reduces things to 50 per cent of the population.

Some wrong numbers love to talk to a *farang* and will go on for hours. This is okay if you need the language practice, although they will call you back at two in the morning with no idea that you aren't too keen on answering the phone when asleep. Other right numbers are not enthusiastic about talk if they have to pay for it. These belong to two types. The first calls you and says immediately, "Call back, no money in phone" (don't). The second are the "one-ringers", who hang up even before you have heard the one ring. They hope you will call them back. If you do, they will ask you to transfer money from your phone to theirs, so they can call you at awkward times, or they might simply cut to the chase and ask you for the money for the operation as they only have two weeks to live (to which the answer is "Call me back in two weeks time"). All in all, it is best not to give your number to one-ringers or suspected one-ringers. You do this by saying you'll call them to give your number, thus saving them the cost of a phone call.

The democratic nature of the mobile phone has taken any cache out of telephone ownership. It is best therefore always to have a secretary make your calls on a "table top" landline phone, putting you on only when you are through to the VIP, not to his secretary. Similarly, only your secretary should receive and filter your calls. If you can trust her.

Bottom line:
Never pick up the phone yourself. If you do not have a secretary to do so, marry one.

84

On Thai is to *Farang* as...

Thai is to *farang* as Jewish is to Goyisch, they can all live better together than living apart, but living together creates some problems.

Farang is a very collective term including all Europeans, North and South Americans of fair skin and occidental features, and all Australians and New Zealanders, although presumably not the Aborigines.

Thai is also a collective term, encompassing peoples who speak a language with some resemblance to Thai (or Lao) who exist in substantial pockets throughout Thailand, Southern China, Northern Vietnam, Laos, Burma, Kampuchea and northern Malaysia (with satellite groups in Washington and California).

The Thai of Thailand break up the ethnic world into *farang* (as above); *Kheck-India* (no distinction between Muslim and Hindu, Pakistan, Bangladesh, Sri Lanka); *Kheck-Burma* (Myanmar); *Kheck-Arab* (all Middle-Eastern and North African nations and peoples, except Israel); and *Africa* (all inhabitants of the continent who are not *Kheck-Arab* or white). Within the *farang* category, they are not so fussy at distinguishing subcategories; thus *Anggrit* covers all British, although there is confusion over whether it covers non-Caucasian British. Besides, there is no point in asking for the "British Embassy"; in Thai it's the "English Embassy". The farther away a foreigner's origins, the less Thais bother with distinctions. The reverse is also the case and Thais have special terms for those near to them, just as the English distinguish Taffies, Paddies and Jocks with terms of endearment that can sometimes be taken pejoratively.

The distinctions are largely geographical, with a large element of skin colour. Thus Americans are *farang*, while "America-dam" or *khon sii dam* to distinguish black Americans specifically or individuals with a dark skin of any nationality. White European types, whether from South Africa, Greenland, New Zealand, the Falklands or French Caledonia are all *farang*.

While occasionally one will hear *"farang"* almost spat out, the terms are usually free of prejudice, and this is best evident in the fact that the terms are all adopted by the people categorised to distinguish themselves from Thais and others. Thus a *farang* will have no problem referring to himself as *farang*, and so on.

> *Bottom line:*
> *Thais think of Thais as a fairly homogeneous grouping and tend to assume other peoples have a similar homogeneity. This is not correct, but there is little to be gained by insisting on being referred to as Scot, or French-Canadian, etc. If it helps Thais to relate to you by categorising you, consider that a useful thing. After all, it is only a step on the way to becoming Thai.*

85

On the Incredible Lightness of Your Being

Your being in Thailand is, and I hope you don't mind my saying this, so light, so very ephemeral, it is like the Thai "r", almost nothing, a whisper in the winds, a tick in the tick-tocks of time, an atom in the aeons of Asia, a sigh suspended in silence, a dot in the dogma, a single grain of sand, a breath in a billion births.

Well, that's put you in your place. It doesn't sound as if it is going to make much of a difference to Thailand if you are around forever or if you've never heard of the country. Of course, one split atom can set off a chain reaction, but there are an awful lot of atoms that don't get split, and just as well too.

Here today, gone tomorrow. Or in 50 years. What's the difference? To Thailand, probably very little. But maybe to you, a lot. Thailand and the Thais might change your epicentre away from yourself towards being part of a larger world. This is not just changing worlds, it is changing you. You were once integrated into a foreign world which revolved around you. Now you are integrating into a Thai world where individuals play different roles, where an individual is not so important. You are learning to flow into a society that is not yours but in which you are becoming part. And to an extent, you are detaching yourself from the society that you used to think of as yours. You are losing your possessive hold.

You are becoming superficial. Beautifully superficial. And one day you will go up in smoke, so lightly. Into the air you now breathe and which will soon breathe you.

No drugs are needed. Not even a beer, although by all means have one if you wish and if you think it will help. You don't have to give up your vanity, but you do need to realise you are vanity. That's all. You can enter Thai society. Come in. There are no barbed wire fences to get through, not even any real doors. It is open to all who want to go there.

You can advance in Thai society but never to being above it, only to realising it is you and you are part of it. Can you ever become Thai? Yes, if you want to be. Perhaps not in this lifetime. But never mind. Aren't you already having so much fun in Thailand as a foreign body? Isn't that enough? Everything you do is a part of you and a part of your learning to become a bit more than you. If you want that, just don't fight it. Become yourself by overcoming yourself. Go where the wind blows. And enjoy the trip.

Bottom line:
The rains fall into the river. The river flows to the sea. The sea gets no greater. All is vanity. Don't take things too seriously. Don't take things. But if you must, never mind.

86

On the Perfect Sleeping Partner

If you ever get the feeling your wife or husband isn't doing much to make the business prosper, look what it would be like without her or him.

You can register as a foreign-owned business in Thailand but you would need to keep at least $50,000 in the bank in case you are a bad boy or girl. You would need to employ at least four Thais, paying at least the going minimum wage. You would need to keep proper accounts and pay all taxes, guaranteeing a minimum tax payment of some $500 per year, even if you make a loss. And of course, before you start you would need to go through the expense and hassle of getting the appropriate visas and work permits, since you cannot open a company, or do any work, on a "retirement" visa or a normal three-month non-immigrant visa.

Marry a Thai and all these problems disappear. Since most farang anyway want a small business — guest house, bar, second-hand bookshop, diving school, language school, Italian restaurant, tour agency — many of which are really supposed to be reserved for Thais, the marriage solution is perfect and, as long as you don't flick off a bottle cap and charge a plain clothes police officer for the beer (work), it is as legal as anything else. Everything goes in your spouse's name, including any debts.

When it comes to working out who is the perfect sleeping partner, it all depends on perspective. Seeing the *farang* man sitting at the entrance of his bar all day and every day, drinking with other expat men, who probably also have Thai wives or Thai boyfriends, apparently doing not a stroke of work while the spouse serves, cooks and cleans, the term sleeping partner is open to interpretation. The foreigner is undoubtedly the one who puts up the initial money, maybe he even has some ideas or dreams, although most small businesses involving *farang* are really small and boring in their repetition, but it is the spouse who is expected to do most of the day-to-day work. Most couples recognise this as fair enough. Typically, the *farang* (almost invariably a man) gets a reasonably happy retirement out of the deal, and after he has gone, the spouse gets a small means of livelihood to supplement whatever pension he left her, if any.

There is, of course, a danger in this perfect partnership. Can you trust your spouse? Can you trust yourself, in the land of temptation, not to give your spouse legitimate reasons to kick you out? The Thai marriage contract is of little use in these situations. Divorce does not lead to a division of the spoils and responsibilities as it does in the West. You can legally sign with your spouse a separate agreement to lend her the money for the business/buying a house, etc. This agreement may be linked to your marriage or not. For instance, if your spouse leaves you for another, or just disappears, she or he agrees ahead of time that the property/business will be sold to pay you back all your loan. Such agreements in writing are made by very few couples and are not appreciated by Thai women and their mothers, since they appear to go against the essence of being in the same family, which is trust.

Homosexual couples do not even have the marriage certificate to fall back on, yet again few make a legal arrangement, feeling that it would be impossible to implement if it came to it. In fact, most couples who run a modest business in Thailand do not break up, and the number of homosexual couples who stay together might approach that of the heterosexual. Having a business together can itself lead to frictions, but the fact of literally living in each other's pockets and being publicly visible as a couple, tends to reduce the opportunities for naughty behaviour. Typically, the male in the partnership, the *farang*, is significantly older than his spouse. Maybe this helps keep the couple together. When both partners are young and working apart, particularly if the man is travelling a lot, the separation and divorce rate is very high.

So, being a careful kind of *farang* and unable or unwilling to go through the requirements of registering your foreign company, you will be looking for a Thai spouse you can trust, no? Well, maybe you have one already — that's often the way; marriage comes first then you look for something to do in Thailand rather than go back home. But for those of you who do things differently — want to stay in Thailand, know what you want to do, need a partner but have difficulty making up your mind, I venture a small contemplation on how to get the right partner for your business. Like everything else in this book, no guarantees. Now, let's start looking.

You can poach somebody. If you plan to open a bookshop, review the girls/boys working in other bookshops; a restaurant, those working in one already. And so on. Of course you first have to establish that the person is free. You do this by asking them, or the Thai way by asking another person working in the same place (who might give a more honest answer!). It is considered very bad form to attempt to poach the wife of the boss of the establishment and this could lead to years of trouble and business failure. Anybody working for a wage can be poached by offering more money. But you don't want a worker, you want a partner. So, in those brief conversations between customers, you have to make it clear that you are free and looking. Your fancy will already be obvious from the amount of time you spend in the place. If you can, make a friend of the boss. At some point, you have to invite her — and her workmates — out. This is a bit of a problem if they work in a restaurant, as they will usually get food and maybe accommodation thrown in and have little free time. But everybody wants to eat something different, particularly seafood. Do not make the mistake on your first date of going to a Western-food restaurant. Menus in English, food your prospective partner probably does not like, no other Thais around except the waiters, and you can bet that one of them comes from near the home village and they have a lot to chat about, leaving you on a forgotten sideline. There are plenty of good Thai restaurants in Thailand and an

increasing number which attempt to serve both Western and Thai food.

The fact that you focus in on somebody working honestly for a small monthly wage suggests that person is not in the prostitution game. Not always so, some girls work in Western or Japanese — or Thai — restaurants as a way of picking up customers. Of course, if you plan to open a girlie bar, you can take endless numbers of girls from endless bars. Unless you are very, very stupid, or very, very clever, this is not advised. Many of those girls make big bucks already and if they go with you, it is either that they consider you potentially offer more, or that they are pregnant, or sick, or that they have two screaming kids and a mother at home that want a regular man around, at least until a better one comes along. Having warned, it is necessary to say that many *farang* men are indeed very, very stupid. If that is your case, try to rent rather than buy premises. You might also consider renting rather than buying a wife of such a background, to see how she turns out. Cost of renting a wife is coincidentally around the same as renting a very small bar — but both will require additional money spent on regular maintenance and refurbishment.

In picking a marriage and business partner in Thailand, you must possess or develop the uncanny ability to consider a person as two people, from a sex-marriage perspective and from a business point of view. Not easy. Almost all reasonably good girls will be attracted by the prospect of marriage with the proper foreigner, i.e. one who wishes to remain in Thailand and has a business. Most can do or learn whatever simple tasks are involved, but if English is important, you might better begin your quest in a language school. One thing is almost certain: the perfect sleeping partner, in both senses of the term, will not be found by looking through the pictures on a romance-wanted website, of which there are many. You have to allow time, and preferably you should, in your own interests, spend some of that time learning Thai; so few foreigners really do.

> *Bottom line:*
>
> *Sex and marriage go together like a horse and carriage. But for the same price you can have a Mercedes-Benz sports convertible.*

87

On Thinking What You Say

Think what you say, preferably before rather than after you say it. Do not always say what you think.

In this the Thais are much more accomplished than you or I can ever hope to be. They can therefore carry out this operation almost automatically. Almost, as it were, without thinking. They are also an extremely proud and sensitive people and do not forgive easily real or imagined slights to their person. So, just watch what you say. By all means *think* whatever you like. Try to keep your thoughts in your head and not let them stray to realisation in your facial expressions or your clenched fist. But even if your face does look like murder, and even if you kick the dog, don't let that murderous thought out in speech. If it is not said, whatever it is or was can be forgotten, it simply never existed. If it is said, it takes a hell of a lot of unsaying.

Diplomats, if any good at their job, have understood this very important lesson. Perhaps this is why Thais make such good diplomats (and such bad politicians).

If you find this difficult, particularly with your "loved ones", try this little trick, if you can do it without a trace of sarcasm (which rarely translates into any language, and is not appreciated by Thais): say the opposite of what you are thinking. So, your wife wastes 1,000 baht in the beauty parlour and comes out looking like a cheap whore. She is expecting some comment. If you remain silent that is better than saying, "Fucking hell! Wasting my money again. You look like a cheap whore." If your wife is Thai (or anything else) such a comment could lead to days of silence or a spiteful repost and ensuing fight, which never gets anywhere and doesn't even let off steam. "Good heavens, I hardly recognised you. You look absolutely stunning. Very sexy. Come here." Lavish praise as liberally as you can, avoiding sarcasm. Thai wives can feel very insecure — no matter how much money you give them, they are afraid you will leave them for something younger and more beautiful, and while flattery sounds fake and demeaning to you, most of them need to hear that they look beautiful. Probably around 100 times a day is enough.

Of course, there are some real limits to how far you can go with flattery. If the mechanic not only failed to repair your breaks but made them dangerously worse, or if you are a foreign wife and your Thai husband is always out with his friends, what's the point in saying the opposite of what you

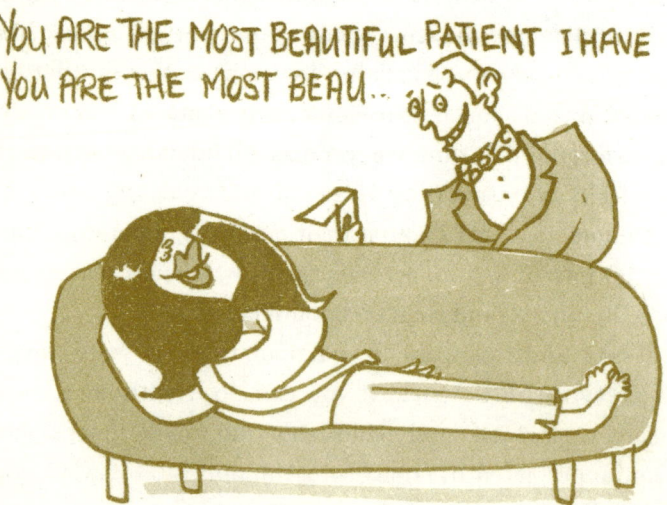

mean? You want some remedial action, and quite right to. But recognise the limitations surrounding you, a stranger in a foreign land, and enlist some aid. Talking politely with the mechanic's boss is likely to achieve more. If he doesn't have a boss, hard luck; you just have to take your car to the garage next door and have the job done properly, after explaining that the first mechanic could not do the job. But for the foreign wife, approaching the husband's boss isn't going to help — unless *you* are the boss! Much better to enlist allies from among the husband's own ranks, primarily his mother of course (and you have always stayed on good terms with her, haven't you?), but also his elder brothers and sisters. Tears get much more sympathy than accusations, which could cause ranks to close against you; and don't forget to tell them how much you love your husband *and* his family, of which you are a part. You are, by the way, in a much stronger position if you have a child; they might not want to lose you, but they would hate to lose the child. Not that you would ever phrase things in terms of an ultimatum.

If you still pride yourself on telling things as they are, saying what you think and doing what you say, your thoughts must be absolutely pure and wish no hurt to any man or woman. If that is not the case, for your own and everybody else's sake, just button your lip and, if necessary, bite your tongue. Or try settling down in the north of England. Oh dear, there I go again, writing what I think.

Bottom line:
If you really can't say something good about a person, say nothing at all.

88

On Time and Money

Thais see no contradiction in holding two totally opposed views of time. One is a leisurely-boating-down-the-river view, the other is a blast-off-to-the-moon view. The first view you will encounter on taking a train from Bangkok to such outlying satellites as Chiang Mai, Hadyai and Nongkhai. The second view is encountered on taking a tour bus to the same cities, and on a Bangkok traffic light turning green.

Whether you go rapid or express (in Thailand, there are no "slow" trains), first-class soft or third-class hard, a train ride is leisurely. No TGV in Thailand. It may seem remarkable that the train from Nongkhai to Bangkok, a distance of 600 km, takes 12 hours; that it regularly arrives two hours late seems almost unbelievable. The bus takes half the time and stops twice for snacks and dinner. Train stations are pleasant places, like their English equivalents (Britain was invited to build Thailand's first rail links), with nicely tended gardens, places to get food and drink and magazines, toilets you don't have to pay for but are maintained anyway, and nice orderly queues forming at little rounded holes, like there used to be at English railway stations before they were replaced with bulletproof glass, through which the attendant will hand you your ticket and answer all your questions, no matter how many people are waiting patiently behind you; bus stations are filthy, complicated, provide homes to socially deranged men covered in tattoos and wearing only old shorts with the backside out, ruinous prices for toilets and whatever recycled refreshments are to be had, and when you find the right desk or counter to provide the tickets you want, they will be up to four times the cost of the train. For the cost of the bus, which on a global scale is already fantastically cheap, you can have a second-class metre-wide seat to yourself, have it let down into a nice bed in an air-conditioned apartment and have enough left over for the carriage attendant to bring you a light meal or a large beer. Stretch out on a train, read a book, have a drink, and turn in for a nice rest to the sound of slow reassuring wheels on rail tracks.

There was a time when the whole of Thailand proceeded at the pace of the train. It was called underdevelopment. Long-distance overnight buses apart, journeys haven't gotten any quicker, but people still buy cars capable of Ferrari performance once a week for 10 minutes on the elevated toll-ways. Such cars lead the pack of Asian-tigers in races up to the traffic lights, to get there before the lights change or to be first away when red changes to green. As you look at the time-clock showing 159 red seconds to go, change into meditation mode and go back to the time of elephants. And glory at Bangkok's average car speed of 4 km/hour, about the slowest walking speed of an elephant, before you complain about the slowness of the train and government enterprises. And wonder where on earth all these people are going as you chug forward in the almost perpetual traffic jam, reaching every hour for the Comfort 400, and the second Comfort 400.

In the old days, and still in that great part of Thailand which is *ban nok*, people didn't worry too much about time and motion, unless there was an important ceremony and a propitious time for doing it. Then, even the farmer who didn't know what day it is and had never worn a wristwatch, could be extremely punctual.

In those good old days, when the Thai way of telling time was adopted throughout the country, a few hours here or there didn't matter much. The Thai day is still divided up into morning (6 am–12 pm), afternoon (12 pm– 4pm), early evening (4 pm–6 pm), night (7 pm–midnight), and night-guard (midnight–dawn). While there are degrees of precision possible within this system by adding the sound of temple gongs and night guards' triangles to the basic time, most people talk as they do in the West, in simple numbers. But whereas the Western 24-hour-day is divided into two blocks of 12 hours each, the Thai is divided up into four blocks of six hours each. In Europe, "see you at 9 o'clock" could mean nine in the morning or evening, although which of the two is most likely to be obvious in the context of conversation. In Thailand, if you are told, "The painters will be at your house at 3 o'clock," you might ask if they can start earlier, but you probably won't be expecting them at 3 am.

So, before the days of fake Rolexes on every wrist, how did people cope? Easy. The little people came early and waited for the big people to be ready to receive them. Accounts of early Ayudhya suggest that many people might be kept waiting days in this fashion, afraid to leave the courtyard unless they were called for the audience they wanted or must endure. The greater the status difference, the greater the waiting time. And always the little people waiting for the big to be ready for them. Just as big men sit at the front and the very little people as far as they can get behind them, if they sit at all, and just as the big man is always higher than the little man, so with time, it had basic social boundaries. In today's world, some vestiges of this are very evident. You are not likely to be kept waiting three days in an outer office, but a 15-minute wait might put you in your place; or you could be received immediately and treated as an equal. If you wait longer than 30 minutes, decide whether the meeting is important enough to you not only to wait but to grovel when finally called. If it is, don't let yourself get angry. Use your time to prepare your grovelling frame of mind, so that your arse-licking will be at its best — it will get you in quicker next time.

Bottom line:

An expression Thai share with farang *languages is "Time is Money"* (wela pen ngeun). *Many* farang *are surprised to hear this.*

89

On Touching Monks

Monks cannot touch woman, women cannot touch monks. *Khatoeys* and others in female drag do not touch monks. *Tom*, females in male drag, do not touch monks. Homosexuals and monks can touch each other but should take no sensual enjoyment in doing so.

Touching Buddhist monks or novice monks is okay for a man, whatever his religion or race, as long as he is dressed like a man. It is taboo for any female or female-substitute to touch any monk, be she Thai, Buddhist, and the mother or daughter of the monk, or be she used to touching a particular monk before he became a particular monk, or be she a baby in arms or a granny in a wheelchair. Touching extends to the robes or anything else a monk wears, and to handing him something or receiving something directly from a monk. The concept of touching is partly in the mind: a monk can happily tie a string onto a girl's wrist, as long as he does not actually touch her. And in crowded buses and at festivals, the chances of a monk's robes brushing a woman are high, although neither party may be aware of the "touch". Handing something need not involve touching, but it is still taboo for the monk and woman. Thus even when placing food and other things in a monk's bowl during the morning alms round, a woman should actually avoid contact with the bowl by dropping her offering a short distance into it. Similarly, the monk may pour or sprinkle sanctified water directly onto a female with no problem.

In the monk's mind, a woman should only exist as piles of skin, bones, nail clippings and hair. Women can help the celibate monk banish naughty thoughts from his mind. If they cannot exactly think of themselves as skin, lard and bone, they can at least dress conservatively when going to the wat, and avoid any direct eye contact. Thai women do indeed not wear their skimpiest clothing when at the wat, but neither do they go into purdah. After all, a visit to the wat is more than a chance to make merit or hear the dharma, it is a social event, so women make themselves up to look nice.

The Thai world is ordered to minimise the touching of monks by women. Front rows of seats at events, the row of seats next to the back door on buses, a roped-off section

of seating at airports, priority boarding, raising the monks physically above the congregation, even if just by a few centimetres. All these things have to do with status, but also, all serve to segregate women physically from monks. A monk shopping will often have a temple boy or man as his companion to handle the money. If not, the monk will pass the money to any man, even a foreigner, who passes it to the woman and handles the change in the same direction.

Monks can talk to women, and women can talk to monks, and they do. Women constitute a majority of people seeking a sort of counselling audience with a monk. Without women, the religion would collapse, as almost all of those placing cooked food into the morning alms bowls are female. However, women cannot ordain in the same way as men. They can decide to become nuns and live as closely as possible to the many rules governing what monks can and cannot do. But however close nuns get to the monastic life, they are governed by the same taboos as other women when it comes to touching monks.

Should a monk or his robes be accidentally polluted by a woman's touch (and it must be added, if he is aware of this), the monk is required to go through extensive rites to remove the pollution. This is not so much that women are thought of as unclean, as a requirement assisting the monk to live a life without temporary sensual pleasures.

Bottom line:
Monks should think of all women as piles of skin and bone. Women can help monks think this way by becoming piles of skin and bone.

90

On Touching Nuns

Nuns live as closely to the monastic path as they can get and as they choose, forming communities within certain temples and accumulating merit through their actions and study of Buddhist dharma. Even if they ordain temporarily for a very short period, all uphold the taboo on sexual activity. But none of the monk's many rules apply to nuns, who do not need to shave their heads or go on alms rounds. Nuns eat what the monks leave over, which inevitably means they pass the noon deadline after which monks should not eat. In many other ways nuns are almost prevented from following perfectly the Buddhist path. Yet many nuns are very, very serious about their calling. There is a current of thought that says nuns should be allowed to ordain in the same way as monks. This occasionally receives public attention, but it is not an issue for public debate in the same way as is the ordination of women in the Catholic Church.

Bottom line:
Go right ahead whether you are male, female or whatever. None of the restrictions on touching monks applies to nuns.

91

On Unpenting Pent-Ups

With all this conflict avoidance, your emotions — indeed anybody's emotions, including those of Thais — can tend to become a trifle pent up. Emotions are bottled inside the body like urine on a shaky long-distance bus with no toilet. And when life's bus does finally stop to allow you a pee-pee break by the side of the road, what happens? Can't go. Blocked up so long, it won't come out. Too many people around, no privacy. So back on the bus with everything pent up as before, with containment an ever greater problem, and the risk of an unintended release ever more likely, just at the time when those around you have unpent themselves and think everything hunky-dory.

Your neighbour's dog shits on your doorstep every morning. Do you complain? No. To do so would risk jeopardising the relationship with your neighbour, big man or small. You either say nothing and clean up — or tell the maid to clean up — or you strategically place a few cactus plants and pepper the doorstep. And your neighbours seem to have lots of people in and make lots of noise all the time. Do you have a quiet word? Unless your neighbours live in a bar, probably not a good idea. Why not? Because people don't do that in Thailand.

It's not really fair maybe, but living in Thailand means you have a lot more to bottle up inside than most Thais.

How come? For the following reasons. Many of the things that play on your nerves will not affect a Thai, or are things that a Thai will barely notice or even like. A few examples. The noise level in any Thai or Chinese restaurant, the loudspeakers at the temple that noise-pollute an otherwise idyllic scene, the TV everywhere you look with nobody watching it. The bureaucracy that requires a foreigner, here legally, to report to immigration every three months, like a paroled prisoner, and don't you forget. The permission needed to buy a car and get a driving license. The crowds of people at any social event, or even when there is no event, making it impossible to get to know anybody really, and when, on occasion you do find yourself having a quiet drink with a Thai and chatting in either language, others will join you or be waved over by the person you want to get to know, or just interrupt without an excuse me. The police who pull your car over when you follow the Thai traffic filtering left where there is no filter arrow but will let you go with a verbal warning for a few hundred baht. "Why me?" you want to shout, "Why not those Thai guys?" But you know the answer, don't you? And why, when a Thai kid smashes his pushbike into the side of your car, causing you to pay for a whole paint job, why do you also have to pay to replace his bike and the hospital bill for his scuffed knuckles?

Is there anything to do about all this? And preferably something other than going back where you came from. There is, but it may be difficult at first. You have to alter your tolerance level and learn to tell yourself *may pen rai* when things seem too much, but there's not much you can do about it. Presuming you want to stay in a Thai world and not retreat into a culture bubble, you have to learn to not notice and not let little things weigh on your mind, making big things. Let things in and through and out. Don't let them get pent up.

If necessary chant like a mantra in your mind, telling yourself "never mind". Of course, some things do mind, but not that much when you think about it — or don't think about it.

Bottom line:

If your mind is pent up with frustration, it's because you trapped it there instead of letting it flow through. Let it drain and you will feel better, smile more, and interact more easily.

92

On Vanishing Virginity

Everybody has to be a virgin sometime. The big question is: when is a virgin not a virgin? The answer used to be: when a girl is married or for the first time sells her body. In the good old days, which are a lot closer to the present time in Thailand than in the West, good girls retained their virginity into their twenties or even longer. Society helped them to do this by making regulations requiring girls in university dormitories to return and retire early, put all their shoes clearly outside their doors when at home, and to keep the door open wide when allowed male visitors were in their rooms, even if it were a stated brother or father. Thailand has never been a place to stone or banish those practising sex without marriage, but it was a place where girls supported each other's efforts to remain intact rather than a place where sexual experimentation among the single set became something of a new norm. Thus, while it is probably true to say that virginity, for girls, remains a Thai value, it is also true to say that it is today something of an ideal. Statistics are understandably damned difficult to obtain and verify, but it seems likely that virginity at marriage is somewhat more realised in Thailand than in the West, although the difference must be small.

This might surprise some of those less perceptive *farang*, who think that all Thais are whores. And it does rather depend on how one interprets "virginity at marriage". It is now the norm to register a marriage by going along to the *Amphur* and signing names in front of officials and witnesses, and picking up a couple of fancy marriage certificates, one for each partner. This certificate is about the most romantic thing in such *Amphur* registrations, where there is no appointment and couples queue up to sign their names. And where, incidentally, at least in the big cities, there will be a handful of *farang* communicating with their Thai girlfriends in the standard ten words of bar-room English. For many Thais, this official registration and recognition of their union comes after what they think of as their real marriage.

Real marriage takes place in the home, and often in the home village in the mother's house (matrilineal aspects are very important — see "On Matriarchy, Mothers and Money"). Traditionally, marriage would follow a *mun*. This is when the two families meet together, with the bride and groom and maybe some of their friends, for a meal and a discussion of the bride price to be paid and the details and date of the wedding. After this *mun*, it is usually socially recognised that the couple will sleep together. (It is not legally recognised as marriage.) The actual marriage will take place some time later, maybe months later, and again will be at the bride's mother's house and involve ceremony and feasting. It is at this home ceremony that visitors bless the couple by pouring water over their hands and expressing their best wishes. It is at this ceremony that the couple dress up, either in traditional clothing or in Western wedding gear. After this, there is no doubt that the couple are married in all eyes. The *Amphur* business is a legal recognition of what has occurred. Some older Thais never bothered with it and possess no certificates of marriage, although their children have birth certificates and full rights. So, at what point do we consider "virginity at marriage"? If at the *mun*, which has been likened to a kind of trial marriage — although one with full expectation of carrying through the process — the incidence of virginity, or almost-virginity would be fairly high. If at the official *Amphur* signing, it could be almost non-existent. Perhaps the important thing to note is that a lot of girls do not have a great deal of sexual experience before their boyfriend-fiancé-husband.

Things are of course changing fast. Many a Thai man now accepts that his wife might not have saved herself just for the day he happened along. This is a logical acceptance of the social consequences of late rather than early marriage. However, there continue to be a number of Thai girls who keep their virginity into their twenties or beyond. This number may be a lot smaller than two or three generations ago, but it remains comparatively significant on a global scale. Higher education and professionalism, along with class structure, play a role here. Definitely, the middle-upper status families keep much more control over their daughters and have the means and motivation to do so. The motivation is a good marital alliance, plus avoidance of the loss of face that a girl brings to her parents if she plays around too obviously and too much. Such families will often expect their unmarried girls to go out "chaperoned" (usually a sister or known friend, but sometimes mother herself), at least until the boy has demonstrated his good intensions. The boy is often happy with this situation, which is taken as a guarantee of virginity.

But a lot goes on beneath the surface. Even the primly, if sensuously, dressed university student might, under the tightly-stretched white starched blouse, have a dagger tattooed on her right shoulder, a rose on her left breast and a no-entry sign on the lower back. Okay, so this is just fashion, like miniskirts and platform shoes, but so is virginity, or the loss of it.

How, in the space of one generation does a charming and innocently virgin teenager, with only the cares of teenage spots and getting back before Thai TV drama starts, become a *gig*, going out to the nightspots, drinking vodka, popping the occasional methamphetamine, covered in more tattoos than a sailor, dressed in whichever revealing way fashion decides this month, smooching in the smart places to be and giving away her status along with her virginity?

Good question, even if I did think of it myself. Some Thais, and some *farang* who watch young Thai girls for a living, think the answer lies in the comparatively new English-language private schools, where the comparatively well-off can get a degree and also have plenty of time to play, and to play without the restrictions of family and the old universities. The old institutions in which these children grew up taught conformity: be like your peers. Schools emphasised the elder-knows-best principle and respect for authority in the shape of role-model Thai teachers, caring but conservative. All, well almost all, girls at school have their hair cut short using a pudding basin on their heads, and all wear and love their uniforms. Those who go on to the state universities have the prestige of being selected from a large pool who want to go there. They continue to wear uniforms, and uniforms which are at once very sexy and very proper, having hardly changed since WWII. They may no longer be locked up at night, but they live in dormitories or with relatives: someone is responsible for their physical and moral welfare, and that someone is above the level of the peer group. The girls in prestigious universities are less likely to wander than those in private English-language universities. They may no longer be saints, if they ever were, but they realise that virginity of girls at marriage, but not of boys, remains a sort of Thai value, a sort of prize for the good boy coming from a good family, a middle-class family with money. Why should those who go to private schools be so different?

Answer, as some Thais firmly believe: English-language universities employ English-language-speaking teachers. These may be Thai who have themselves studied overseas and have a more flexible concept of social boundaries, but they are often *farang*, who lead a very different lifestyle to that of traditional teachers and lecturers. Being teachers, the students recognise and respect them as elders and betters, even if they are *farang*, because they have been brought up to do so. But if the teachers go to nightclubs, discos and parties, the message gets through: it's okay, it's cool.

The same social group of friends that kept a girl in line, *might* now countenance her drinking alcohol and possibly experimenting with drugs, making out with a number of partners, having an affair, taking the pill or having an abortion. The correlation between drinking alcohol at parties and first sexual experiences is well documented and such behaviour is dripping down into high-school years (although drinking alcohol occasionally was never forbidden to girls, especially in the village environment). Fashion is paramount. The new message is self-assertion, and what better place to do that than within one's peer group subculture? Platform shoes, wearing black to parties, miniskirts — none of it Thai. Thai girls have, thankfully, stopped short of rings through nose and vagina... at the moment...

Bottom line:

Bottom line: Friendship and family groups can maintain norms and values and they can change them. Simple as that. But has that much changed in terms of morality? If it has, the Thais don't seem too concerned.

93

On Visiting Thais at Home

On visiting a Thai at home, it is a reasonable certainty that you know them, or if not, that you have at least telephoned to say you are coming and given some sort of reason. Chances are then that you have had some previous social interaction with the visited. So, if they have invited you to visit them at home, that's a pretty good sign that you did at least something right last time you met. Well done.

But you don't have to wait to be invited. You don't even have to let them know you are coming. It's okay to just drop by, alone or with a friend, who may be somebody they don't know but should never be somebody who might make you and your hosts lose face or feel uncomfortable. You will most likely be received in the "room to receive guests" if there is one — sounds a bit Victorian England or Hungarian, but Thais do not automatically show visitors all over their home American-style.

If yours is a casual "I was in the neighbourhood anyway so I thought I'd drop in..." visit, that's okay, but no need to say it. To Western ears it sounds like you are politely excusing yourself and such a statement might well be followed by, "...but I won't stay long." To most Thai ears it sounds confusing, as if you would only come to visit if it is convenient to you. And while you do not have to stay long if you have other things to do, saying so suggests that you don't want to spend long in the company of those you have come to visit. So, why visit at all? On such "drop-in" visits, it is not necessary or even normal to bring a gift. However, if invited to visit, you can be pretty sure you are going to eat there, or possibly in a restaurant at the host's expense, so bring along something to hand over. Whatever you give, you will not get instant status points with the host or other guests for your generosity, because the other guests will not see what you hand over. Your present — usually nicely wrapped — will be put aside for the hosts to examine after everybody has gone. So, what to bring?

No need to think expensive; to do so might embarrass your hosts or send some wrong signals, or involve them in expected reciprocity. On the other hand, nothing too cheap. Taste doesn't come into it — your taste is likely to be different from that of your host. Giving flowers or fruit is okay, but give some nice ones and make sure the presentation is the best. Very commonplace and cheap fruit is out, so no bananas unless they form just part of a nicely arranged fruit basket, which will possibly contain Chinese apple and tins of fruit cocktail. Basket arrangements for flowers are also available and save your hosts the trouble of putting things in water in vases. Flowers not cut to size, badly arranged and wrapped in newspaper straight from the market stall are not acceptable. And make sure you do not hand your hostess flowers which might be a blaze of fresh colour to your eyes but are only given when there is a death in the family! Such flowers should not be brought into the house, so you not only give an inappropriate present, but place your hosts in an awkward situation. Flowers and fruit, for practical reasons, are usually not wrapped other than the presentation covering or basket.

Chocolates are always acceptable, if they are in a nice box and gift-wrapped. If they need refrigeration, say so, your host won't really appreciate getting dripping chocolate out of a table cloth. Don't forget any small children; Thais often hand them small bank notes — 20 baht is fine, 100 is too much unless it is the child's birthday or children's day or a newly born baby. Do this only if you see others do it, do not put such small money in envelopes and do not ask the parents first, as you would in the West. However small, wait there while the child gives you a *wai* of thanks. But if he doesn't, don't take the money back! Small change to children is usually given at goodbye — if they bother to send you off.

A few printed photographs of normal size are cheap, so hand these over as small supplements to the real gift. They provide conversational material, a link to a past occasion you shared with the host, and you can be sure they are appreciated. But they do not constitute the stuff of the brightly wrapped gift. On the other hand, a single nice enlargement of the host family in a nice frame is a present and can be wrapped. In fact, while not expensive, it makes a very nice present: Thais have an inexhaustible capacity to spend hours looking at themselves. Giving such small gifts is quite a Thai thing to do, and therefore you get social points far in excess of the cost and effort involved.

If you are visiting somebody you fancy or care for, a well-framed picture of that person (*not* a picture of you), together with a bunch of roses, wrapped bouquet-style for you at the market stall or shop where you bought them, will make your intentions obvious without saying a word, and will help establish you as a nice sort of person. Give such gifts personally but not in front of a large group, which might cause embarrassment. If really serious, get the picture touched up to remove warts and nascent moustaches and provide a fairness of skin. This is quickly done at the photo shop using their computer programme appropriately called Photoshop; the Thai version can even remove unwanted *phi* at no extra cost. The bigger the framed picture you give, the bigger the impression. Your Thai love will gaze at this picture of herself or himself for hours, even ignoring the Thai Drama of the day, until her or his thoughts transmit psycho-waves to your inner being and make you reach for the smaller version, unframed, that you had printed for yourself. At that point, if in the rainy season, there will be a huge clap of thunder and your entwined thought patterns will pop up to the God of Thunder for his approval. If visiting somebody you are serious about, you will score high points for giving flowers to the girl/boy — but do be aware that Thais will take this as a sign of romantic interest of the serious sort, particularly a nice bunch of roses. If you really have such interest, an additional bunch of flowers of the same size to the mother will greatly advance your cause. Never mind the father.

Whatever your reason for visiting Thais at home, if you are shown family snapshot albums, however awful, show the greatest interest you can manage. Find something to compliment or flatter, and at least try not to yawn. In viewing, but not lustfully ogling, a picture of Somboon's wife, or even when Somboon's wife is standing in front of you in the flesh, it is quite all right to say to Somboon, "Why, you certainly have a beautiful wife, Somboon." This is a compliment to Somboon as much as to his wife. Don't smack your lips as you say it, and don't follow through as you might to your American buddy, "Can't see what she sees in you."

And even if you *have* just come from a funeral, and never mind that it's fashion, a lot of Thais will not like it — so don't go dressed in black. Dressing all in black or with a black shirt or blouse is not the way to make people feel comfortable, and being comfortable and making others feel comfortable should be your primary consideration.

Well, that's got you in the front door. Now, where do you go from here? Possibly nowhere. You will be brought a glass of water or a soft drink, and the host or hosts will come and sit with you. You talk. If after ten minutes you have had enough or have run out of Thai, you begin to say goodbye. Here if you want, you can offer an excuse for such a short visit. Or you can do what Thais do and withdraw slowly, as if compelled to leave although you would love to stay. It is fully in order and polite to say you must be going. The host may or may not say "don't go yet". You don't go the first time but continue talking, even perhaps going into a new subject, punctuating every few minutes with the fact that you must be going. If nothing becomes of your visit like the leaving of it, you have done well. Sometimes the goodbye can take longer than the visit itself. Finally you stand up, your host stands up and you move slowly to the door, stopping on the way briefly, then at the door your final goodbye and "thank you". This is one time when Thais often say "thank you" when they mean goodbye. In other countries, it is usual for the host to thank the visitor for the visit; in Thailand the visitor thanks — implication, not usually stated, thanks for receiving me. The host may also thank or may not. There, you have been on your best behaviour and left a good impression.

If your visit is going to be a longer invited one, be prepared for maybe quite a lot of people. Thais rarely invite just one or two people to a sit-down meal. There will certainly be somewhere to sit and it is now usual to have a choice of sitting in a circle on the floor or on chairs around tables. Often, weather permitting, eating will involve an outdoor buffet, which certainly helps if there are some things you'd rather not have on your plate. It is fully in order to compliment the food.

People will come and go, so reception and leave-taking is not so protracted and you cannot expect to take up all your host's attention. Such occasions are usually "relaxed smart casual". Your hosts may tell you to keep your shoes on. If they and the other guests are wearing shoes, keep them on; but look out for points, perhaps passing through an internal door or going up a floor, where shoes suddenly come off. If eating buffet outdoors, shoes will be kept on, but having taken your food in hand, if you sit on a mat, shoes off before treading on the mat. With a plate and drink in both hands, slip-on shoes are great assets and if you are unused to them, try again.

Bottom line:

Group occasions are supposed to be fun, so don't talk too seriously about the latest war coverage on TV, who's died, or problems in the south. Smile, wai your hosts on entry and departure only, and if you find you are not really enjoying yourself, have another drink and smile again.

94

On *Wai*, Why, When, Who

Everybody knows that when in Thailand you *wai*. True, but a generalisation. And all generalisations are dangerous. There, I just made another one, probably the most dangerous of them all. Nothing will happen to you if you return the *wai* to the doorman and reception girl who greet you at the Oberoi Hotel. You won't break a leg. You won't offend them. Even if you *wai* the checkout person at Tesco, a thunderbolt of culture shock won't strike you dead — after all that person *wai*'d first, didn't he or she? And if, after *wai*'ing all the cleaners and car park attendants and the bar steward, you turn and *wai* the big man you are trying to impress... Well, you certainly screwed that one up. You have just shown that your knowledge of Thai culture stretches not one page further than the cover of a book on Thailand or the Thais; and almost all publishers seem to think that a pretty girl making a *wai* is the way to sell a book.

Thais certainly do *wai*; but that's a 50 per cent statement. In any social situation, they are as likely *not* to *wai* as to *wai*. What's the good of a 50 per cent rule on social interaction? Absolutely none at all if it stops at 'In Thailand you *wai*'. Might as well say, "In Thailand, you don't *wai*". In fact, that might be closer to reality.

Flashing the *wai* everywhere you go will certainly get you noticed. In precisely the wrong way. You want to present an image of a foreigner who knows Thai ways and respects Thai culture and the Thais, and you want to impress those in a social position above you. The last thing you want is to appear as a buffoon, harmless but ridiculous. But, the last thing you want is the first thing you get. And in Thailand, at least as much as anywhere else, first impressions, superficial as they are, are important to a culture played out largely on the surface.

Like just about everything else in Thai culture, the *wai* is part of the deference system, which you might think of as a *defence* system for those at society's bottom. For once, the historical origins give a clear pointer as to correct contemporary use. By putting your palms together, you show they are empty. No sword. No gun. Not in the best position for a karate chop to the throat. By bringing your head down to meet your hands (the real *wai* of respect lowers the head as much as it raises the hands), you give your social contact the chance to bonk you on the head while you are not in a position to defend yourself. This is most unlikely to happen, even to a harmless, ridiculous buffoon, but it does show you trust your social superior (or are pretending to do so). And it obliges him or her to acknowledge this. The acknowledgement will always be a grade or two below yours and you might not merit a *wai* in return, although many Thais will snap you one to keep the *farang* happy. Those of high status, monks, etc., will not, or should not, *wai* you in return. They may give a smile or a small nod, maybe, and many men in such a position might prefer a Western handshake and be done with it (not women 'though).

When the girl or boy packing your groceries or taking your money after you pay a bill gives you a *wai*, no return gesture is expected. Sure, if you think they're cute, give them a smile — try not to be too lecherous 'though, people are looking. Overuse of anything devalues its meaning; this is very true of the *wai*. There has been a certain devaluation in Thai culture, even without the bumbling *farang* intervention, and it is quite okay for two more or less equals to *wai* each other on meeting and departure. But, being equals, they might as easily do nothing. Nobody wants to receive devalued currency. *Wai* all the big man's social inferiors, then turn and give him the same *wai* and you might as well insult him to his face. Probably no insult will be taken, but you could be written off as yet another foreigner who doesn't know how to behave. And you're not, are you?

A *wai* is not just a way of saying "hi" without speaking. Economise your use of it and you will discover its meaning.

Bottom line:
If you go into the chapel of a wat and wai the Buddha image, which is about the most respectful wai you can give, three times, face touching the ground, you don't really expect the Buddha image to wai back, do you?

95

On Watching Thai TV as a Guide to the Thai Middle Class

If you marry a Thai, you will be allowed perhaps half an hour to watch the news in English. Most of the rest of the evening will be given over to serialised Thai dramas. These will be watched by the whole family, indeed pretty much by the whole nation, so if you don't want to be left out, you have to watch. But even if you have no intention of marrying a Thai, are quite happy with your farang spouse, are a dedicated homosexual or a confirmed bachelor, in your efforts to integrate into Thai society and understand its structure, ambitions, motivations and fears, you can pick up a lot from a few passive doses of Thai TV.

Of course it helps if you understand Thai or are learning the language, but even this is not essential as plots are thin and few in number, and actors tend to play the same roles, which is what the Thai viewer wants to see. Bear in mind that these actors and actresses are very well known and are constantly interviewed on screen and in magazines. They lead fashion and while being Westernized materially, they are all very Thai in the threads of morality that hold the plots together and make them easily predictable. They are very much a part of everyday life for the ordinary Thai and may be considered a unifying part of modern Thai culture. Their words are listened to, whether they are extolling the virtues of a whitening cream or talking sensibly about how to avoid AIDS by wearing condoms.

In addition to what you see on the screen, you will gain a lot from the audience reaction (if viewing with Thais), and learn something about what makes Thais laugh and cry. If watching with a Thai audience, particularly if your parents-in-law are part of it, try not to laugh at the blatant visuals: the over-use of make-up poorly applied (particularly blood substitutes), the hairstyles, and the sudden appearance of monsters or phi to disturb the idyllic harmony. Laughter, when there is any, will be spontaneous and all will laugh at exactly the same time. When the beautiful little teenager who wouldn't slap a mosquito is transformed into a blatantly over-embellished phi with a long cardboard stick-on farang-looking nose, don't chortle and say, "How ridiculous". Remember, you are the odd one out and you are the student. And if I were you, I'd also avoid any unnecessary attention to noses.

While there are some more or less straight cops vs baddies dramas, sometimes remodelled from Western TV, the majority of Thai dramas involve a very Thai adaptation of good vs bad, with *phi*, good and bad, spinning and resolving the plot by flinging back and forth balls of kinetic energy. In some dramas, *phi* are replaced by beings from space; these are also good and bad and also rely on throwing fireballs — which have the great advantage of requiring no clouds of censor's haze (it's quite okay to zap somebody with a fireball). Whatever the script, the physical and social background hardly changes. Absolutely all main characters are middle-class, including the *phi*, and live in enormous houses, wear clothing suggestive of an air-conditioned temperate climate, wear hairstyles which are absolutely the latest style in Bangkok (which sets such things for the rest of the country), speak Central (Bangkok) Thai, drive very expensive cars and occasionally travel to remoter parts of the Kingdom to emphasise their centricity. There will perhaps be a maid, often speaking a Thai regional dialect, who is pretty, good, under-educated, very well treated by the family to whom she is completely loyal and devoted, and who often provides comic relief a la Shakespeare's fool. Those old enough to remember will recognise early TV settings and characters from their foreign childhood, before the "kitchen-sink dramas" introduced the working class to TV as something more than audience or scenery.

A typical drama will include characters that everybody can identify with, and their opposites, the protagonists, with maybe just one who yo-yos between good and evil: good when in the family and a Buddhist milieu, evil when taken by a bad spirit. Don't be surprised when the heroes are cornered in an impossible situation by baddies, most of whom will be able to transform themselves into physical manifestations of evil and possess miraculous and deadly powers, and when there is no way out at all, in pops a good *phi* and zaps all the baddies. Sometimes it is a Buddhist monk who suddenly appears and by his presence, or a few chants, renders the bad *phi* helpless.

There are actors who have risen to fame dressed in the Gaudy guise of a *phi*, always a good one. One *phi* even has a fan club and is the hero of the show, which is named after him. Of course it is very hard to completely destroy a bad phi but they can be checked until the new script is ready. There is a strong element of formal religion vanquishing the dark pre-Buddhist days when vampires and all kinds of nasty spirits had it all their own way. The wat (like the church) is considered a safe place — if the heroes can get to it in time, the large Buddha image will prevent bad *phi* from following. And just as the vampire is about to bite, the victim's dress is torn, revealing the Buddha image on a chain around her neck. All very passé in Western cinema or TV, but very much a part of Thai contemporary drama. The great difference is that Western audiences might like to be scared by ghosts and vampires, but most people in the West do not believe these things really exist; in Thailand practically everybody believes. This is evident in Thai life every day, in the Buddha images worn on the person and placed respectfully in normal Thai houses that will not be a scrap on the little palaces of the TV middle-class. Anyway, on Thai TV, good always triumphs in the end. Do good and you'll come back middle-class with a Mercedes-Benz. And the TV police are always good guys and gals.

Police and villains on Thai TV actually do not use guns and knives to intimidate or terminate each other, they use little clouds of thick smoke. These float around the TV screen looking for any weapons that get close to a victim and obliterating it. The same little cleansing clouds will rush over to a cigarette or cigar raised to a person's lips, thus visualising the health warning that smoking may obliterate half your face in a greasy little cloud. The screen can become a complete cloud when a cigar-smoking villain grabs a hostage and threatens her neck with what is maybe a knife, but may well be a cigar. And while Thai and international fashion models may wear as little as required for the function of their work, any bare breasts bring on the clouds immediately. This cloud therapy helps counter the passive effects of too much television by encouraging the viewer's imagination to come out of hibernation.

So, apart from a large dose of cloud therapy, what does Thai TV teach us? The imagery at first may seem to be complete fantasy, unreflective of Thai material culture.

Your Thai family and friends in the audience like it that way. They may be sitting on the floor in a one-room bamboo shack, but they have a TV turned on and can dream and, of course, imagine. And they dream middle-class TV dreams: big house, beautiful car, quiffy hairstyles, beautiful boy- and girlfriends, faithful partners, family norms and values, the aid of friendly phi and the destruction of evil. They dream of the same sort of things you do: they just don't let too much reality spoil their dreams. And if reality looks like it might come on too strong, the little clouds will drive it away.

Bottom line:
The perceived middle-class is the way to go. Behave like a good character in a Thai drama and you will soon develop a fan club.

96

On Watching the Boat Races

Tip had mentioned several times that the boat races would take place on Thursday. Husband John said it was lucky they now had a house by the river as Tip could see everything from the top balcony and this year, they wouldn't have to fight through the crowds, and they could have all they wanted to eat and drink from the fridge.

An hour into the races Tip was doing the washing. Considerate John asked if she was not coming up to watch the boat races. She replied no, it was boring. Actually, John was delighted to hear that, as he found the heat and crowds and even the races very boring indeed. He was glad his wife seemed to be maturing in her interests, and the washing did need doing.

Then the bell rang. Two young girls from up the road. Coming to the boat races, Tip? Tip was off like a shot.

When she came back, hot, tired and sweaty, John asked if she had enjoyed herself. Yes, she had had a really good time. John was a bit confused. I thought you said the races were boring, he said.

Well, said Tip, they would be boring if I didn't have any friends.

Anyway, who won? John asked.

No idea, said Tip.

Tip had enjoyed an event because she was with her friends. Had she watched the same races alone, or if she had dragged along reluctant but considerate John, than she might as well do the washing.

Bottom line:

Doing things alone is no fun. The more the merrier.

97

On White and Black

When tripping along the aisles of a Tesco-Lotus supermarket looking at the girls, or the boys, hover around the toiletries shelves awhile, not the chemical alley of cosmetics but the normal deodorants and skin cream section.

If and when you use deodorant, to where is it applied? Armpits? And a second place? Can't think of one. So armpits then. Now look at the labels on 99 per cent of deodorants. In the West, the most powerful word in advertising is NEW. In Thailand, the most powerful word is WHITE.

Extra White. Super White. Extra Super Whitening. Who in the whole world would buy a deodorant because they want extra super white armpits? To judge from the democratic shelves of modern supermarkets, that's exactly what the Thais want. This is in spite of a demographic survey at Tesco on four consecutive Sunday afternoons which covered all attractive female deodorant shoppers between the ages of 17 and 21, and 1 in 100 young men of the same age range, a grand total of 4.7 million young bits of stuff. The partial survey showed conclusively that not only did 100 per cent have no idea what a survey was, but 50 per cent also had no real idea what colour their armpits were. But the other 50 per cent knew they had black armpits. Furthermore, the 50 per cent unsure of the present colour of their armpits definitely did not want to develop black armpits.

Of the same people, when asked why they bought the Extra Whitening face cream, 100 per cent said it is because they have black face skin. Not honey-coloured, not sugar-coated, not even bronzed, but black. Their arms and legs and breasts and all the bits in between are black. And all require UV Filter #3 million, and walking around under umbrellas, to prevent them becoming even blacker. Hand cream: Extra Whitening. Breast cream for firming up after a baby or a heavy night: Deep Whitening. Body cream: Super Deep Whitening to get you Stunningly White. Who is looking at all these body parts? I mean, maybe Patpong bar-top dancers do need a touch-up or two, but these kids at the supermarket, these are normal kids, aren't they? Yes they are and nobody had a spray tube of Durex Play in her black little hands. But then that's about the only cream that did not claim extra-terrestrial whitening powers. Without the whitening agent, one can only tremble at the possible effects of daily use of Play.

Well, it certainly seems that Thais have a thing about White. If the supermarket experience left any doubts in your mind, try an evening of Thai TV without switching between channels as soon as the adverts come on. Absolutely every product that comes into contact with any part of skin, and many that don't, can guarantee white skin. My favourite is the special hermetic basement where, for six months, all meals, white rice and white bread only, are delivered through an opaque feeding tube direct to your intestines, and where the only colour, including hair and defecation waste, that you see during this period is white. This basement will be fitted under your existing house by men wearing white masks and white suits. When you emerge after six months in your white cocoon, you are Snow White, and this is what the seven dwarves will call you as they follow you around singing about how deeply white you are.

So, how do Thais get on with *The Colour Purple*? Few have read the book. And even fewer realise why the popular Darkie toothpaste, which advertises sparklingly whiter teeth, was renamed Darlie and the top-hatted black and white minstrel face on the packet was changed to black and white instead of being all black. Nobody, it seems, thought black people might be offended. Same with Golliwog marmalade. In fact, the Thais have much in common with their brothers and sisters in central Africa, where exactly the same whitening products enjoy not only an experimental playground but very substantial sales, to people who really cannot afford it. (End of lesson: sorry for the brief diversion into morality, won't happen again.)

White is not the colour of status in Thailand. At the time of writing the most popular colour is yellow, as this is the colour of the day on which the King was born. Next in line might be the various shades of saffron-brown worn by monks. But no Thai has yet to declare that he or she wants yellow or saffron-brown skin. They want super-white skin, the colour of the robes worn by nuns, who get no seat reserved for them on a bus or at the airport and who do not get to go first-class on the train unless they pay the full fare.

The same young things that want every day, in every way, to get whiter and whiter, will go to the parties of other young things dressed in fashionable black, whenever black is fashionable, breaking all social taboos.

Of course the Thai fixation with white needs a bit more perspective. Thai beauty queens are judged or selected by people more important than the average Somboon. Those selected tend not to come from the darker regions of the south or from over by the Cambodian border. They are white if anybody is white. So, if ordinary people are fixed on turning paler than pale, they are only following what their biggers and betters are doing — which is a Thai way of doing things. But white perhaps goes beyond simple fashion. Most of the farang who come to Thailand are white, at least until they attempt to become bronze gods and goddesses by lying out in the sun, where they go various blotchy shades of lobster red. Why the farang have this fixation on becoming brown is as perplexing as the Thai love affair with the colour white. And why are farang gods bronze and Thai angels white?

Does the white-imperative spill over into racism? It does in the sense that Thais will almost always compare their one-shade darker skin negatively with the beautiful white farang skin. If it were not for all the very real efforts (and disappointments) to become white, we might be able to dismiss this as Thai flattery. We can't. A fair-skinned Thai may be best of friends with a dark-skinned Thai and will extol

her or his beauty; but if somebody the same Thai doesn't care for has a dark skin, this will be stated as a negative about the person, along with all the other negatives.

The idea that white is good and black is bad is, of course, not uniquely Thai, but is found throughout East Asia. Certainly, Thai language contains expressions of this idea. So does Thai drama (although not the modern TV dramas, conceived by more globally sensitive writers). But, let's face it — English is also full of such expressions, which, in both countries pre-date any noticeable presence of black-skinned people. Perhaps the real test is how black people are received. Here the Thais do rather well. Africans and black-Americans do not feel any of the prejudices they tolerate in the West. They are aware that Thais are curious about the colour of their skin, but to my knowledge none have suffered hostility.

So, how do the Thais really score in black and white terms? Well, most of them are probably whiter than their Asian neighbours, except for the Chinese, Vietnamese and their own hill peoples. This might well be because of the very large amount of intermarriage that has taken place between Thais and Chinese. (The average Thai is considered to be one-quarter Chinese, those in Bangkok and other cities, rather more.) This certainly draws the national colour line towards the white pole of the black-white continuum. But it also shows the tolerance of Thais when it comes to intermarriage. It is perhaps impossible to find any nationality or type which is rejected by Thai families as undesirable marriage partners for colour or religious reasons. Far more important than skin colour is status, including wealth. Given that only a small minority of the millions of foreign guests visiting or working in Thailand each year is black, Thai-black marriages are probably proportionate to the number of blacks in Thailand. Realistically, then, the freely-stated Thai preference for white, backed up by the commercial success of whitening products, and the Thai perception of their own skin as "black", does not seem to be in any way realised in attitudes to black people. It might even be that Thais feel at ease with blacks precisely because real blacks pose no competition in the skin-game — but that is merely speculative hypothesis.

Bottom line:

In Thailand, as all over the world, the white chess pieces move first. This gives a one move advantage but does not guarantee the game.

98

On X-rated Literature, Cinema and Internet

While the bars and backstreets of Thailand are witness to live shows of the erotic, and while under-the-table video pornography leaves nothing to the imagination, and while prostitution is available at the bat of a 1,000 baht note, the public exhibition of X-rated books, magazines and films is subject to savage censorship and prohibition. Naughty sites on the Internet are not forgotten — look one up and you will see a message from a Thai authority saying the site is off limits.

Thus, legal soft-porn video compact discs (VCDs) have clouds of haze hanging around the pubic regions, and legal girlie and "boyie" magazines have little white sticker rectangles over nipples and anything a tad more raunchy. Thai TV extends the smoke screen to guns and knives when pointed at other people, and cigarettes when in the mouth. Can't get much more thorough than the Thai censor.

Some Thai book and magazine sellers rip off the front page, or half the front page. This does not necessarily indicate an attempt to circumvent censorship. With Thailand now committed to stamping out piracy of legal products, at least superficially, this vandalism of the product suggests it is being sold second-hand, and therefore not subject to royalty payments.

Bottom line:
If in doubt, cut it out.

99

On You!

On being addressed by a complete stranger as "You!", offer no words or actions in reply. Certainly do not smile. Certainly do not enter into an English lesson with the caller. Certainly show no anger. Do not yell, "You!" or even "*Khun!*" in return. This crude and lowly attempt to attract your attention by a man (99 per cent chance such callers are men) must fail. Ensure it does. Stare the man straight and unswervingly in the eye. He will not say, "Who do you think you're looking at?", for one simple reason: he knows only one word of English, and that word is, "You!" He must of course be punished for disturbing your peace, but leave that to the loss of face that will follow as you walk straight past him and, speaking perfect Thai, buy an identical article to that which he is selling from a different seller who's command of English idiom does not stretch to "You".

If calling your attention for a ride in a *tuk-tuk*, and presuming you actually want a *tuk-tuk*, do not grace his vehicle with your backside, but, take a 1,000 baht note from your breast pocket, rustle it in the air, and jump in the first *tuk-tuk* that jams on the brakes in front of you. As you pass the first, confused and humbled *tuk-tuk* driver, resist the justifiable temptation to say, especially if you can say it in absolutely fluent Thai, "And wash your armpits".

Bottom line:

Never, ever, acknowledge with anything other than unspoken disdain the appellation "You!" If, however, you have been hailed with "You Crap", treat the caller appropriately.

100

On Zenith Attainment

On reaching the zenith of full social integration, or on realising this is as close to it as you are ever going to get, dig yourself in, and with the tenacity of a crab louse, hang on to what you have and where you are.

It is pay-off time. The arse-licking, the crawling, the self-abasement, the exaggerated *craps*, the practised smiles, the prolonged waits, the serving as dust beneath another set of feet, all is suddenly and miraculously reversed. While you have spent years preparing for this moment, it may take you by surprise, arriving like nirvana when you have finally ceased to lust after it. You will need a period of adjustment. Your behaviour can become once again something like what it was before you set course for integration and eventual assimilation. You can stop bending over backwards to ingratiate yourself into Thai society and reverse deferential convention on all matters that do not affect your funeral, subsequent deification and posterity.

Like Superman, Spiderman and Batman, pick early on the outfit that will make you instantly recognisable as *the* foreigner-Thai. It should be as individual as you are, kindly allowing lower folk to recognise your illustrious presence and adopt appropriate positions of grovel. As a real big man, you *might* decide to stamp your mark on the world wearing jodhpurs, a monocle, riding boots, swagger stick and a shaven mahogany pate. That particular attire has of course been tried and didn't in the end ensure a happy posterity, so maybe something a tad humbler for your new role in Thailand. How about a blue serge neck-less Thai farmer's shirt and a general's haircut? But come to think of it, that has been done too. The point is, it's up to you. Even when caught up in a counter-counter-coup and tied to a post in front of a brick wall, make sure you call the shots.

You are now a *Big Man*. Of course, you know don't you that you are still mountains and sky from real nobility. You can never achieve real nobility since there is an insurmountable birth qualification which requires your death and metempsychosis, for which you are not immediately ready. Indeed it is strongly advised not to attempt transmigration of the soul until you have built up a whole lot more merit than you currently have on the credit side of the ledger. You can most happily agree to this defining social cap on your own quasi-mystical ambitions. It does not hurt at all to be reminded that even you have your place and there will always be some above you, to whom you will defer more enthusiastically than you ever did on your way up. It's good for your soul. And besides, you need the exercise.

You will be Thai enough by now to realise that everyone needs to be part of a group if he or she is to survive. Thus, contrary to the Western zenith, it is not lonely at the Thai top. Not that you want to be too crowded up there. Enough people to hold hands and keep each other in place while keeping the place to yourselves, not so many people as to risk the intervention of elbows and bad breath or, heaven forbid, a fall from grace.

While most of your public time will be spent in the company of your group, to make sure nobody is plotting your ouster, your private time, as long as it is private, remains yours to tinker with at will. You may, in the cloistered privacy of your own palatial domain, or in the back rooms of a gentleman's club, allow yourself the occasional romp with those of inferior status. But apart from such private occasions, you must save your smile for press conferences, when it is to be used undiluted to sidestep any and every question and take the place of words. The smile thus used is better than a million words, as later it never has to be denied.

Bottom line:

Here endeth it all, your zenith is all part of the great design. Enjoy it while it lasts.

Words That Must Not Be Said

You are strongly advised not to practise these words in public, or even in private. If you hear them coming in your direction, it is a good time to practise fleeing the scene.

ai tua	male prostitute (ok sometimes, but not as address)
chok wow	male masturbation (fly kites)
daak	arse
dao	movement (of penis in vagina)
falang ba	mad *farang*
falang khinok	birdshit *farang*
falang khwai khwai	the *farang* has a buffalo's penis
goo	"I" (use only when speaking to somebody in a straightjacket and well fastened down)
ham-hiao	withered penis/testicles
hee men	smelly cunt
hee	pussy (not a cat)
hii-hiao	withered vagina
hoy	an edible mollusc that lives between female thighs
ii-doke	female slut
ii-tua	female prostitute
isa cream	blow job (okay in the correct environment; not)
jew	penis of a small boy/little dick
kai-ham	testicles

luuk gali	son of a whore
moyi	pubic hair (ok between close friends)
mun/meung	you/he/she (pronoun okay when used for animals, although we don't know if the animals would say the same)
na beau	you bore me to death
na giat	your ugliness takes me away
*naa ye*t	fuckable
ru-daak	arse hole
sup buri	see *isa cream*
yet mae	motherfucker
yet man	fucker
yet	fuck

Thai Words in the Text

The following words are frequently heard by foreigners. Some are English in origin but do not retain their original meaning in contemporary Thai. All Thai words here are in the text.

ajarn	teacher
Amphur	District Office
ang	large jar/ reservoir (water)
Anggrit	British/ English
apamen	apartment
aray na	what (added politeness)
aray	what
aroy dii maak	really very tasty
aroy dii	very tasty
aroy	tasty
bahn nok/ ban nok	in the countryside/ village/ country bumpkin
bang/ thanakhan	bank
boon/ boun	merit
chay/ may chay	correct/ incorrect, yes/ no
chop mai	do you like it?
chuay duay	help
clap ma	come back/ return
crap/ cap/ khrap/ *craphom* (M) *kha/* *ca* (F) *dharma*	particle of respect/ yes Buddhist scriptures/ teachings
fan	boy/girl friend, fiancée, spouse
farang/ falang	Caucasian

galaman	large flat water vessel (washing clothes, etc.)
gap gam	snack (often with alcohol)
gig	young person who is "with it"
gin khao/ kin khao	eat/ come eat
gin layo	eaten already/ thanks but no
hello	hello (on phone)
hong nam	toilet
im layo	full (stomach, of food)
jai yen	literally cool heart meaning even tempered
jinjok	cute little lizard
jup hom	sniff kiss
Kamnan	administrative head of a group of villages
karma/ ka'ma	fate/destiny
ker/ keu	spacer word in conversation, like "er..."
ker wa	that is to say
kha	see *crap*
Khao Phansa	beginning of Buddhist Lent (July)
khao phiak	rice noodles
khatoey	male with strong female inclinations
khay luak	egg with formed chick inside
Kheck-Arab	person from Middle East
Kheck-Burma	person from Myanmar
kheck	sub-continental
khi niao	mean with money
khon Africa	African
khon dii	good person/ "dear"
khon sii dam	black person

khor thort	sorry/ excuse me/ please punish me
khrap	see *crap*
khun	you
khun ying	well-placed woman of official rank
khwai	means buffalo, cake and a naughty word for penis
krengjai	fearful respect
kuti	monk's quarters
kwaytiaw nam	noodle soup
kwaytiaw	noodles
ler	Is that so?
leu	Really?
lip	lift/ elevator
lok	contrary (particle of speech)
lung	"uncle"/ elderly man (elder brother of father)
luuk krung	child of mixed parentage
mae	mother
may pen rai	never mind
meu teu	mobile (cell) phone
mia noy	minor wife
mia	wife (informal)
mor duu	fortune teller
mor lam	traditional singer
mor nuat	masseuse
mun	engagement
Nai Amphur	District Officer
nam dang	water with red syrup (popular drink)
nam jai	giving with no thought of reward
nam jim	sauce in separate dipping dish

nam pla	fish sauce
ngeun	money
nit-noy	tiny
ock phansa	end of Buddhist Lent (October)
pa	elder sister of mother/father
pai (falling tone)	sign/ bus stop
pai (mid tone)	go
pen	"is"
pen array	opposite of *may pen ray*; something's up
pheuak/ puak	social/ friendship group
phi/ nong	elder/ junior
phi	spirit/ ghost
phom	hair/ I (M)
phor/ mae	parents
phra phum	spirits of the land
phuut len	joking/ pleasantries
reu	or
sakti na	power (of land)
sanuk	fun
san-wit	sandwich
satem	stamp
sawatdii	hello (usual verbal greeting)
say thung	put it in bag (take away leftovers)
serm suay	beauty parlour
sia	broken down/ out of service
sin deuan	month's end/ pay day
soi	lane/ small road
som na na	better luck next time
than	prefix used for important people
thao ni/ thao nan	that's all
thio/ tio	trip/ outing
toh pit	wrong number (on phone)

tom	female with strong male inclinations
tookger	big ugly lizard
tuk-tuk	also called *samlor*, a motorised trishaw
tung yang	plastic bag/ condom
urh	yes/ I agree (informal)
wai	nose to hands act of greeting/ deference
wan phra	day set by moon for making merit
wat	Buddhist temple
wela	time
yaa dom	menthol inhaler stuck up the nose
yaa mong	tiger-balm or similar pain-relieving ointment
yok thort	apology accepted

About the Author

Robert Cooper is an Englishman who has lived most of his life in Asia. He speaks Thai, Lao, French, Malay and Indonesian. Awarded a doctorate for his studies among the Hmong of Thailand, he was elected a Fellow of the Royal Anthropological Institute in 1979 and lectured in anthropology at the University of Singapore before joining the United Nations High Commissioner for Refugees. Often stationed in remote hardship stations, where he witnessed all too frequently man's inhumanity to man, he escaped from the hardships and dangers into the world of writing. While recognising that he can never quite equal the black comedy of the real world, he considers 19 years within the hullabaloo of the UN the best apprenticeship for a writer of humour.

Taking a very early retirement from the UN, he joined the British Foreign and Commonwealth Office in 2000 as Head of the British Trade Office in the Lao People's Democratic Republic. In 2006, he opened Book-Café Vientiane, the largest second-hand book outlet in the Lao PDR, where he continues to live and write.

Robert Cooper has written widely on Thailand and the region, including the well-known *CultureShock! Thailand* and *Thais Mean Business*. He has also written cultural guide books to Bahrain, Bhutan, Croatia, Indonesia and Laos, and the ethnography *The Hmong*. Under the name Robert Fox, he has published two novels, *Red Fox Goose Green* set in an English village, and *Red Flag Blue Member* set in Laos. He is currently working on a third novel, *Professor Dog,* a comedy set in Singapore.